Weaving Generations Together

Weaving Generations Together

Evolving Creativity in the Maya of Chiapas

Patricia Marks Greenfield

Photographs by Lauren Greenfield

Foreword by Evon Z. Vogt

❖ A School of American Research Resident Scholar Book ❖
❖ Santa Fe, New Mexico ❖

School of American Research Press
Santa Fe, New Mexico

Director: James F. Brooks
Executive Editor: Catherine Cocks
Copy Editors: Jane Kepp, Kate Talbot
Production Manager: Cynthia Dyer
Designer: Cynthia Dyer
Proofreader: Peg J. Goldstein
Indexer: Jan C. Wright
Spanish edition, 2010: *Tejedoras: Generaciones Reunidas*, printed and bound by Tien Wah Press, Singapore
Tzotzil edition, 2015: *Jolobil Xchi'uk Xchanobil,* printed and bound by Editorial Fray Bartolomé de Las Casas, San Cristóbal de Las Casas, Chiapas, Mexico
Production, third printing: Jack Nelson
Printed and bound in Malaysia by Tien Wah Press

Library of Congress Cataloging-in-Publication Data

Greenfield, Patricia Marks.
    Weaving generations together : evolving creativity among the Mayas of Chiapas / Patricia Marks Greenfield; foreword by Evon Z. Vogt.
        p. cm.
    "A School of American Research Resident Scholar Book."
    Includes bibliographical references and index.
    ISBN 1-930618-28-X (pbk. : alk. paper)
    1. Tzotzil textile fabrics—Mexico—Zinacantán Region. 2. Tzotzil women—Mexico—Zinacantán Region. 3. Tzotzil weavers—Mexico—Zinacantán Region.
    4. Textile design—Mexico—Zinacantán Region. 5. Zinacantán Region (Mexico)—Social life and customs. 6. Zinacantán Region (Mexico)—Economic
    conditions.
I. Title.
    F1221.T9G695 2004
    972'.7500497'4287—dc22

2004000152

Front Cover: Rosy Xulubte' leans back into the backstrap as her mother passes the bobbin through the shed. Nabenchauk, 1991.
Herding sheep. Nabenchauk, 1991. Inside front and back covers: Details from baby's baptismal blouse, Nabenchauk, 1991.
Frontispiece: Saturday market, Nabenchauk, 1991. Dedication: Embroidered band from Zinacantec blouse, 1991. All photographs: © Lauren
Greenfield/VII.

weaving-generations.psych.ucla.edu

For Jerome Bruner, mentor, friend, and inspiration

In memory of Evon Vogt, with thanks

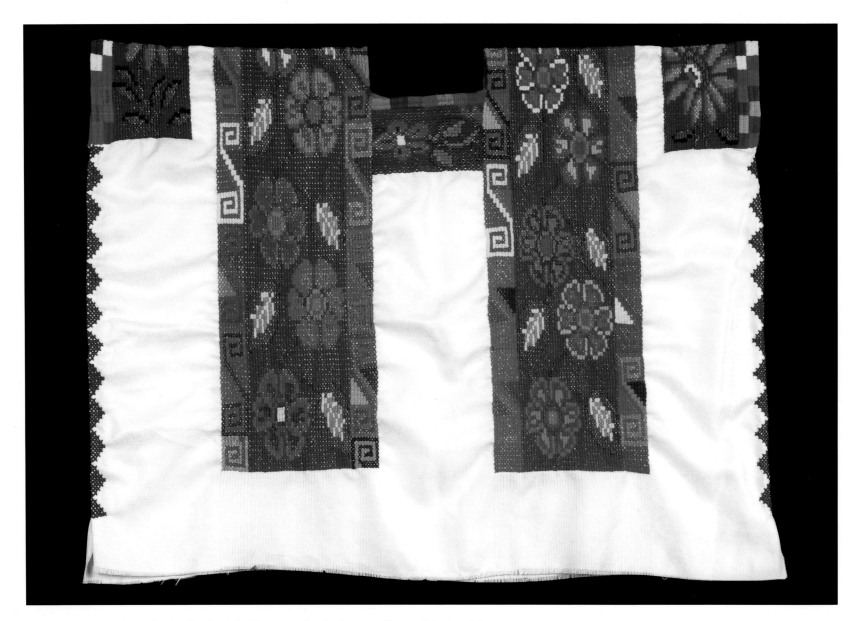

Figure 1. Lupa Z'us designed and embroidered this blouse in Nabenchauk, 1992. Photograph by Don Cole.

Table of Contents

Figure 2. Xun-Mol-José throws a plastic spider as a flock of birds fly by. Nabenchauk, 1991. ©Lauren Greenfield/VII.

Foreword

The Zinacantec hamlet of Nabenchauk (literally "the lake of thunder and lightning") has been the site of the remarkable field research that is the basis of this outstanding book. The hamlet lies in a small valley on the south side of the Pan-American Highway at an altitude of seven thousand feet in the highlands of Chiapas, Mexico. It was here that Professor Greenfield initiated her fieldwork in 1969 on an innovative project that has evolved into a long-range study of two generations of Zinacantec mothers teaching their daughters to weave on the backstrap loom. As Greenfield points out, the Maya have used this backstrap loom for at least one thousand years. For the Maya style of life, the loom has many advantages: it is easily portable and can be used at the same time the busy Zinacantec woman attends to other duties. If she is tending the family's small herd of sheep, she can tie one end of the loom to a tree and continue her weaving. In the patio just outside a Zinacantec house, the loom can be tied to a house post, and the woman can weave while keeping an eye on her small children playing in the patio.

From the beginning, Professor Greenfield's project has been collaborative and multidisciplinary in the most productive way. Greenfield was trained in cognitive development and cross-cultural psychology, her supervisor and mentor in graduate school at Harvard being the celebrated Professor Jerome Bruner. She was invited to go to Chiapas by Dr. T. Berry Brazelton, a distinguished pediatrician who was studying Zinacantec infancy in a developmental and cultural context. As director of the Harvard Chiapas Project, I was able to provide Greenfield with a talented assistant, Carla Childs, an undergraduate student in anthropology who had become fluent in Tzotzil. Greenfield later added sociologist-anthropologist Leslie Haviland Devereaux, who had a house in Nabenchauk and was also fluent in Tzotzil and familiar with the customs of the community, as a collaborator.

The research design combined the traditional anthropological methods of participant observation of the flow of life and informal interviewing of key informants in the culture under study with the psychological methods of experiments, standardized interviews, and making videotapes for quantitative microanalysis, as well as merging ethnographic field notes and quantitative treatment of behavioral data.

Professor Greenfield has wisely focused her research over the years on weaving, an activity par excellence of Maya womanhood. With this sharp focus, it has been possible to ask important general questions such as the following: How are children socialized? What generates innovative as opposed to traditional behavior? What is the effect of globalization on the weaving and sale of Zinacantec textiles? Professor Greenfield then was able provide convincing answers by posing and either accepting or rejecting specific hypotheses as she analyzed the data.

Among the crucial findings of the research is the discovery that periods of heavy dependence on subsistence agriculture in Zinacantec history favor traditional stability in clothing styles. Contrasting periods of dependence upon commercial activities are times of innovation and change in clothing styles. Greenfield describes how during the seven years between 1991 to 1998, the pace of change in styles of clothing and methods of teaching weaving to the new generation of young women exceeded that of the thirty-year subsistence agricultural period from 1940 to 1970.

During the 1990s the clothing styles underwent drastic changes from the plain, red-striped clothes of the agricultural period to clothing with more red and a riot of other colors and designs in the elaborate embroidery of flowers, animals, and geometric figures.

Greenfield shows in detail that these style changes were related to weaving with acrylic yarn, which could be purchased in stores, replacing the cotton and wool of older textiles, and to the weaving of textiles targeted for sale to tourists in stores along the Pan-American Highway or in San Cristóbal de Las Casas.

Finally, I am impressed with three remarkable features of this volume:

[1] The demonstration, using iconographic images from pre-Columbian sites (Bonampak and Yaxchilan) as well as pictures from the *Florentine Codex,* that the Mesoamerican form of elite women's dress persists from the Maya Classic to contemporary Zinacantán. Especially notable is the square form of textiles that results from weaving done on the backstrap loom.

[2] The excellent use of stunning still photos (some taken by Professor Frank Cancian and most by Professor Greenfield's daughter, Lauren) to show stages of weaving and changes in style of clothing.

[3] The videotaping of the complex weaving process, which permitted close study of the behavior of mothers teaching their daughters how to weave.

This was the first video field study of cultural apprenticeship that had ever been done. Careful, intensive study of the videos revealed that the basic body skills needed for efficient backstrap weaving are threefold: (1) restrained movement of the arms, which are kept close to the body; (2) kneeling comfortably on the ground for long periods of time; and (3) maintaining balance when leaning forward. Some of these basic movements are part of the early socialization process, for example, keeping the arms close to the body; others Zinacantec girls learn at an early age, for instance as they carry firewood on a tumpline, wash clothes, grind maize for tortillas on *manos* and *metates,* or bake tortillas on the grill that rests on the three traditional hearthstones around the cooking fire in the Zinacantec one-room house.

The still photos and videotapes also provided convincing data for the changes in teaching styles as mothers and older siblings taught young girls to weave. During the periods of subsistence farming and stability in cultural patterns, daughters quietly observed their mothers weaving and proceeded to imitate them. There was also more active intervention on the part of the mothers. During the periods of commercial activity and innovation in cultural patterns, there was much less intervention on the part of the mothers and less imitation on the part of the girls. In families in which mother and daughter were actively involved in textile commerce, girls learned to weave through a more independent, trial-and-error process, well adapted to producing innovative textiles for the markets both internal and external to the community.

In the final chapters, Professor Greenfield takes up the problem of creativity and the shift from community values to individual values and provides an interesting cross-cultural comparison between the Zinacantec weavers and the Pueblo and Navajo artists in the Southwest.

In my judgment, Patricia Greenfield's pathbreaking book is a clear-headed model of multidisciplinary research at its very best.

Evon Z. Vogt
Harvard University

Figure 3. Approaching Nabenchauk from the west, 1991. ©Lauren Greenfield/VII.

Acknowledgments

In many ways, this book is a story of mothers and children studying mothers and children. I therefore begin by acknowledging my own children, Lauren and Matthew, who were participants, witting or unwitting, at every stage of the work. I first took Lauren and Matthew to Chiapas in 1969, when I went to begin my fieldwork. Lauren was three; Matthew was ten months old (fig. 4). They came back with me a year later, again for two summer months (fig. 5). Years later, when I was applying for a grant in 1989 to study the next generation of Zinacantec children and mothers, Lauren, then a struggling photographer living in London, said she wanted to go back with me to photograph. When my grant from the Spencer Foundation was funded, Lauren was part of our team. At that point, I told

Figure 4. Greenfield and her children. Nabenchauk, 1969.

Figure 5. Lauren and Matthew Greenfield a year later. Nabenchauk, 1970. Photograph by Sheldon Greenfield.

Matthew, a film major at Wesleyan University, about our return trip to Chiapas, and he wanted to join us as well. I felt gratified that their associations with Chiapas were so positive, and I was excited about their participation.

Supported by a generous contract with *National Geographic* magazine, where she had served as a photography intern, Lauren took pictures for most of the five months of our 1991 fieldwork. Her pictures are beautiful, and they are central to this book. Lauren had a very special relationship with the girls of Nabenchauk, and this relationship is visible in her pictures. But the photographs are more than illustrations. They became unexpected data upon which several key arguments rest, particularly those in chapter 2. Lauren also helped collect some of the weaving videos and run the pattern representation experiment.

Matthew came to Chiapas with his friend Hannah Carlson for his birthday in September 1991 and stayed to help me organize my video database until the end of the fieldwork in November. Hannah skillfully helped me make weaving videos. Sometime after our return to Los Angeles, Matthew set up our computer database and coded and input data until February 1995; this was his "day job" as he established a career in independent film.

As a mother, I made a lot more sense to the Zinacantecs than I did as a researcher. Working with my children was more understandable than working with students or colleagues. Not only that, but when Lauren returned in 1991 with a fiancé and Matthew with a girlfriend, they added to my prestige. This was especially true of Matthew's girlfriend, because in Zinacantán married boys traditionally live near their parents, whereas married girls live near their in-laws. Working with one's children is as complex as it is satisfying. I am grateful to Lauren and Matthew for undertaking the challenge and for helping me do things I could never have done without them.

This project goes back to 1968, with an invitation to go to Chiapas, Mexico, from T. Berry Brazelton, a fellow fellow at the Harvard Center for Cognitive Studies and my children's distinguished pediatrician. Berry invited me to follow up his pathbreaking research with Zinacantec babies. The task he set—to place Zinacantec infancy in a broader developmental and cultural framework—was challenging and took years to accomplish. But Berry's contribution was far more than a scientific one. If I had not had my pediatricians with me in Chiapas (Berry for one month, John Robey for the other), I would never have dared go into the field with a baby who had been seriously ill most of his short life.

Nor could I have accepted Berry's invitation were it not for another person, Jerome Bruner, to whom I dedicate this book. Jerry had provided me with the incredible opportunity to do a psychology dissertation on culture and cognitive development in Senegal a few years earlier. It was through him that I met Berry at the Center for Cognitive Studies, which Jerry had cofounded and was codirecting. I am grateful that he was willing and eager to continue supporting me as I embarked on a new cultural journey in Chiapas, Mexico.

Berry's invitation to Chiapas depended on still another person, who had made Berry's Maya research possible and was soon to facilitate mine: anthropology professor Evon Z. Vogt, director of the Harvard Chiapas Project. At a time when my cross-cultural research had been cut off by family responsibilities, the context provided by Vogtie and the Harvard Chiapas Project made meaningful short-term cross-cultural research possible, allowing me to continue in the field of cultural developmental psychology. I feel honored that Vogtie has written the foreword to this book.

The Harvard Chiapas Project provided language and cultural training for its undergraduate students (and me) who were about to go into the field. Even more important, Vogtie assigned me one of these students, Carla Childs, then an anthropology major and a junior at Radcliffe College, as an assistant. In 1969, my first summer of research in Nabenchauk, Carla was already an experienced fieldworker in Zinacantán with excellent Tzotzil Maya

Figure 6. Xun Pavlu and his daughter Loxa look at her 1970 weaving video, made twenty-one years earlier. Nabenchauk, 1991. ©Lauren Greenfield/VII.

language skills and a strong interest in child development and education. Carla has been a mainstay of the project from beginning to end. Her 1970 honors thesis provided the first wave of experimental data on pattern representation (chapter 5).

Neither of us returned to Chiapas for twenty-one years, but in 1991 we returned together. Now a wife and the mother of three children, Carla came to Chiapas with her family for two months of collaborative fieldwork in 1991. Later, aided by her knowledge of backstrap loom weaving and Tzotzil, Carla expertly coded videos of girls learning to weave in 1970 and their descendants learning to weave in 1991 and 1993. Similarly, she carefully coded pattern representation data from 1969, 1970, and 1991. Her patience and willingness to recode all of the 1969 and 1970 data made possible reliable comparisons across the two generations, the heart of our research design. Since that time Carla has been a steadfast collaborator on papers, always ready to help when needed. Her careful reading of chapters in this book made many technical points concerning weaving and our experiments much clearer.

In 1969 Vogtie and Stanford anthropologist George Collier selected the highly respected elder Xun Pavlu to be my assistant in Nabenchauk. With his extensive network of family and *compadres* (co-godparents), he was the perfect choice (fig. 6). Xun was devoted to Carla, to me, and to the project until his death in 1997. I am particularly grateful that Xun was ready and willing to help in 1991, after a period without contact that had lasted twenty-one years.

Even before Xun's death, his daughter-in-law Maruch Chentik had become a valued assistant and friend to all members of our team. Lauren selected Maruch as her assistant because of her understanding of the photography project—even though it meant Lauren would have to communicate in Tzotzil (and learn it fast!) rather than in Spanish, which she already knew. Despite having a young family (four children from three months to nine years of age), Maruch was enthusiastic about having a regular job—in this, she was exceptional in her culture. With her husband, Telex, and her children, Maruch not only helped us with our work but also opened her home with warmth, humor, and generosity to me, Lauren, Carla, and, a few years later, my collaborator Ashley Maynard. In particular, two of the Pavlu children, Paxku' and Rosy, grew into important friends and helpers. The relationship was really family to family, a kind of informal *compadrazgo* (co-godparentship) —witness the presence of Lauren's wedding pictures on the wall of the Pavlus' one-room house. The youngest child, Patricia, is named after me, and as I complete these acknowledgments, I am in Chiapas to be the godmother of Paxku's first child, born in May 2003.

I must also express appreciation to Xun's daughter Katal, who, like her late mother, cooked wonderful lunches for us for months on end. Her whole family was a major help in our project. Finally, I want to express my gratitude to all the people in Nabenchauk who participated in experiments or interviews, were videotaped while learning to weave, or were photographed in their everyday lives. Their participation was our sine qua non.

In 1991 Carla and I were joined by two more members of the field team, Leslie Devereaux (formerly Haviland) and Tsuh-Yin Chen. Leslie helped both Lauren and me to understand Zinacantec culture more profoundly. She taught me what to

talk about—gossip and jokes about sex— so that I would seem a sophisticated conversationalist, despite my rather basic Tzotzil language skills. A number of Leslie's observations became themes of my later quantitative explorations. Leslie also helped in collecting video data and introduced us to the Vásquez family, to whom I offer many thanks, particularly to Paxku Vásquez, for friendship to me and Lauren and for offering me the opportunity to acquire the family's fifty-year collection of ritual cloths and other textiles (chapter 4), an invaluable source for tracing historical change in Zinacantec textiles.

Leslie's 1991 field notes and her 1978 dissertation, the result of forty months of living in Nabenchauk over a period of nine years, provided added historical perspective at many points in this book. Her method was to learn the skills and lead the life of a Zinacantec woman. She learned to weave and embroider in Nabenchauk and was an early innovator, embroidering butterflies on a poncho and flowers on her own blouse in 1973; girls in Nabenchauk watched. Not only a researcher, Leslie may well have been one of the many forces that led to the sprouting of flowers on Zinacantec blouses.

Tsuh-Yin Chen, then a UCLA graduate student, pursued a parallel study in San

Figure 7. Lauren Greenfield and Paxku' Pavlu, age nine. Nabenchauk, 1991. Polaroid by Patricia Greenfield

Pedro Chenalho, comparing weaving apprenticeship in families belonging to weaving cooperatives with those who did not. Tsuh-Yin's study makes an important contribution to chapter 3. Josephine Moreno, then a textile graduate student at the University of Iowa and now a professor at Rhode Island School of Design, helped and gave advice at a crucial moment of the 1993 textile elicitation study.

Ashley Maynard infused new life into the project. As a graduate student in developmental psychology, she transferred from Berkeley to UCLA in 1995 in order to work with me in Zinacantán. I introduced her to the Telex Pavlu–Maruch Chentik family, and they hosted her as she learned to speak Tzotzil, to weave, and to know our families. Out of this experience she developed a general model of the Zinacantec ethnotheory of learning and teaching; this ethnotheory is discussed in chapter 2. Her experience in Nabenchauk, combined with two years of statistics study, enabled her to carry out some of the sophisticated data analyses that are endnoted in chapters 3 and 5. Her participant observations as an apprentice in all the tasks of Zinacantec womanhood also contributed to chapter 2. My collaboration with Ashley has been a source of comfort and joy as we lived together in Chiapas and worked together in Los Angeles. She followed up our collaborative work with an award-winning dissertation on learning to teach in Nabenchauk, and we have completed a new collaborative study of the cognitive development that underlies learning to weave, briefly described in chapter 2. Together, we have written a number of papers on the data presented in this book. Most importantly, Ashley will carry on the long-term study of culture, development, and learning in Nabenchauk. We plan for her to study

the next generation, some of whom have already been born.

In San Cristóbal, I am grateful to Marcy Jacobson and the late Janet Marren for their warmth, hospitality, and conversation. Also in San Cristóbal, the late Nancy Modiano, a pioneer in the study of Maya Indian education, offered friendship, hospitality, encouragement, and help to me and my team. Thanks to Mimi Laughlin, who found my team wonderful housing for our return in 1991, and to Judith Aissen for her friendship and interest in the project. The Stanford Medical Project and George Collier, respectively, generously made their census data from Nabenchauk and Apas available to me. Lourdes de León was a source of intellectual stimulation as she carried out insightful research on language socialization in Nabenchauk. My thanks go also to Steven Lopez, my UCLA colleague and director of a National Institutes of Health Minority International Research Training (MIRT) program in Mexico, and to Pablo Farias, then director of El Colegio de la Frontera Sur (ECOSUR) in San Cristóbal de la Casas. In the summer of 1997, MIRT provided funding and ECOSUR offered a strong and very useful institutional base in San Cristóbal. Chip Morris, a founder of the weaving cooperative Sna Jolobil, provided valuable

feedback on my research, and Pedro Meza, director of Sna Jolobil, re-created a wonderful drawing of an ancient Zinacantec pyramid (see fig. 4.56).

Were it not for nine months without other responsibilities, this book would never have been written. Had the nine months been any place other than the School of American Research (SAR), an institute for advanced study in Santa Fe, New Mexico, the book would have been very different. The School's programs and facilities introduced me and gave me access to many Native American arts. This experience gave me the material for the coda that concludes the book.

Unexpectedly, among my colleagues at SAR, it was the archaeologists, with their interest in material culture, who influenced me the most. My analysis of historical change in Zinacantec textiles was greatly enhanced by discussions with Berkeley archaeologist Kent Lightfoot, a resident scholar with me at SAR. Kent pointed out that I was trying to document change in the rate of change of Zinacantec textiles and that logically I needed at least three data points to do so. In addition to this theoretical help, I received unique material help at SAR. The resident photographer, Katrina Lasko, showed me how to shoot photographs on a copy stand, and SAR's Indian Arts Research Center provided the facilities to do so; the reader will see a few of these photographs in chapter 5. Roberta Haines served as my assistant and friend during the year I spent at SAR. And where else could a scholar find an academic press that knows how to do art books and can accept a book with more than two hundred color photographs? Thanks to Joan O'Donnell for her enthusiasm in acquiring this book for SAR Press, to Catherine Cocks for her careful editing, and to James Brooks for overseeing it all. Special thanks to Cynthia Dyer for a sensitive and beautiful design that is highly responsive to the scientific and aesthetic content of the book. I feel extremely grateful to SAR for the opportunity to write this book, to publish it, and to get the kind of help I needed to do so.

Many thanks to the Spencer Foundation and to the National Geographic Society; their financial support made the follow-up study possible. I would also like to acknowledge Robert LeVine and the late Sylvia Scribner; both were not-so-anonymous reviewers of my grant proposal who advised the Spencer Foundation that this historical study was a worthwhile project. Detailed historical comparison would not have been possible without technical support from Bill Worthy, owner of Channel One Video in Venice, California. Bill

rescued the 1970 reels of weaving video and transferred them to VHS; this rescue operation enabled us to recode the 1970 videos and make a quantitative comparison with the next generation. Thanks, too, to Millier Loeb, who was a supportive presence from beginning to end; to Van Do Huynh, who faithfully administered my grants; to Linda Fitzgerald, an extremely supportive program officer at the Spencer Foundation; to Katie Callan, Sheila Masson, and Ryan Beshara from Lauren Greenfield Photography, who helped me with the photographs; to my sister, Terry Marks-Tarlow, for the book's subtitle and scholarship on creativity; and to Victoria Scott and the late Peter Furst, who encouraged and aided me greatly in Santa Fe and afterward. More thanks to Janet Tomiyama, who helped with manuscript preparation and with Jonathan Flanigan completed the catalog of my textile collection, central to chapters 4 and 6; and to Nick Breitborde, who aided in the completion of the SPSS database. The 1993 interview and textile study (chapter 6) was made possible by a grant from the Wenner-Gren Foundation for Anthropological Research. My thanks to Elinor Ochs for her help in developing that proposal.

As the data analysis and writing phases of the project outlasted the major funding

sources, the UCLA Center for the Study of Women, the UCLA Latin American Studies Center, and the UCLA Academic Senate filled in with small but highly significant grants. The first wave of fieldwork was supported by the Harvard Center for Cognitive Studies, the Harvard Chiapas Project, the Milton Fund, and the Radcliffe Institute.

The interest of a number of valued colleagues along the way sustained my confidence in the project and provided opportunities to present and publish pieces of the whole, which made a book-length project much less daunting and more manageable. For this I thank Michael Cole, Giyoo Hatano, Elliot Turiel, Lee Munroe, Isabel Zambrano, Vera John-Steiner, Susan Seymour, Deborah Best, Suzanne Gaskins, Joanne Derevenski, Anastasie Tryphon, Heidi Keller, Geoffrey Saxe, Larry Nucci, Thomas Csordas, Pierre Dasen, Grace Johnson, the late Rodney Cocking, and the researchers at CIESAS in San Cristóbal.

The intellectual thread upon which this book rests is the notion of social change. I can credit my interest in the implications of social change for individual psychology to the class "Social Relations 10" that I took at Harvard and the book *The Passing of Traditional Society*, by Daniel Lerner, which was assigned in that freshman course. But inspiration for this particular study of social change came from Frank Cancian, professor emeritus of anthropology at the University of California, Irvine, and an alumnus of the Harvard Chiapas Project. After completing and publishing studies from our first wave of fieldwork, I never expected to return to Zinacantán. However, while I was a fellow at the Bunting Institute, Radcliffe College, in 1986–87, Frank came to Harvard to give a lecture in the Anthropology Department on economic development and changes in the *cargo* (religious office) system in Zinacantán; I attended. He spoke of Zinacantec men halting their agricultural work as corn farmers to become entrepreneurs in the transport industry.

Based on the first wave of fieldwork and its cross-cultural context, I had developed a theory of two modes of cultural transmission, one adapted to the maintenance of the status quo, one adapted to producing change and novelty (chapter 3). Frank had mentioned entrepreneurs, and I recognized that a basic value of entrepreneurship is innovation. After the lecture, I therefore asked Frank if there was any sign of novelty in the weaving, and he told me that flowers were now appearing everywhere. I had preliminary evidence for novel design elements in weaving. Now I want-

ed to see whether apprenticeship—the method of transmission—had also changed in accord with my theory. I saw a unique chance to test this theory in a controlled manner by going back to Nabenchauk and studying the next generation.

My appreciation goes to Frank for the inspiration and for subsequent encouragement to pursue both my research and Lauren's photography. I also owe Frank a debt of gratitude for giving me access to his wonderful photographs of Zinacantán, which have added a systematic historical dimension to the analysis and beauty to the presentation in this book. Many thanks to Frank, to Stacey Schaefer, and to Jane Kepp for their extremely insightful reviews, which both encouraged me and led to great improvements in my manuscript. At the last stages, I had the good fortune to work with a wonderful textile photographer, Don Cole, at the UCLA Fowler Museum of Cultural History. Don not only took extraordinarily beautiful photographs of the textiles from my collection, which appear in the following pages, but he also helped a complete novice tie up absolutely every loose end that remained on her side of the production process, including work on the video stills (to which Bill Worthy, Sherry Lam, and Chris Quilisch also contributed).

Finally, I express my gratitude to Sheldon Greenfield for joining me in the field for a month in 1969 and 1970 and for taking the photographs that document those field seasons.

As this book comes to fruition, new issues in my relationship with our participants in Nabenchauk have presented themselves. I wanted to give credit to the families who had shown commitment to the project, and I wanted to give credit to the creators of the beautiful textiles shown in the pages that follow. Yet it was equally important to preserve anonymity where appropriate or desired by our participants. I tried to thread a careful and responsible pathway through these complexities. For the three families who were committed to helping with the research and photography over the life of the project, I showed them all the photographs in which they appeared and asked if they wanted their names to appear with the pictures. Two families did and one did not; the wishes of all have been granted. For participants who had a more fleeting relationship to the project, I decided to present their photographs without their names. For the textile photographs, I also give credit by name to the weavers and embroiderers in those same families, as well as where I was very sure that the maker would be proud

Figure 8. Girls searing chickens for a ritual meal. Nabenchauk, 1991. ©Lauren Greenfield/VII.

of her product. For other participants in my textile study and participants in our pattern representation study, I have preserved anonymity by using first names plus family I.D. numbers. (At the time of our research, a first name was not very revealing of identity, as there were few names, and every nuclear family contained many of the same first names.) I hope that these guidelines for when to provide anonymity and when to provide identity will satisfy every one of the hundreds of children and adults in Nabenchauk who made this project possible.

Venice, California
July and December 2003
San Cristóbal de las Casas, Chiapas
November 2003

Preface

When a woman goes to the field in a society with strict gender roles, she has two options: be a woman or be an honorary man. Although I made no conscious choice, my interest in mothers and children made me a woman in Zinacantán, with the rights, privileges, and limitations thereof. In 1969 I was highly involved in the still new women's movement, rebelling against traditional female roles in the United States. Yet as I sat around with Zinacantec women in highland Chiapas, Mexico, peacefully weaving the late afternoon away, I couldn't help feeling that their roles were preferable to what Zinacantec men were doing: working in the fields. Much to my surprise, I was happy to function as a Zinacantec woman. Zinacantec women, with their outspoken pride in women's work, led me to understand the cultural relativity of the women's movement as I knew it.

Figure 9. A young girl helps the author pat a tortilla. Day of the Dead, Nabenchauk, 1991. © Lauren Greenfield/VII.

The Harvard Chiapas Project had taught me and my colleague, Carla Childs, to wear Zinacantec clothes, which helped to normalize us as women and make us members of the community. In terms of our relationship with participants, it also helped that the long-term focus of our study was weaving. Weaving was important not only to us but also to Zinacantecs, particularly Zinacantec women. It made sense to them that we would be interested in learning about something so important, yet lacking in our own culture, and this reaction made the research easier and the data more reliable.

Another important aspect of our relationship with the community was that we always paid our participants for both their participation and their textiles, no matter how small or playful. Paying participants is a tradition in psychological research; it differs from the traditions of both anthropology and photojournalism. Consequently, my daughter, Lauren Greenfield, who took many of the photographs for this book, did not pay her photography subjects in money, but National Geographic generously made thousands of dollars' worth of color prints for Lauren to distribute as thank-you presents.

❖　❖　❖

With this book I have tried to make a new, interdisciplinary synthesis in both content and methodology. In the anthropological tradition, my research team and I worked in the Tzotzil language and spent time sharing the everyday life of Nabenchauk, a small-scale, nonindustrial village. In the psychological tradition, we carried out experiments, conducted standardized interviews, and made videotapes for quantitative microanalysis. In this volume I combine ethnographic field notes from the anthropological tradition with quantitative treatment of behavioral data in the psychological tradition.

Most importantly, in the pages that follow, I present the story of the research visually. Indeed, the heart of the research data was visual: videotapes of two generations of girls learning to weave; striped patterns constructed out of sticks to represent culturally central woven patterns; woven and embroidered textiles. I have tried to develop methods to present the visual data in visual terms. The ways in which I have done this do not quite fit the categories of visual anthropology,[1] but neither do they fit neatly into the methodology of cultural or developmental psychology.

Though Jon Wagner, in a 2004 article, notes the fine line between documentary photography and social research, he also sees a definite divide.[2] I have tried to create a methodological synthesis that eliminates this divide. For example, the photographs by Lauren Greenfield and Frank Cancian serve simultaneously as ethnographic, artistic, and scientific materials, especially in chapters 2 and 4. Chapter 4 also presents a quantitative analysis of Cancian's Zinacantec family photos from 1961 and 1962. In chapter 3, I use video frames to create a multi-generational case study of weaving apprenticeship and its historical transformation; this case study dramatizes more general points made through quantitative microanalysis of the videotapes. In chapter 5, I have re-created and, with the expert help of Don Cole, photographed the striped wooden designs participants originally created in the pattern representation experiment. These photographs can be seen both as scientific data and as aesthetic productions. Indeed, this project satisfied my inchoate wish to integrate science and art.

As I investigated changing models of creativity—the movement away from community tradition and toward individual innovation—my textile collection, an unplanned by-product of the research, emerged as a primary tool for documenting and communicating these historical changes; photographs of this collection form the backbone of chapter 4. Textiles from my collection are also used in chapter 6 to document the nature of the creative process in Zinacantec textile design.

All of these methods are ways of studying implicit rather than explicit cultural processes. An important subtext of the book is that cultural values and adaptations are reflected, expressed, and transmitted both in everyday practices and in automatic cognitive processes. Rather than studying cultural values as they are explicitly told through myth and ritual, my colleagues and I have studied them as they are implicitly expressed through the interactions and artifacts of everyday life on one hand, and through problem-solving approaches to experimental tasks on the other. Casual conversations and formal interviews complemented these external ("objective") data sources with our participants' subjective perspectives. I hope and believe that this methodological complexity provides greater texture and a deeper sense of the developmental, social, and cultural realities than would otherwise have been possible.

Throughout the book I have put technical aspects of the research, especially statistics and bibliographical references, in endnotes, where they will not break the thematic flow. I think this approach will help the general reader to understand better and the academic reader to enjoy more. It will also aid in interdisciplinary communication, because one field's technicalities are another field's gibberish. At the same time, the researcher who wants to evaluate methodology and quantitative results can use the endnotes to do so. Someone who wants to read further will be aided by the bibliography at the end of the book. With interdisciplinary barriers lowered, I hope the book will speak to readers with diverse academic interests: anthropology, psychology, textiles, indigenous peoples, the Maya, and social history. Hopefully, the visual presentation will make complex ideas and research findings clearer to specialists and more accessible to a general audience.

Last but not least, I designed this book to serve as a catalog for a museum exhibition of textiles, photographs, videotapes, and weaving artifacts from Nabenchauk. The exhibition plan highlights a changing textile tradition, the role of childhood in cultural transmission, alternative models of creativity, the techniques of backstrap loom weaving, and use of the textiles in everyday life. By joining the exhibition to the book, I hope that the many years of many people's work will reach far beyond academe to those who love children, weaving, photography, the Maya, or Mexico. As I complete this preface, *Weaving Generations Together* has just appeared in the catalog of ExhibitsUSA, a nonprofit organization that curates traveling exhibitions; the exhibition is now available to museums everywhere. Our participants in Nabenchauk were motivated to bring an understanding of their weaving to our land; I share in this goal.

Venice, California
July 2003

San Cristóbal de las Casas
November 2003

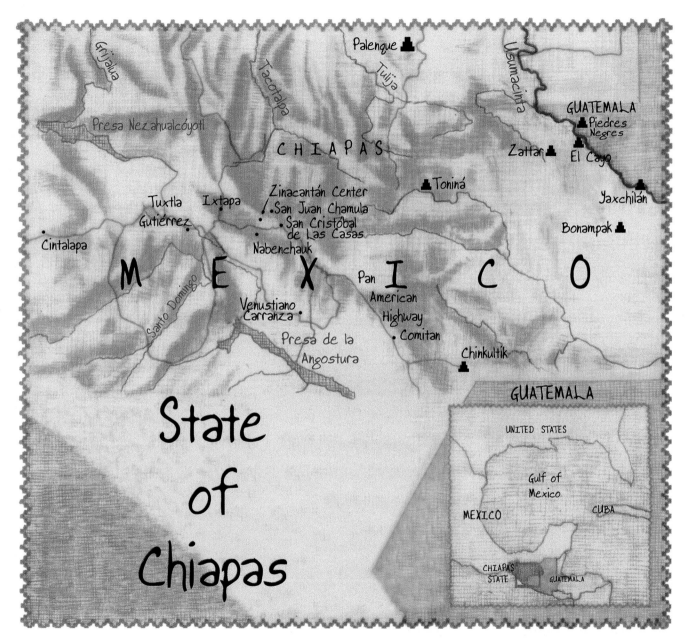

Figure 1.0. Map of Chiapas, Mexico.

CHAPTER ONE

Changes in the Fabric of Life

In 1991, the author and her colleagues
returned to the Maya village of Nabenchauk
to study two decades of change. ❖

Approaching the valley of Nabenchauk from the road, I saw a large concrete structure next to the highway and stopped the car. Clothing and other handwoven textiles hung from every rafter of the open-sided building. It was 1991 and, full of uncertainty, I was back in Nabenchauk, a hamlet of the highland Maya community of Zinacantán in Chiapas, Mexico, after an absence of twenty-one years. In 1970 anthropology student Carla Childs and I, a developmental psychologist, had spent the second of two summers of fieldwork in Nabenchauk studying how Zinacantec girls learned to weave. Now Carla and I wanted to use weaving as a measuring stick with which to answer questions about the psychological effects of social and economic change.

"Mi li'ote," I said—are you here?—trying out the customary Zinacantec

greeting in my rusty Tzotzil. "Li'one"— I am here—answered a teenage girl. I entered the store with my daughter, Lauren, the team photographer, and two of Carla's children, Dan, age ten, and Jean, thirteen. I was wearing 1969-model Zinacantec clothes (fig. 1.1), relics of our earlier field research. The girls taking care of the shop stared but did not know what to make of us. The clothes I was wearing—a long blue woven cotton skirt, a white cotton blouse, and a woven red-and-white striped cotton shawl—bore little resemblance to what they were selling in their shop, to what gringas usually wore, or even to what the Zinacantec girls themselves were wearing.[1]

Hanging from the rafters and racks was a rainbow of textiles in bright, even fluorescent colors, with fancy embroidery and decorative woven borders (fig. 1.2).

Figure 1.1. The author wearing her old Zinacantec clothes. Loxa K'o and her son Chepil Xulubte' each hold a photograph we had given to them two decades earlier. Nabenchauk, 1991. ©Lauren Greenfield/VII.

Figure 1.2. The Xulubte' shop, with woven and embroidered items hanging from rack and rafters. Servilletas (napkins), an item developed for sale to outsiders, are on the rack. Loxa K'o makes a sale as her young daughter Octaviana Xulubte' looks on. Nabenchauk, 1991. ©Lauren Greenfield/VII.

Figure 1.3. The author's blouse, from Nabenchauk, 1969. Photograph by Don Cole.

Special tourist items obviously predominated. When I had last been in Nabenchauk, the only things weavers had been willing to give up for sale to tourists were their mistakes.[2]

Even more astonishing than what the Zinacantecs were selling to tourists was what they themselves were wearing. My blouse, of plain white cotton with a thin line of purple stitching (fig. 1.3), had spawned progeny adorned with wild geometric or figurative embroidery in profusion (fig. 1.4).

Twenty years earlier, weaving and textile production, along with farming, had lain at the heart of Zinacantec subsistence. Since our departure in 1970, subsistence had clearly expanded into commerce. To build stores and houses along the road, rather than in the protected valley, was a new phenomenon. It symbolized increased commerce with the Spanish-speaking world and the Mexican national economy.

I had come to investigate whether entrepreneurship had begun to introduce the foreign value of innovation into what had been a traditional way of life based on respect for the authority of elders. In the arena of clothing and textiles, the answer was obviously yes. Although a clearly defined traditional dress code still existed, individual creativity had definitely entered the scene.

A Zinacantec woman came in and said, "Usos," apparently remarking in her

Figure 1.4. Detail of embroidered blouse with geometric design. Nabenchauk, 1991. ©Lauren Greenfield/VII.

visible, standing with him, a boy of five, his mother, father, and grandmother, was the Carla Childs of two decades earlier. "She is my godmother," he said in Spanish, pointing to Carla's picture. "These are Carla's children," I replied, pointing to Dan and Jean. I introduced Lauren, whom the woman remembered as a child of three or four. The man was thrilled at the prospect of seeing his godmother again. My fear that it would be difficult to reestablish contacts in Nabenchauk was allayed. But I still had no idea who these people were.

Carla, who had not come with us to the store, later solved the mystery. In the summer of 1970, she had been selected as the godmother, or *madrina,* of a baby in Nabenchauk and went to hold the infant for its baptism in a San Cristóbal church. When the mother took the baby off her back and unwrapped it to be baptized by the priest, she found the child dead. It was a traumatic experience for the family and for Carla, one she had preferred to forget. Together, we had attended the baby's funeral, sleeping overnight on a cold dirt floor in the family's house. This man with the photographs was Chepil Xulubte', the dead baby's older brother.[3] The woman was Loxa K'o, his mother. In absentia, Carla had become Chepil's godmother when he was confirmed some years later.

limited Spanish that I was wearing used clothing. "I bought the clothes in Nabenchauk," I answered in Tzotzil. The woman looked surprised. "I bought the clothes in Nabenchauk twenty years ago," I continued. Her reaction turned from surprise to astonishment. "I am your *comadre*," she replied. Clearly my rusty Tzotzil and Spanish had deserted me; I

must have misunderstood. How could I be the godmother of her child, when I did not even know who she was?

But I had indeed understood her words, if not her meaning, correctly. A younger man dressed in European-style clothes appeared with two photographs (the ones he and his mother are holding in fig. 1.1). The photos were old and worn, but clearly

For the family, it was a way of maintaining symbolic ties with someone they perceived as important. And by association with Carla, I had become Loxa's comadre.

The Xulubte' family was clearly in the vanguard of social change. Its members had left the protected valley core of Nabenchauk four years earlier to buy land on the road in order to construct a store. They were meeting and selling to the public for the first time. Yet they were primarily selling textiles woven on the traditional backstrap loom, which dates back to the ancient Mayas. The Xulubte' women and teenage girls wove not only to clothe their family but also for profit. Living next to the store, the whole family was in contact with people from all over Mexico and indeed the world who might happen to stop and buy a soda or a piece of weaving at their store. In addition, Petul Xulubte', Loxa's husband, owned a Volkswagen van, which his son-in-law drove as part of the innovative transport system that had sprung up since our earlier stay, when not a single resident of Nabenchauk owned a vehicle or knew how to drive.

Figure 1.5. Xunka Z'u preparing food. Nabenchauk, 1971. Photo courtesy of Frank Cancian.

RECONNECTING WITH FAMILY

The day before, Carla, Lauren, and I had started out by car from San Cristóbal de las Casas to make our first contact with Nabenchauk after twenty-one years. In 1969 and 1970, Carla, then a Radcliffe undergraduate in anthropology, and I, a young researcher at Harvard's Center for Cognitive Studies, had traveled every day to Nabenchauk from San Cristóbal in a second-class bus, along with chickens and loaded baskets. Because life in Nabenchauk, with its dirt-floored houses and cold nights, was hard for an American child used to modern comforts, Lauren, then three and four, had been only an occasional visitor to Nabenchauk, remaining most days in the colonial city of San Cristóbal with her baby brother, babysitter, and household help. Now, at twenty-five, Lauren had returned as the team photographer, under contract with *National Geographic*.

Lauren was at the wheel of the car, all three of us a bit nervous about navigating the twisting road with its sheer drop-off. Carla and I were trying to memorize the conveying of condolences in Tzotzil, because Xunka' Z'u, the wife of Xun Pavlu, our Zinacantec assistant of two decades earlier, had died at Easter time. Xunka' (fig. 1.5), then the mother of eight and grand-

mother of three, had provided familial warmth and lunches for us during two summers of work. While Carla and I practiced Tzotzil, Lauren drove us literally through the clouds as we climbed in our approach to Nabenchauk (fig. 1.6). We were full of uncertainty about our return, having been out of touch with the community for so long. How much had changed? How would we be remembered? Would photography be accepted? Who would be willing to work with us?

Two decades before, we had walked down the mountain from the highway every day, carrying our equipment. Now there was a road from the highway into the village. We found it and descended a steep lane paved in stones to provide traction when the way became muddy. We reached the church in the middle of the village, then tried to mount the hill to Xun's house by car. Going up a bumpy dirt road, we reached a place where only a foot of dirt separated the car from a drop-off of about twenty feet. Imagining ourselves sliding off the cliff, I strongly suggested turning back and walking up the hill.

We parked at the church and set off again by foot. Children yelled "Alemán!" (*foreigner*, from the Spanish word for German) to each other as we passed and then followed us. We told them we were

looking for Xun Pavlu, and they led us to his house. At first Xun did not recognize us, although we had sent word that we would be coming that morning. A daughter-in-law was patting tortillas, a scene that remained exactly as I remembered it from two decades earlier. Maruch Chentik and her husband, Telex Pavlu, one of Xun's sons, had moved in with Xun after his wife's death; a Zinacantec man cannot live alone, with no woman to pat his tortillas. When we asked Xun how he was, he sadly told us about Xunka'.

Xun was now seventy, still handsome and spry, many of his teeth capped in gold. Like the Xulubte' family, he and his family were in the vanguard of social change. When we left Nabenchauk in 1970, Xun had been a corn farmer. No one in the village owned or drove a motor vehicle. When we returned in 1991, Xun was head of a small transportation dynasty and a large extended family. His late wife had borne him two more children, for a total of ten living children. They had given him thirty-nine more grandchildren; two deaths brought the total to forty-one. He had six great-grandchildren as well. (fig. 1.7).

Three of Xun's children now owned large trucks, and he and one of his sons-in-law each had a Volkswagen van, part of

Figure 1.6. Nabenchauk, 1991. ©Lauren Greenfield/VII.

Figure 1.7. Most of the Pavlu clan. Nabenchauk, 1991. ©Lauren Greenfield/VII.

an innovative community bus service to and from San Cristóbal. In addition, one of his sons—three years old when we had last seen him—was working for the government as the driver of a huge new dump truck, which he proudly drove around the village upon occasion. Indeed, transportation lay at the heart of the entrepreneurial development that had occurred in the last two decades.

We went out to the courtyard and were offered the tiny chairs usually reserved for Zinacantec males. By this time we were surrounded by some twenty women and children. Xun's daughter Katal brushed her hair and put bright new ribbons in her braids as she talked to us. I had a photograph of her as a nine-year-old in Nabenchauk, brushing Lauren's hair (fig. 1.8). Katal and her older sister Loxa remembered us with great pleasure, and we, them. Petul, one of Xun's two unmarried sons, arrived. Born after our departure from Nabenchauk in 1970, he was dressed in rather trendy, European-style attire. He wanted to speak to us in Spanish rather than Tzotzil.

We were there to study how the development of entrepreneurship in the intervening two decades had affected weaving—not only the weaving itself but also the way weaving was taught and

Figure 1.8. Xun's daughter brushing Lauren's hair. Nabenchauk, 1970. Photograph courtesy of Sheldon Greenfield.

learned and the nature of weaving as a representational enterprise. Because entrepreneurship requires and encourages innovation, both in practice and as an ideology, I had predicted that pattern innovation and creativity would be among

the spin-offs of entrepreneurial development.

I was now seeing the first confirmation of my prediction. Twenty years earlier, all clothing, for toddlers up to adults, conformed to a closed stock of about four patterns; two were variants of red-and-white stripes. Now I was seeing the innovation and creativity I had predicted, but the variety and elaboration of the weaving and embroidery exceeded my wildest imagination. I asked which was better, the old or the new. I was told that the new was better because it was redder.

Someone brought out an old *pok mochebal,* the Zinacantec woman's red-and-white striped shawl, and asked me to put it on and stand up. Now surrounded, I did so and turned around to model it, to enthusiastic laughter. The girls examined our clothes carefully. They asked if we still had our old Zinacantec clothes and asked us to wear them when we returned to the village. It was on this return that we met our comadre at the roadside store.

Carla showed the audience a piece of weaving she had done using a Zinacantec backstrap loom, working with her students at Germantown Friends School in Philadelphia. When we carried out our original weaving study twenty-one years earlier, she had said that we wanted to know how the Zinacantecs learned to weave so that she could teach people in our country. She had done so, and here was the proof.

But perhaps on the whole we had not been so responsible about meeting our obligations. Sometime later, Maruch remarked to me that I had returned too late—after the death of Xunka', who had been looking forward to seeing us. Her comment drove home the recognition that in Zinacantec culture, relations with outsiders, exceptional occurrences, were assimilated into permanent family ties. In Western culture, people are more accustomed to ephemeral ties with multiple strangers. I had assimilated my relationship with Xun's family according to that model. Therefore, I had meant more to them than they had to me. At that point, I realized that I was part of the Pavlu family, and I made a commitment to return regularly. After 1991, I returned in 1993, 1995, 1996, 1997, 2002, 2003, and 2004.

STUDYING INNOVATION, LEARNING, AND CREATIVITY

Now, in 1991, we wanted to study the daughters of our prior weaving learners, to see how they were learning to weave in the new, more commercial and entrepreneurial environment. In 1970 we had videotaped fourteen girls at various stages of learning to weave. Through microanalysis of the videotapes, we had concluded that the way in which weaving was transmitted from mother to daughter reinforced adherence to and continuity of basic Zinacantec textile patterns.[4] Our methods and results for that project are described in chapter 2.

We expected weaving apprenticeship to have changed. We thought that weaving learners would have become more independent and experimental in the apprenticeship process, and we planned to test this hypothesis by videotaping the next generation of girls learning to weave. An important part of our planned sample was the daughters of our 1970 weaving learners. Again using video microanalysis, we hoped to study the interaction between learner and teacher and the ways in which it had changed from 1970 to 1991. At the moment of our return, we did not realize that a few descendants of our 1970 weaving learners were still a little too young to have started weaving. Therefore, we came back in 1993 to videotape two daughters of our 1970 weaving learners who by then were judged by their mothers to be old enough to weave. Our video comparison of two generations learning to weave is detailed in chapter 3.

We also expected that any historical movement toward a more experimental learning process would be reflected in innovation in the woven textiles. Our first days back in Nabenchauk confirmed this hypothesis. What we did not expect was that our study of textile change would continue for twelve more years. But with the later help of Ashley Maynard, who conducted fieldwork in 1995, 1997, and 2000, along with my own subsequent field trips in 1993, 1995–97, and 2002–4, I documented accelerating innovation and individuation in woven and embroidered textiles through 2003. Chapter 4 presents these findings.

We thought that innovation in the woven textiles would both reflect and help develop increased cognitive skill in mentally representing novel patterns. To test this hypothesis about cognitive change, we planned to repeat, with the next generation, an experiment on pattern representation we had carried out in 1969 and 1970. Again, an important part of our planned sample was the children of participants in the 1969–70 experiment. Unlike the weaving sample, the participants in this experiment included both boys and girls. Many of the girls were weaving learners who had been videotaped for the study of weaving apprenticeship. I compare the pattern representations of the two generations in chapter 5.

As a result of the 1991 fieldwork, I became curious about the nature of the creative process that was generating innovative textiles and the way in which girls and women saw their own weaving and embroidery. Consequently, during my

1993 stay in Chiapas, I interviewed fifty-six of the fifty-eight weaving learners whom we had videotaped, as well as thirty of their mothers, about the process of creating their best woven and embroidered textiles, which I photographed. I also elicited their worst textiles, to see whether I could discover their own criteria for evaluating their weaving and embroidery. These interviews and photographs became the basis for chapter 6, in which I analyze the nature of collaborative creativity in Zinacantán.

Chapter 2 was conceived almost last. It grew out of the serendipitous discovery of play weaving and toy looms during the 1991 fieldwork season. This discovery led to a longitudinal study of play weaving (continued in 1993 and 1995). It also led to an ethnographic analysis of young girls' preparation for weaving in their everyday lives, before they ever get inside a real loom. The heart of the evidence presented in this chapter is Lauren's beautiful and revealing photographs. I use them to offer an explanation of how weaving on the backstrap loom has been so reliably transmitted from generation to generation since pre-Columbian times.

Also relevant to chapter 2 is Ashley Maynard's field research in 1995, 1997, and 2000. In each of those years, Ashley

stayed with Maruch Chentik and Telex Pavlu, and Maruch served as her assistant, as she had for Lauren four years earlier. In 1995 Maruch's daughter Paxku' taught Ashley to weave. Ashley's experience as a participant observer tested and extended the model of weaving apprenticeship developed through our earlier video studies of weaving apprenticeship. Ashley also served as an apprentice in making tortillas and carrying firewood, the two other major tasks of Zinacantec womanhood. This experience enabled her to find out whether the model of weaving apprenticeship could be generalized to other cultural skills.

In 1997 Ashley returned to the field to ask, How do Zinacantec girls develop skill in teaching as they grow up? The answer to this novel question about the development of teaching also appears in chapter 2. Finally, in 2000, she returned to carry out an experiment in cognitive development that tested my theory about the cognitive processes underlying winding a warp on a toy loom and a warping frame; this experiment is also part of chapter 2.

The coda to the book places changes in models of Zinacantec creativity in a broader perspective. It grew out of the opportunity I had to write this book at the School of American Research, an anthropological institution in Santa Fe, New Mexico. The School and the region afforded me many precious opportunities to meet and talk with Native American artists and to see the incredible native art of the area. I began to see parallels between the changes Zinacantec textiles were undergoing—from a model of community creativity to a model of individual innovation, and from social value to cash value—and processes of historical change in Pueblo Indian and other indigenous arts in the Southwestern United States. The parallels between social changes in Maya textiles and indigenous arts in the U.S. Southwest are the topic of this brief coda.

WORKING IN NABENCHAUK

When we arrived in 1991, we were relieved to find Xun Pavlu ready to help us carry out our studies, much as he had two decades earlier. On our first visit, Carla Childs brought out the family trees of the children who had originally participated in our project. In order to study the next generation, we first had to locate our participants of 1969 and 1970. Such a task would have been virtually impossible in the mobile, urban society to which we have become accustomed in the United States. Nabenchauk was, by contrast, a remarkably stable, in-marrying community,

and Carla had kept good genealogical records. She questioned the Pavlu family about who had married whom, who was still living, and what children they had. The assembled group took great interest in helping Carla update the family trees.

Carla and I were particularly interested in finding the fourteen girls who had learned to weave in front of our video camera, so that we could study how their daughters were learning two decades later. Xun utilized his network of extended family and compadres (partners in godparenthood) to find our 1970 weaving learners. Some of the original sample had died, moved away, not married, still had very young children, or had no girls of an appropriate age. But we ultimately succeeded in finding and studying fourteen daughters of our 1970 weavers, descended from seven of the original fourteen girls. Every weaving descendant of appropriate age and gender living in Nabenchauk elected to participate. Using Carla's family trees, we also looked for and found the descendants of children (also members of Xun's network) who had participated in our pattern representation experiment in 1969–70. They, too, were willing to participate. At the same time, we expanded our samples beyond direct descendants to nephews, nieces, and godchildren of

our original participants.

Despite Xun's desire to work with us and his prestige in the community, we had initial concerns about a potential barrier to our work: traditional beliefs and attitudes about visual images. In 1970, before there were any television sets in Nabenchauk, Carla and I had videotaped fourteen young weavers at various stages in the learning process. After we finished the fourteenth tape, a baby died in the village, and people said we had caused the death with our camera. Xun forbade us to make more tapes. We had been told that to take away an image of someone was to take away a piece of his or her soul. In a society with a high rate of infant mortality, people logically enough considered the souls of babies to be especially fragile.

Now we wanted to videotape the next generation of girls learning to weave. Television had arrived in the meantime (fig. 1.9). How much would its advent have changed people's feelings about being videotaped? I wanted them to feel as comfortable as possible. Two decades earlier, we had coped with the fear of soul loss by giving away Polaroid pictures of each girl at her loom, hoping in this way that our subjects would feel we had returned pieces of their souls to them. When we returned to videotape the next generation, we

Figure 1.9. Boy watching television. Nabenchauk, 1991. ©Lauren Greenfield/VII.

Figure 1.10. Mother with Polaroid photograph of herself in 1970, given to her by our research team. Nabenchauk, 1991. ©Lauren Greenfield/VII.

found that one mother had kept her Polaroid portrait all those years, and she brought it out (fig. 1.10). This technique had reassured people, but only up to a point, as the sudden end of our study in 1970 attested.

Now, Xun's oldest son, Chepil, had his own Betamax videotape player. In addition to making the modest payment customary for participation in psychological studies, I decided, therefore, to return all soul parts in the form of a copy of each videocassette. After we had filmed about forty weavers, however, money seemed to

become more important than soul loss. First the requested payment doubled from 5,000 to 10,000 pesos, plus a charge of 10,000 pesos for a follow-up interview (10,000 pesos equaled US $3.33 at the time). Then the president of Zinacantán accused me of stealing from the people, because, he said, an American had come to Zinacantán Center and offered 50,000 pesos ($16.65) for five minutes of video-tape. I responded that with the cost of the videotape ($12), I was paying more than 50,000 pesos each and offered to pay sub-sequent weavers 50,000 pesos in lieu of a copy of their tape. In all but one case, my offer was accepted. With each cassette, I had thought I was giving back a piece of a soul. I began to wonder.

In fact, this preference for money reflected a number of changes that had taken place in Zinacantec society. First, the need for money had grown. Zinacantecs were using many more items that had to be purchased—everything from eggs, soft drinks, and clothing to insecticides and fertilizer. Second, picture taking had left the realm of the purely spiritual and acquired a political and economic aspect. Politically, restricting picture taking at public events was a way of asserting control in a community that had been exploited by European outsiders since

the Spanish conquest. Economically, Zinacantecs had concluded, perhaps from seeing Indian postcards for sale in San Cristóbal, that photographers sold their pictures and made money at their expense. If so, why should not they, the subjects, also be paid?

Third, the advent of television meant that pictures were not just being taken; they were also being received. A young man from the bilingual (Tzotzil-Spanish) community of Nibok (Ixtapa in Spanish) put it this way: "We don't mind others filming us for television. We watch television and see other people and their lands. We understand that they want to see us." For him, television had created a new two-way relationship with the visual image. It had also expanded his world. This two-way relationship had gone full circle by March 2002, when one of Xun's sons phoned me from San Cristóbal. He proudly told me that he had recently per-formed a cargo (held a ritual office) in Zinacantán Center and wanted to send me the videotape of it.

But some people, especially older ones, had very different attitudes. At one taping session in a peaceful courtyard high on a hillside, an old woman, the weaver's grandmother, who was also Xun Pavlu's older sister, moved around the corner of the house as soon as the camera came out, saying, "I'm going to get out of the way of this photographing." The weaver, her teenage granddaughter Loxa Sanches Peres, asked how many people had been photographed like this. "More than one hundred, more than one hundred," Xun answered hyperbolically. Because he had not moved out of the direct line of the camera, she then asked, "Have you been photographed a lot, too, then?" He answered, "Lots," to which his sister responded, "How will you feel when this puts you in your grave?"

Despite occasional reactions like this woman's, it turned out that the tradition of videotaping weavers was now well established in the older generation. Still photography, however, was quite another matter. We hoped our relationships with the community would make it possible for Lauren to photograph life in Nabenchauk, but the project clearly had to be approached with care and sensitivity.

A new member of our team, sociologist-anthropologist Leslie Haviland Devereaux, had a house in the village, on a plot of land given to Leslie's daughter by her Zinacantec godfather, Petul Vásquez. Leslie, fluent in Tzotzil as well as in the customs of the community, was put in charge of making the arrangements for photography. We decided that she would approach Xun

Pavlu. In addition to being our research assistant and the head of a large extended family, Xun was also the father of Leslie's godson, Manvel. In Mexico, the most important relationship of a godparent is not, as in the United States, that between godparent and godchild; it is the relationship between the biological parents and the godparents, who can be called upon for myriad favors, including loans.

Leslie made an appointment to speak to Xun at his house. Lauren purchased supplies suitable for an important formal request: five Cokes, five Fantas, and a bottle of Bacardi rum. Probably expecting a godmotherly visit, Xun had his son Manvel present. His daughter-in-law Maruch Chentik, who lived with him, was there, too. Following the protocol of a formal Zinacantec request, Leslie first chatted, then told Lauren to put the rum at Xun's feet, followed by the ten soft drinks. When he saw the bottles, a look of astonishment filled his face as he realized the purpose of the visit. The abundance of gifts revealed a weighty request. He started laughing and said, "Ask me quick; I'm getting terrified." Leslie proceeded to explain that Lauren's work was photography and that she wanted to photograph the village extensively to document the Zinacantec way of life. Maruch and Manvel support-

ed the idea. Maruch's understanding of and enthusiasm for the project led Lauren to suggest that Maruch work with her as her guide.

In a formal Zinacantec request, the deal is sealed when the person being asked opens the bottles to drink. Lauren and Leslie breathed a sigh of relief when Xun called for a can opener. Custom obliged everyone present to drink one bottle. Because all the soft drinks had to be drunk, Lauren passed them out to the various children present. Two decades earlier, it would have been necessary for everyone to have drunk *pox,* the rumlike sugarcane liquor made by the Chamulas, a neighboring Tzotzil-speaking Maya group. With the success of the formal request, we thought we had crossed the last major barrier to our projects.

As it turned out, whereas anyone could agree to be photographed at home, taking photographs in public places or at public events required official approval. Although Xun was a powerful elder in the village, things were not always under his control. Through his son Chepil, who was a local church official, Xun succeeded in getting permission from the church officials for Lauren to photograph the fiesta of Santo Domingo. But he had not dared to ask the town officials.

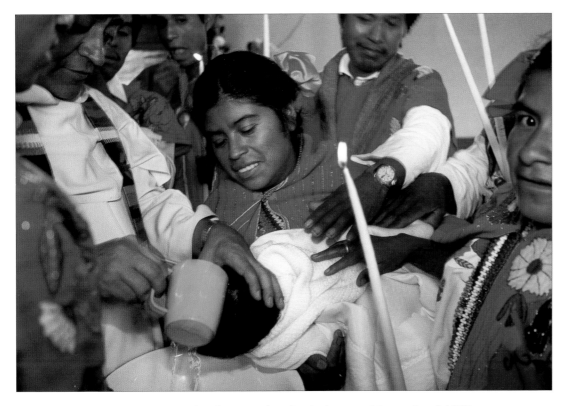

Figure 1.11. Baptism (literally, in Tzotzil, "taking water"). Nabenchauk, 1991. ©Lauren Greenfield/VII.

After the baptism, a parade suddenly appeared outside the church. Children were dressed up as monkeys in costumes and masks; men were dressed up in deer frames with sparklers shooting from them; and clowns cavorted alongside.

While Lauren was photographing the parade, a man motioned to her to stop taking pictures. She pointed to the band, who had asked her to take pictures of them. The man then grabbed and released her camera several times in a menacing way. We later found out that he was the mayor of Nabenchauk. Xun straightened things out. The upshot was that public photography was out, but photographing families and individuals in private situations was permitted.

For Zinacantecs, there is a big difference between private and public spheres. The Zinacantec woman's world is primarily private. The public square, with its fiestas and political gatherings, is predominantly male. Whereas people are sometimes quite relaxed and free in the privacy of their homes and courtyards, in public they are always restrained, careful not to provide fuel for local gossip.[6] Public actions are also subject to review by the local government.

Shortly after the camera incident, Maruch Chentik sent her daughter Paxku' to invite us to join the family for a gather-

Photography went smoothly inside the church, where Maruch had asked Lauren to photograph the baptism of her daughter Xunka', Xun's newest grandchild, and where another baby was also being baptized (fig. 1.11).[5] The Catholic priest, present only because of the holiday, began the mass. He paused in the ritual while the lay religious officials danced to the music of traditional Zinacantec musicians. As Leslie pointed out, "traditional" Zinacantec singing is in fact Renaissance music accompanied by Zinacantec versions of instruments from sixteenth-century Spain. For Zinacantecs, as for peoples everywhere, change has been the rule, not the exception. The novelty of one generation becomes the tradition of the next.

ing after the christening. We followed Paxku' to the godparents' store on the town square. There, Maruch began distributing pox to drink "for Juana Maria," baby Xunka's baptismal name. She poured the pox out of a soda bottle, serving the men first in order of seniority: her father-in-law, Xun Pavlu, who left after drinking his; then Lauren's fiancé, Frank Evers, who impressed Maruch by imbibing the pox in a single swallow, in true Zinacantec style. Without a Zinacantec male in the group, we became, effectively, a ceremonial group of women, unusual in this society. Leslie prompted everyone with the interactive toast, "Kich'ban" (I take it first). The response is "Ich'o" (Take it!). The women were given sodas with which to cut the pox after the first gulp.

"Juana Maria has changed places with her grandmother," said Maruch. Xunka', now four months old, had been born just after her namesake grandmother had died. Maruch broke down in tears, talking about her mother-in-law's death.

The feeling of a group of women together toasting a baby—a feeling of warmth, understanding, and mutual support—was very special. Not being in the habit of drinking, I felt the one glass of pox go to my head, and my Tzotzil rapidly improved.

Xunka's three-year-old sister, Rosy, usually in conflict about growing up, was ecstatically grown-up that day. Still, having recently been displaced as baby of the family, she was happy to have a lap—mine—to sit on. As the summer wore on, I came to feel that for Rosy, I was the one who had changed places with her late grandmother. Rosy became my best friend in Nabenchauk. She reappears throughout this book, particularly in chapter 3. I had developed an understandable familial role in a society where work relationships are first and foremost family relationships.

That day there seemed to be something universal, something easily transcending vast cultural barriers, about women caring for each other's children, celebrating a ritual occasion in honor of bringing a new life into the world, and at the same time mourning the loss of a maternal tie.

SIGNS OF SOCIAL CHANGE

The fiesta of Santo Domingo, although Lauren had to forgo photographing it, not only gave me a new friend but also brought with it an important development in changing roles for women in Nabenchauk. Normally, women are conscious bastions of cultural conservatism in Zinacantán. They avoid speaking Spanish, for example, even if they have learned it at school.

Their voices dominate at rituals of family continuity, such as the Day of the Dead. But at the fiesta of Santo Domingo in 1991, for only the second time, women danced in Nabenchauk.

For weeks, the young girls had been asking Carla, Lauren, and me, "Are you going to dance at the fiesta?" Now it was clear why: they wanted moral support. Up until a few months earlier, only men had danced in Zinacantán, and then only during ceremonies. In Zinacantec custom, men and women have no physical contact with each other in public, even in groups, let alone in couples. To introduce boy-girl dancing was a radical departure in a society in which, through the 1960s, girls over the age of ten had to be accompanied by their mothers, older female relatives, or other girls.[7] Yet this foreign custom had not been imposed from outside; it had been brought in by a decision of the elected local government—men elected by men.

On the first night, five Zinacantec couples actually danced to the Ladino (Mexican) dance band.[8] Virtually all the vanguard were Pavlus, cousin dancing with cousin or young uncle. The girls had been practicing in their houses with their stereos for weeks. They danced confidently, dressed in their shawls and big hair ribbons

Figure 1.12. Poncho made to be worn by an outsider. Nabenchauk, 1991. ©Lauren Greenfield/VII.

Figure 1.13. Poncho (pok k'u'ul) *made to be worn by a Zinacantec. Nabenchauk, 1991. ©Lauren Greenfield/VII.*

with rosettes. Their arms stayed demurely under their shawls, in proper Zinacantec fashion, but their shoulders and hips moved to the music.

The second night of the fiesta, the number who dared to dance multiplied. Xun Pavlu asked Carla to dance first, as an icebreaker. To patch up the incident of the day before, he also got the drunken mayor to dance with Lauren. Soon there were perhaps sixty couples on the dance floor. Little girls and middle-aged couples

danced for the first time. Xun said to Carla, "We are dancing the way you do in your country."

As in dancing, younger women, and particularly teenage girls, turned out to be the leaders of innovation in weaving and embroidery. One teenage girl brought out a blouse she had just made and proudly told us it was the first of its kind. She had woven the material rather than buying machine-made fabric, and she had woven in flower designs rather than embroidering them. Others also started to weave their blouses, harking back to a much more ancient practice.

Studying weaving in Nabenchauk in the 1970s, Leslie Devereaux had found that women were bartering to family members textiles that formerly would have been given as part of unpaid subsistence obligations.[9] By 1991 fewer women knew how to produce the increasingly elaborate textiles necessary for modern Zinacantec clothing, and those textiles took much more time to make. This situation created pressure for more weaving and sewing "to order," that is, for payment. The payment was no longer in corn but in cash. Zinacantecs, poor as they are, now pay each other more money for a fancy blouse to wear to a fiesta than a tourist ever would.[10]

Correspondingly, the creativity and workmanship displayed in the Zinacantecs' own clothing is much greater than that seen in the simpler items made for tourists.[11] Compare, for example, the poncho made for tourists in figure 1.12 with the poncho made to be worn by a Zinacantec in figure 1.13. The former is plain woven in a simple striped pattern with no embroidery and only a simple brocade border. The latter features ornate embroidery above a border of elaborate brocade weaving; the background pattern is a red-and-white stripe. Innovation in textiles, then, is tied not only to external commerce but also (and perhaps more so) to the development of cash value for women's subsistence labor.

Although the weaving and embroidery done for the general public are simpler, the public is also unconstrained by Zinacantec ideas of proper attire and acceptable design. A new item has been created for this market: the *servilleta*, or napkin (seen hanging from the rack in fig. 1.2). It is small and can be woven quickly. Although its appearance is novel, its design "rules" are actually based on those of a traditional ritual cloth (*tovalya* or *mantrex*; refer to fig. 4.21). One woman even called the servilleta a *kox mantrex*, or small ritual cloth.

Although it can have a brocaded border, the servilleta's small size makes it suitable for beginning weavers. We found beginners who had woven and sold a servilleta as their very first piece; commerce beyond the community had become part and parcel of learning to weave. Servilletas, something Zinacantecs themselves would not use, permitted a certain degree of originality, for they could be of any color; the borders could take a variety of geometric designs; and the warp, or vertical, designs could be multicolored stripes. The Vásquez family told Leslie that they enjoyed weaving to sell on the highway, to non-Zinacantecs, because "you could weave whatever came into your head."[12] This assessment suggests a direct link between commerce and innovation—creativity in the Western sense.

Selling thread was part of this web of relations between innovation, entrepreneurship, and a cash economy. Twenty years earlier, women in Nabenchauk had to go to San Cristóbal to purchase their commercially made thread—then cotton—at retail stores. Mainly two colors were used: red and white; the red cost double the white. By the mid-1970s, women had discovered the cones of acrylic yarn—synthetic thread made as a by-product of the petroleum industry—that San Cristóbal knitters were using and began to experiment with them in weaving. Once people in Nabenchauk had trucks, local entrepreneurs began to sell flowers in Mexico City and to bring back goods such as acrylic thread to sell in Nabenchauk. By 1991 acrylic thread, in every color of the rainbow, had become a local business.[13]

Entrepreneurs in Nabenchauk were buying thread wholesale in Mexico City, winding it into smaller lots, and reselling it to women in the village (fig. 1.14). We noticed that girls whose mothers sold thread had a great variety of materials to "play" with and that that they tended to develop new styles and techniques in textile design. The materials were not only accessible but also available at a lower price, leading to greater freedom in their use. According to Leslie, the ethos of not wasting, which had been strong twenty years earlier, was no longer applied to thread because of its new accessibility and Ladino source. Thread was now available as a material with which to play and experiment—all the more so if your mother ran a thread store.[14]

The practice of buying thread wholesale and selling it retail in the village had introduced wage labor for children. Winders, usually orphans or children of single mothers, were paid between 5,000 and 20,000 pesos per day ($1.66 to $6.66). One of the apparently wealthiest families in Nabenchauk was in the thread business. This family had a truck that it used to buy acrylic thread wholesale in Mexico City. It also had the only two-story house in town. The bottom story housed thread-winding machines operated by young employees (fig. 1.15).

It was easy to see how child labor resulted from the transition from a subsistence economy to a cash one. Like children in other subsistence societies, Zinacantec children grew up helping their parents farm, cook, and weave textiles. Once

Figure 1.14. Thread store in Nabenchauk, 1991. ©Lauren Greenfield/VII.

Zinacantecs began to develop businesses, what could be more natural than for children, accustomed to doing what their parents did, also to work for cash? But wage labor for children is very different from subsistence labor: children no longer work alongside their parents but at someone else's house. They are paid by the hour, so the unscheduled nature of subsistence work evaporates.

As a cash economy develops, schooling becomes increasingly important to prepare children for adult work. We noticed that the son of the owner of the thread business in Nabenchauk went to school, whereas the boys who worked for wages did not; they spent their time winding thread. It was as if the modern industrial class system was being born again in front of our eyes —harking back to the era before child labor laws.

The survival of a society depends on its being able to raise a new generation that will have the conditions and skills with which to flourish and re-create themselves. Effective strategies for doing this vary according to the ecology and economy of a particular society. Social scientists have long recognized that in the transition from subsistence to cash, children go from being economic assets to being economic liabilities. It was astonishing to see the

Figure 1.15. Young employees winding thread. Nabenchauk, 1991. ©Lauren Greenfield/VII.

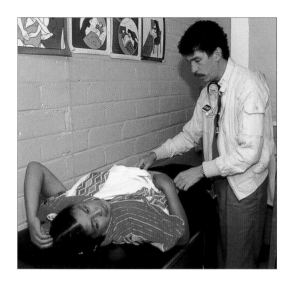

Figure 1.16. Doctor examines patient in the Nabenchauk clinic, 1991. ©Lauren Greenfield/VII.

dawning recognition of this fact among people for whom large families were still the norm. As we visited households to observe weaving, our own reproductive behavior became the object of many questions. For Zinacantecs, with their strong belief in the value of large families, Leslie, Carla, and I were strange because we each had only two or three children. "They work too much and they love money, that's why they don't have a lot of children," Xun once answered. But Zinacantec women did not just want to know why our families were so small; they also wanted to know how. And so the questions turned to our birth control practices.

The issue had more relevance to Nabenchauk than we at first realized. Before we left the village, three members of one family, all in their twenties and thirties, told us of a wish to limit their families in some way. One, a woman, had taken contraceptive injections at the local clinic, run by the Stanford Medical School, in order not to get pregnant again until her youngest child was old enough to help with a new baby. The reasons offered by the other two, both men, were identical: children cost money. The ideas and ideals of family planning had begun to change, reflecting the larger change from a subsistence to a cash economy, as well as the spread of medical facilities. When I returned to visit Nabenchauk in 1995, two young mothers in this extended family had obtained elective sterilizations after their fifth child each. I have never seen two happier women. In 2002 the eldest daughter of one of them, recently married at around age twenty, told me on the telephone that she was waiting to have her first child until she and her husband had more money.

Along with birth control, other types of medical care had become increasingly available in recent years (fig. 1.16). One young man, stabbed during a political quarrel, had had his life saved by surgery.

His youngest sibling, out of ten, was the first to be born in a hospital. But the medical doctor has not replaced the Zinacantec curer. In Nabenchauk, Western medicine exists side by side with Zinacantec curing ceremonies, referred to as "taking candles" (fig. 1.17). People kill chickens, light hundreds of candles, and stay up all night to heal a sick person—but when it is all over, they might also take the patient to a medical clinic to see if there is any medicine that will help as well. For Zinacantecs, Western medicine is simply a recent addition to their armamentarium of healing.

ZINCANTECS IN A GLOBAL WORLD

Other signs of social change involved interactions beyond the limits of Mexico. When we arrived in 1991, we heard about two cousins from Nabenchauk who had gone to Oregon to pick fruit. One cousin had mysteriously died the night after his arrival; the other came back with a camper truck, a color television, and a videotape recorder. Other young men in the village seemed to remember the latter's success rather than the former's tragedy. From our first day back in the village, young men wanted to talk to us about how to get to the United States. It was hard to persuade men used to camping out in rented corn-

Figure 1.17. Curing ceremony ("taking candles"). Nabenchauk, 1991. ©Lauren Greenfield/VII.

fields that it is much more expensive to live in the United States and that four or five dollars an hour would not go as far as it did in Mexico.

But Zinacantecs no longer had to travel to see the world. Television had brought the world to Nabenchauk. More than 45 percent of the children in our studies had a TV in the home. Manvel, Xun's next-to-youngest son, turned out to be an avid television viewer. He watched film and music videos, including some in English. At one point he asked me to translate phrases such as "I love you" that he heard frequently in movies from the United States. Shortly after our arrival, his father, Xun, expressed a desire for a videocassette recorder. "Why?" we asked. "To watch war and people killing each other," he said. Perhaps the appeal of televised violence is in fact universal. *Lucha libre* (free fight), an extremely brutal form of freestyle TV wrestling with masks and fighting in the audience, was a favorite for men and boys in Nabenchauk.

Television had indeed taken hold. It had even created a postmodern recycling of images: the favorite TV wrestler was called Octagon; Manvel had a basketball team named Octagon; his father's Volkswagen van was called Octagon; boys wore Octagon masks and drew pictures of

wrestlers in the dirt.[15] They pretended to be lucha libre wrestlers as they banged each others' heads against the ground. The anthropologist Evon Vogt, in his book *Zinacantán,* commented on the replication of traditional cultural elements such as the older brother–younger brother relationship throughout the Zinacantec worldview in the 1960s. Now we were seeing the replication of a television image that unified newer domains of activity.

Whereas the Pavlu men and boys watched wrestling and war movies, Leslie Haviland Devereaux's predominantly female family, the Vásquezes, watched Mexican soap operas, or *telenovelas.* Watching with them, Leslie found them fascinated by this behind-the-scenes look at the feared Ladino society, presented in a form comprehensible even to people who understood little of the Spanish in which it was broadcast. Watching a telenovela with another family in 1993, I found that the young women, who understood only a little Spanish, grasped everything about the characters' relationships with each other—who was married to whom, who was cheating on whom. In the United States, it is said that there are more televisions than toilets. This is definitely the case in Nabenchauk, where, as of 2004, the first flush toilet had yet to be built.

By 2002 globalization had reached textile commerce. A friend in the village discovered a beach near Cancún, the Yucatán resort city, full of Americans to whom his wife and daughter could sell their handmade textiles. He and his daughter wanted to talk with me about financing this enterprise next time I came to Chiapas. I was sure that a formal request would be forthcoming.

Could the Zinacantecs incorporate cash, entrepreneurship, and innovation into their lifestyle while maintaining a distinctive Maya identity and way of life? Zinacantecs seem to have a special talent for guarding their cultural integrity, one from which other minority groups, both indigenous and nonindigenous, could learn important lessons. The Mexican government's policy of allowing local self-government and treating indigenous peoples as communities rather than as individuals has undoubtedly served as a necessary precondition for cultural integrity. Zinacantecs' wariness about the presence and activities of strangers must also contribute to their cultural continuity. But just as they had done for years, Zinacantecs in the 1990s were skillfully selecting elements from outside their society to enhance, rather than diminish, their distinctive cultural tradition.

Even the development of a transportation industry involved incorporating material goods from outside Zinacantec culture into traditions that were centuries old. Well before the twentieth century, Zinacantecs provided transport and commerce for the highlands of Chiapas. "The Zinacantecos were popularly known as independent muleteers and petty traders in the region," Leslie Haviland Devereaux wrote. "They ran strings of up to 20 mules, carrying agricultural goods to the towns and manufactured goods to the villages, food and money and gunpowder to the contending armies of the revolution, and even mail. Some residents of Nabenchauk today [the 1970s] remember carrying on this activity well into the 1930s."[16] By the early 1980s in Nabenchauk, mules had simply become trucks and vans. The Zinacantecs were using new materials to support an old tradition.

Leslie sensitized me to the ways in which the new means of transport and communication had changed the world of space and time for the Zinacantecs: When the Vásquez grandparents first married, they had to get up at one in the morning to walk to San Cristóbal, a seven-hour walk. They would have only an hour in town before walking back. Fear of being captured into forced labor or encountering bandits on the road made them determined to return before dark.[17] In 1991 Xun's son Manvel made the half-hour trip to San Cristóbal several times a day, charging passengers the equivalent of sixty cents for a one-way trip in his father's van.

Two decades earlier, Mexico City was a foreign country that few Zinacantecs had ever visited. With their own trucks, they now took the eighteen-hour trip nonstop, bought and sold flowers at the market, and returned to Nabenchauk in the space of two days. Xun had bought a truck and made this trip weekly for five years. Mexico City had become part of the Zinacantec world. Indeed, Xun now spoke of Los Angeles, my home, as "near." The referent of "far" had become Australia, Leslie Haviland Devereaux's home.

Communications technologies, as well as transportation, were involved in this psychological shrinking of space. By 1991 one telephone had come to Nabenchauk. That year, Xun spoke on the phone for the first time from my house in San Cristóbal. He spoke to Carla, who by that time was back home in Philadelphia. After he hung up, his comment was, "Wonderfully near."

Eleven years later, as I was finishing the last revisions of this book, I received a phone call from the home of one of Xun's sons. He had the first private telephone in Nabenchauk and used it as a tool in his business, to communicate with the people from whom he bought and to whom he sold in distant places. Communication and commerce, the motor of the historical changes I went to study in 1991, remained tightly linked as they developed hand in hand. Some months later, in July 2003, Ashley Maynard, during a research stay in Chiapas, received an e-mail message in Tzotzil from one of Xun Pavlu's nephews. The Zinacantec world had now reached into cyberspace, but at the same time, the written language was Tzotzil rather than the Spanish learned at school.

Already in 1991 the effects of transportation on Zinacantecs' sense of space were clear. Xun preferred to drive to a neighboring house, rather than walk. The stereotype of the Los Angeleno's abhorrence for walking even short distances was beginning to apply to the modern Zinacantecs. One day when Lauren was at the wheel of our car, Xun asked whether Carla and I knew how to drive. Women do not drive in Zinacantán, and older men like Xun never learned. To have the young men of Nabenchauk possess skills unknown to their elders was a mark of change in a society where the elders had

Figure 1.18. The author's blouse. Photograph by Don Cole.

together with their baby in Nabenchauk.

Yet despite the expansion of the Zinacantec universe, Nabenchauk was still very much its center. One man told me that if in the future, more education became available and Zinacantecs began to practice professions outside of Nabenchauk, they would still keep houses in the village. "Why?" I asked. "Because there they were born, there they were created, and it has been so by custom, from long ago."

As I talked to my acquaintances in Nabenchauk, I came to understand that they did not see change as a threat to Zinacantec culture and society. There could be change, so long as there was always a distinctive Zinacantec way. Carla and I saw this attitude expressed in terms of textiles during our 1991 stay, when machine-embroidered blouses made by Guatemalans were first offered for sale in Zinacantán.[18] Women had started to put a value on their labor, so these blouses were of interest to women in Nabenchauk because their own fancy, hand-embroidered blouses took so much time to make (mine, shown in fig. 1.18, took a busy mother of five more than two months to complete). Some people even admired the look of the machine-embroidered Guatemalan blouses, especially their colors and the perfection of the embroidered flowers (fig. 1.19).

traditionally been the teachers.

Xun's son Manvel seemed a portent of other social changes to come. Whereas his eight older brothers and sisters had married and raised their families in Nabenchauk, Manvel was courting a young Ladina woman in Cintalapa, a Ladino city that twenty years earlier had lain beyond the perimeters of the Zinacantec world. Xun's oldest son, Chepil, sold flowers at the Cintalapa market every week; working with him, Manvel had met his Ladina girlfriend. By 1997 Manvel had married Ruby, and they were living

The Guatemalan blouses interested me because they were the first commercial products I had seen that were explicitly tailored to the requirements of Zinacantec culture. The Guatemalans were conforming to the distinctive Zinacantec custom of embroidering a design down the left and right side of the blouse's front. Compare the Guatemalan blouse in figure 1.19 with both the old (see fig. 1.3) and new blouses (see figs. 1.4 and 1.18) made in Zinacantán. For the first time, Zinacantecs were being catered to as a commercial market.

Indeed, the blouses had been designed through an interesting dialectical process of market research. On the first blouses brought to Nabenchauk for sale, the makers had carefully copied the location and configuration of the embroidered flowers on a conventional Zinacantec blouse (fig. 1.19). Some Nabenchauk women said they liked the blouses but wanted broader bands of flowers. A few weeks later, blouses made to such specifications (fig. 1.20 is an example) were brought to the village. Later, I saw embroidered birds, which were also popular in locally made, hand-embroidered blouses, appear on Guatemalan blouses for sale to Zinacantecs.

My first, romanticized reaction to the Guatemalan blouse was that machine-

Figure 1.19. Blouse made by Guatemalans for the Zinacantec market. Nabenchauk, 1991. Photograph by Don Cole.

made embroidery undermined the essence of Zinacantec womanhood. This was not necessarily the Zinacantec view. Clothing identified a Zinacantec in the urban mar-

ketplace of San Cristóbal just as well in the 1990s as it had in the 1960s and 1970s. Of the future of Zinacantec clothes, one Zinacantec woman said,

Figure 1.20. Close-up of blouse made by Guatemalans for the Zinacantec market. ©Lauren Greenfield/VII.

"Who knows what women will be wearing twenty years from now? But you can be sure it will be distinctively ours." Her underlying philosophy ensures that the Zinacantecs will endure as a distinct Maya people with their own way of life. "It is good that each land is different," she said. "It would be bad if each land were the same."

Figure 2.0. Baby Xunka Pavlu watches her older sister Paxku' embroider a poncho. Nabenchauk, 1991. ©Lauren Greenfield/VII.

Foundations of Cultural Continuity

Features of child development and transmission of knowledge in Zinacantán have enabled the backstrap loom to last for thousands of years. ❖

For more than four thousand years, indigenous people of Mesoamerica and the Andes have created textiles on the backstrap loom (fig. 2.1). Girls and women in Nabenchauk, like their counterparts across the region, still use backstrap looms today (fig. 2.2). Although the Zinacantecs' economy, ritual life, and weaving have shifted cyclically, the backstrap loom, along with other aspects of household culture, seems to have remained a constant throughout their history.[1]

How has this weaving tradition been maintained over the centuries? The answer lies in the ways in which weaving is taught and transformed from one generation to the next, and it revolves around child socialization and child development. The answer also highlights the rather underappreciated role of women, particularly mothers, in cultural transmission.

Figure 2.1. Ceramic statue of a woman at backstrap loom, Jaina, Campeche, 700–900 C.E., 16.5 cm. high. Courtesy of the Instituto Nacional de Antropología e Historia, Mexico City.

Figure 2.2. Zinacantec girl at a backstrap loom. Nabenchauk, 1991. ©Lauren Greenfield/VII.

THE BEGINNING

The tradition of weaving on the backstrap loom has been securely maintained over the centuries in Zinacantán because a Zinacantec girl's body and mind are prepared for weaving from birth. When a

baby girl is born in Zinacantán, family members immediately place cooking and grinding utensils, weaving tools, and flowers in her newborn grasp to reinforce her future feminine role. This early introduction to weaving is itself mirrored early in

Mesoamerican history. In 800 C.E., the same ceremony was performed for the newborn Sac-Nichim (White Flower) in highland Chiapas. Seven centuries later, Fray Toribio de Motolonía, in a book completed in 1540, told of a similar Indian practice in New Spain, although the precise region of which he wrote is unclear.[2]

Zinacantec babies are born with distinctive patterns of movement and visual attention, which are then co-opted for weaving apprenticeship. The pediatrician T. Berry Brazelton, with his colleagues John Robey and George Collier, found that in comparison with Euro-American babies born in the United States, Zinacantec infants displayed an overall lower level of motor activity and a higher level of visual attention from birth. Their characteristic of resting the arms close to the upper body was especially striking in comparison with Euro-American babies, who displayed more expansive arm movements.[3]

This Zinacantec body style provides an innate foundation for the use of the body in backstrap loom weaving.[4] I use the term *innate* in its literal sense of "born with." There is no way to establish the relative roles of genetic factors and prenatal environment in these behaviors; most likely, both sets of factors are important. The point is that the behaviors appear at birth

Figure 2.3. A woman kneels to weave as a little girl looks on. Nabenchauk, 1991. ©Lauren Greenfield/VII.

and are stable over time. This stability depends on a match between the baby's temperament and the social environment, so that people reinforce newborn behavior.[5]

Low motor activity in Zinacantec newborns is indeed reinforced by the culture in which they mature. For instance, infants' movements are restricted by swaddling, or

wrapping the baby in cloth. Newborns are encouraged to nurse at the slightest sign of motor activity, a practice that further lessens infant movement. Girls observe their mothers and other women exhibiting restricted motor movements; women do not move their arms far from their bodies. According to cultural norms, this is the way they are supposed to move. The *is* of

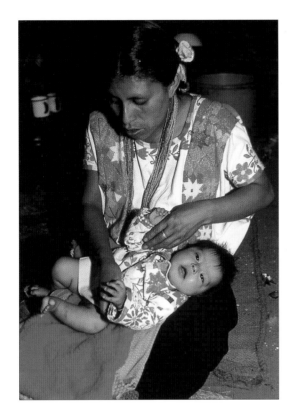

Figure 2.4. Maruch Chentik kneels to change and dress her baby, Xunka. Nabenchauk, 1991. ©Lauren Greenfield/VII.

newborn temperament has become the *ought* of culture. Even when girls dance— a recent phenomenon—I have observed that their arms remain close to their upper bodies. Culture takes the easy path; it moves with biology, not against it. In weaving, this low level of motor activity, and especially upper-body stillness, is cen-

tral to providing a solid anchor for one end of the backstrap loom. The confluence of organism and culture-specific environment creates a "local biology."[6]

As Zinacantec infants mature and become children, they learn other motor behaviors proper for their culture. Girls grow up watching their mothers and other older females use a kneeling position in weaving (fig. 2.3) and many other daily tasks. For example, women and older girls kneel to change babies on their lap (fig. 2.4), to prepare and cook tortillas, and to wash clothes. Putting a tortilla on a grill (fig. 2.5) and washing clothes (fig. 2.6) use the same basic motion and body position as lifting up the heddle of a loom (fig. 2.7). Girls learn to maintain this position, essential for backstrap loom weaving, through traditional cultural practices as they themselves make small weavings (fig. 2.8), kneel to put wood on the fire (fig. 2.9), or help shear sheep (fig. 2.10).[7]

As the paleontological record shows, kneeling at a young age shapes bone development so that the capacity to kneel is maintained into adulthood. There is a "sensitive period" in development during which experience is critical to maintaining the ability to kneel for long periods of time. Such experience is culturally shaped; indeed, cultures define certain stages of

motor development. One example is squatting. Although infants universally assume this position, squatting is considered a developmental stage only in cultures that elaborate this position in adulthood. Similarly, I would expect kneeling to be considered a stage for female children in Zinacantán, although it is not considered a developmental milestone in European-based cultures.[8]

Balance is another quality important for the daily activities that Zinacantec girls and women perform, including weaving. Girls and women frequently must carry heavy loads of firewood hanging from their heads on tumplines (fig. 2.11). Good balance is crucial for carrying such cumbersome loads, often for long distances. Practice in carrying wood, beginning with a single piece of firewood around age five, can help girls develop the balance required for weaving.[9]

Thus, innate capabilities, both universal (such as kneeling) and culture specific (such as upper-body stillness), are strengthened by cultural values and practices. When girls are introduced to weaving, these practiced motor habits surface and place Zinacantecs at an advantage. Like people learning their mother tongue, they are "native learners." The native learner needs less instruction in

Figure 2.5. Two teenage girls and a young woman kneel to cook tortillas on a grill. Nabenchauk, 1991. ©Lauren Greenfield/VII.

Figure 2.6. A woman and a teenage girl kneel to wash clothes. Nabenchauk, 1991. ©Lauren Greenfield/VII.

Figure 2.7. Kneeling at her loom, Paxku' Pavlu, daughter of Maruch Chentik and Telex Pavlu, lifts up the heddle (which raises every other warp thread) with her left hand. This action creates a space to insert a weft thread (pink), using a bobbin (lying on the ground). Nabenchauk, 1991. ©Lauren Greenfield/VII.

Figure 2.8. Octaviana, age five, daughter of Chepil Xulubte' and Loxa K'o, kneels in a backstrap loom. Nabenchauk, 1991. ©Lauren Greenfield/VII.

body technique and has less trouble weaving because of her ability to kneel for long periods of time, her gentle and controlled motor activity, and her balance.

Native learners of Zinacantec weaving also differ from non-native learners in their ability to use their relatively long visual attention span to learn through observation. Opportunities to observe adult activities are plentiful in the daily lives of Zinacantec children from an early age. In figure 2.0, for example, baby Xunka' Pavlu watches her older sister Paxku' embroider a poncho. Learning by observation is an

Figure 2.9. A young girl puts wood on the fire from a kneeling position. Nabenchauk, 1991. ©Lauren Greenfield/VII.

Figure 2.10. The girl on the right kneels to help shear a sheep. Nabenchauk, 1991. ©Lauren Greenfield/VII.

important component of Zinacantec weaving apprenticeship (fig. 2.12).

The relatively long visual attention spans present in Zinacantec newborns are manifested by first-time weavers. In our 1970 study of weaving apprenticeship, we videotaped two girls weaving for the very first time. Microanalysis of the video records showed that these girls spent 53 percent of their time observing their teacher weave, rather than working on the weaving themselves.[10]

Among our 1991 weaving learners was a seven-year-old weaving on an adult-sized loom for the first time (see fig. 2.45). She showed a visual attention span and level of concentration hard to imagine in an American child of the same age. Through-out the hour of our weaving video, her attention never wavered from the task at hand. Persistence and a lengthy attention span are important qualities for weaving. A large weaving, such as a shawl, could take several weeks to complete, and indi-vidual weaving sessions often range from fifteen minutes to one or two hours.

Non-native weavers may have more trouble using observation to learn. In the United States, we often consider "learning by doing" to be most effective and employ trial-and-error methods of learning.[11] A dramatic example of the trouble someone

Figure 2.11. Carrying wood. Nabenchauk, 1991. ©Lauren Greenfield/VII.

from another culture might have using observation as a mode of learning comes from U.S. college student Marta Turok's description of learning to weave in Zinacantán. She had been watching weaving for two months, something her teacher called learning and she herself called observation. She wrote: "Many times she [the teacher] would verbally call my attention to an obscure technical point, or when she would finish a certain step she would say, 'You have seen me do it. Now you have learned.' I wanted to shout back, 'No, I haven't! Because I have not tried it myself.' However, it was she who decided when I was ready to touch the loom, and my initial clumsiness brought about comments such as, 'Cabeza de pollo [chicken head]! You have not watched me! You have not learned!'"[12]

Figure 2.12. Maruch Chentik's niece (left) watches Maruch wind warp threads on a warping frame (komen), *to be transferred later to a backstrap loom. Her daughter Paxku', occupied with her baby sister, Xunka, is also in position to watch the warping when the baby does not need her attention. Nabenchauk, 1991. ©Lauren Greenfield/VII.*

PLAY WEAVING

Although the anthropologist Francesca Cancian, a former member of the Harvard Chiapas Project and currently at the University of California, Irvine, had commented in her 1963 dissertation on "make-believe" weaving on toy looms in Zinacantán,[13] I discovered the toy loom only in 1991, and then quite by accident.

With our assistant, Xun Pavlu, Lauren and I were paying an unplanned visit to the family of one of his sons, Xun. There in the courtyard, Xun's granddaughter Rosy Pavlu, age five, was working on a toy loom (fig. 2.13). So long as I was doing a formal study of weaving, play weaving *(tahimol holobil)* had remained hidden from me. Most likely, Zinacantecs did not

consider it worthy of display. My belated discovery of play weaving revealed one reason why our 1970 weaving learners, even the first-time weavers, seemed so expert: they had had prior experience with play weaving and the toy loom.

At first, Rosy's warp seemed a tangled mess, unweavable. But a closer look (fig. 2.14) showed that the warp had been wound in the figure-eight configuration necessary for "real" weaving to take place. Although it was taking place on a toy loom, the weaving was actually not make-believe at all.

We discovered that play weaving was an almost universal phenomenon in Nabenchauk. It was part of the learning experience of girls growing up in the 1990s, just as it had been part of their mothers' experience. In our 1993 interviews, we showed a play weaving (fig. 2.15) and asked both girls and their mothers whether they had ever done anything like this. The mothers often put their hands over their mouths and giggled—seeming to say, "How did you find out about this?" Nearly all of them, it turned out, had done play weaving when they were little: 86 percent of the mothers and 98 percent of the girls.[14]

Although the rate of play weaving for mothers was high, the increase between

Figure 2.14. Close-up of Rosa Sanchez Perez's warp on her toy loom. Nabenchauk, 1991. ©Lauren Greenfield/VII.

Figure 2.13. Rosa Sanchez Perez, age five, weaving on her toy loom. Nabenchauk, 1991. Tragically, Rosa died in 1994. ©Lauren Greenfield/VII.

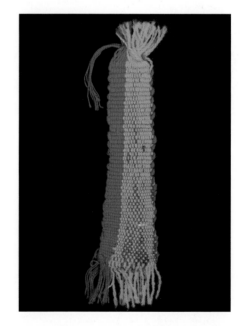

Figure 2.15. Play weaving done by Paxku' Pavlu for the author's 1993 interviews on play weaving. The weaving is 1 inch wide and 5 1/2 inches long. Photograph by Don Cole.

the earlier and the later generation is probably also meaningful. One mother said that they did not have play weaving before, but now girls learn that way. Another mother said that she did not do play weaving because she spent her time watching sheep. That job has virtually disappeared with the diminution of the herds that has gone hand in hand with human population growth and the radical shrinkage of grazing land.

Play embroidery was also familiar to everyone—sometimes in the form of tiny, doll-sized embroidered blouses and sometimes as practice designs on used, worn-out weaving. All of the girls we interviewed and 91 percent of the mothers had done play embroidery. In one family I

Figure 2.16. A "make-believe" play weaving, Nachig, Zinacantán, 1971. This photo by Frank Cancian appeared in his book Another Place: Photographs of a Maya Community. *Reproduced courtesy of Frank Cancian.*

was able to validate my notion that learning had become more independent. The mother volunteered that she had learned to do play embroidery by watching her mother. Her daughter, in contrast, did not watch her mother but learned on her own.

How had we missed this first stage of learning to weave in 1970? Perhaps it was because we had asked to see girls learning to weave. For Zinacantecs, play weaving was probably considered play rather than weaving. By analogy, if researchers wanted to study how girls learn to cook in the United States, they would probably be shown girls helping their mothers make a real meal, not making mud pies or Playdough cookies.

In 1971 Frank Cancian photographed a Zinacantec girl making a play weaving (fig. 2.16). By the time of our 1991–93 study of weaving apprenticeship, she would have been about the same age as the mothers we interviewed. Like the play weavings Francesca Cancian had observed earlier, the one in this photograph was "make-believe." The "warp" lacks the figure-eight structure (fig. 2.14) that would have enabled the weaver to place a weft thread over and under alternate threads. In cases like this, a girl incorrectly wraps an unweavable set of threads around the endsticks, drawing on general impressions she

Figure 2.17. Menencia Xulubte', age seven, daughter of Petul Xulubte', tries to help her niece Rosy make a heddle out of a piece of red thread. Rosy participates by holding the stick that will be used to attach the thread. Nabenchauk, 1991. ©Lauren Greenfield/VII.

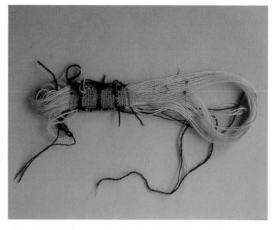

Figure 2.18. Play weaving by Rosy Xulubte', age three, daughter of Chepil Xulubte' and Katal Aliax. This is the product of the process shown in the photo to the left. Nabenchauk, 1991. This weaving is the smallest in the author's collection. ©Lauren Greenfield/VII.

has gained from observational learning.

At the other extreme, a girl might receive careful instruction about how to weave the threads. The youngest subject in our video database, Rosy Xulubte', age three, daughter of Katal Aliax and Chepil Xulubte', was given her first experience in play weaving on a toy loom for our camera in 1991 (fig. 2.17). The warp on the toy loom on which Rosy was learning was about 1 inch wide, and the final weaving about 6 inches long (fig. 2.18)—a small piece of cloth suitable for such a young beginner lacking strength and weight.

This task simplification was complemented by help Rosy received on parts of

the weaving process that she herself was unable to accomplish. One of these parts was making the heddle. The heddle, made from a string looped around a stick (shown in fig. 2.20), picks up every other warp thread, enabling the weaver to place the cross-threads (the weft) over and under the individual warp threads. At first, Rosy's young aunt, Menencia Xulubte', age seven, tried to help her make the heddle out of a piece of red thread (fig. 2.17). Rosy participated in this cooperative enterprise by holding the stick to which the heddle thread would be attached.

Menencia herself, however, was just

Figure 2.20. Markarita lifts up every other white warp thread and winds the red string around warp thread and stick to make a heddle for Rosy. The heddle allows the weaver to raise every other thread, creating a space, or shed, through which she will pass a horizontal weft thread. The triangular space can be seen in the photo. Nabenchauk, 1991. ©Lauren Greenfield/VII.

Figure 2.19. Aunt Markarita (left), age ten, Menencia's next oldest sister, steps in to make a heddle for Rosy. Menencia (center top) stays involved, and their younger sister, Octaviana, age five (right), is also part of the scene. Nabenchauk, 1991. ©Lauren Greenfield/VII.

learning to weave and did not know how to construct a heddle either. When she was unable to complete the task, Rosy's next older aunt, Markarita, age ten, stepped in to help (fig. 2.19). Menencia stayed involved, probably learning both how to make a heddle and how to teach. Even the youngest aunt, Octaviana, age five, was part of the scene, although she was not watching at the moment Lauren took the photograph (see fig. 2.19).

We know from Ashley Maynard's brilliant dissertation that learning how to teach is an important developmental process in Zinacantán—probably equal in importance (although not in awareness) to learning how to weave.[15] The energy spent in learning how to teach, systematically documented by Maynard and seen in this example, is another key to the sureness with which backstrap loom weaving has been transmitted across the generations.

Markarita, during her turn at making a heddle for Rosy, carefully lifted up every other white warp thread and wound the red string around the warp thread and a stick (fig. 2.20). She successfully completed the heddle, and Rosy was ready to weave. In this way, Markarita provided a scaffold of help for Rosy, carrying out parts of the task that Rosy herself was not yet able to do.

This example reveals four keys to the successful transmission of weaving: beginning with a tiny weaving, well adapted to the body size and skill of the learner; involving slightly older members of the extended family; dividing the teaching labor according to skill level; and giving girls practice not only in weaving but also in teaching.

Play weaving also constitutes a native learner's first opportunity to practice directly the body techniques needed for weaving. Rosy, at only three, demonstrated her knowledge of body technique with many of her movements.[16] Her kneeling position, of course, was well practiced. As for movements more specific to weaving, Rosy had seen some of these before, observing other girls and women in her family while they were weaving. For example, on her next day of weaving, when she was working on a different piece on a real loom (fig. 2.21), she demonstrated her knowledge of body techniques by keeping the backstrap low on her back and usually leaning back into it at appropriate times (figs. 2.21 and 2.22). Rosy also tried unsuccessfully to pull back on the threads

Figure 2.21. Three-year-old Rosy Xulubte' beats down a warp thread while leaning into the backstrap of her real loom. Nabenchauk, 1991. ©Lauren Greenfield/VII.

to create a space for the bobbin (a wad of weft thread)—again, an action she must have observed many times. A photograph of her shows that she is now holding the beater in the appropriate position and leaning back into her backstrap. But she did not yet possess the dexterity to pass the bobbin through its space, so her mother stepped in to insert the bobbin (fig. 2.22). In addition, the undivided attention Rosy shows in the photographs was typical of her first two weaving sessions, as was her body position, with arms close to her sides. Both characteristics

Figure 2.22. Rosy Xulubte' leans back into the backstrap as her mother passes the bobbin through the shed. Nabenchauk, 1991. ©Lauren Greenfield/VII.

reflect developmental continuity with the visual attention and body position typical of Zinacantec newborns.

Sometimes even younger girls begin to practice using their bodies in play weaving. When Paxku' Pavlu temporarily left a small loom she had set up to make a play weaving in 1993, her youngest sister,

Xunka', only two years, four months old, came over and got inside it. Xunka' knew to pull the backstrap up over her bottom (although she pulled her skirt up at the same time, to laughter from older girls watching). She demonstrated not only some basic knowledge of what to do with her body but also her motivation to

weave: she got angry when her older sister returned to the loom and wanted to weave the warp herself.

Rosy Xulubte' gave me the opportunity to follow the development of her play weaving over a period of four years. In 1993, two years after she began her play weaving career in front of our camera, I interviewed Rosy and her mother about her weavings. The interview was part of a study about the process of creation and the criteria Zinacantecs use to judge their weavings and embroideries. In addition to conducting interviews, I photographed what weaving learners and experienced weavers considered their best and worst woven and embroidered pieces. Rosy was then five years old. She and her mother showed me the only weaving Rosy had done since our video study; it was a little mess (fig. 2.23, top). Clearly, trial-and-error learning had shown its head away from the camera's gaze. After that, Rosy herself became interested in showing me her weaving progress—probably because I always purchased her play weavings—and she set up a better warp for me (fig. 2.23, bottom). When I returned in 1995, Rosy's mother asked me to come and look at the play weavings that Rosy had done for me in the intervening two years (fig. 2.24). Rosy was now seven, and in line with her greater size and strength, these pieces were much larger than her first play weaving at age three. And for the first time, she had tried out embroidery on these pieces.

Play weavings come in a variety of forms. Sometimes they are miniatures of real woven clothing. Lupa 235 (the number assigned to her family in our study) sold me, for ten pesos ($3.33), a miniature poncho she had woven and embroidered years before (fig. 2.25).[17] In 1993 Lupa was about twenty-one, already a young mother. A play weaving by Maruch 231 (fig. 2.26, left) is fully woven, but the weft lines are far from straight. This tiny play weaving contrasts greatly with Maruch's first real weaving, a striped bag (fig. 2.26, right). Although it is small for a real weaving, the bag not only is much larger than the play weaving but, unlike the latter, is utilitarian and has a complex design created in winding the warp.

In the social sciences, a common interpretation of play is that it constitutes practice for adult skills. Play weaving is no exception to this generalization. More recently, Lynn Fairbanks has given a neural interpretation to play; her theory is that a play activity takes place just as the relevant brain regions are maturing, and play stimulates the neural activity that will make the adult activity possible.[18]

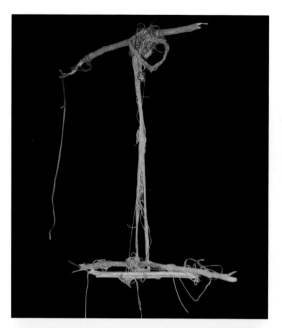

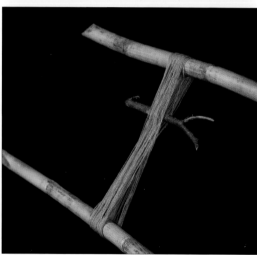

Figure 2.23. Top: *Play weaving done between ages three and five by Rosy Xulubte'.* Bottom: *Warp set up for the author by Rosy Xulubte', age five. Top photograph by Patricia Greenfield, bottom photograph by Don Cole.*

Figure 2.24. Two play weavings with embroidery done by Rosy Xulubte' between ages five and seven. The top bag is a weaving 5 3/4 inches wide and 11 inches long, then folded in half. The bottom, a miniature servilleta, is 14 inches long and 8 3/4 inches wide. Photographs by Don Cole.

Figure 2.25. Play weaving with embroidery: a miniature poncho by Lupa 235. The poncho is 4 by 4 inches; unfolded, the weaving is 8 inches long. Photograph by Don Cole.

Figure 2.26. Play weaving (left) and first real weaving (right) by Maruch 231. Photograph by Don Cole.

THE TOY LOOM

If we define play weaving in terms of its miniature size, then it is the case that much (but not all) play weaving is done on a toy loom. The toy loom is much easier to set up than the real loom. But interestingly, its ease of use is not so much physical as conceptual. Most remarkably of all, the toy loom seems to embody an implicit cultural understanding of cognitive development.

But although much has been written about the adaptive functions of play, far less has been said about the adaptive functions of toys, the technology of play. This brings us to the toy loom.

The small but important difference between the toy loom and the real loom lies in the ropes that run between the two end-sticks, one rope on either side (fig. 2.27). A real loom (fig. 2.28) does not have such ropes. By holding together the two end-sticks, these ropes permit the warp threads (the white threads in figure 2.27) to be wound directly on the loom. A photograph of a young weaver kneeling in her toy loom (fig. 2.29) shows how the end-sticks that constitute the loom are connected by (in this case) a loop of ribbon that goes around the weaver's back to the post. The tension necessary to keep the loom from collapsing is provided by the weaver, who leans back against the backstrap. On a real loom, only warp threads hold the two end-sticks together. These threads cannot be wound directly

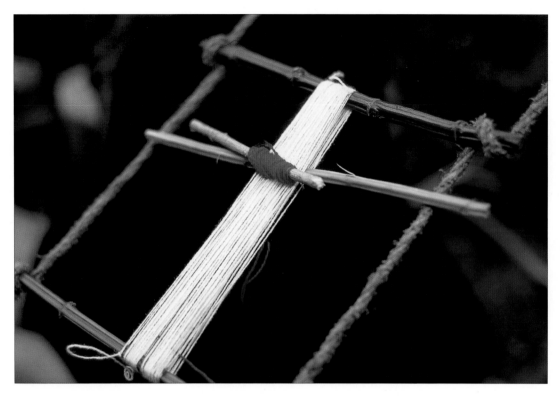

Figure 2.27. A toy backstrap loom. The side ropes hold the two frame sticks together while the warp (white threads) is being wound. Nabenchauk, 1991. ©Lauren Greenfield/VII.

Figure 2.28. A real Zinacantec backstrap loom. Note the absence of side ropes; the warp (multicolored threads) holds the loom together. The warp cannot be wound directly onto the loom, however, because the loom does not exist as connected sticks before the warp is wound. Nabenchauk, 1991. ©Lauren Greenfield/VII.

on the loom, because without the warp threads, the loom would collapse—it has nothing to hold the end-sticks together before the winding of the warp threads begins. In one of our videotapes, a relatively inexperienced weaver, Markarita Xulubte', age ten, tries to wind a warp directly on a real loom for her younger sister Menencia. Finally she gives up and uses the loom to weave a warp that

has been prewound.

Indeed, a real loom must have the warp prewound on a separate apparatus, a *komen,* or warping frame (fig. 2.30). My thesis is that winding the warp on a komen requires thinking at the level of concrete operations, a stage described by the Swiss developmental psychologist Jean Piaget. Piaget saw the essence of concrete operational thinking as the ability to

transform images in one's mind. For example, one sees a glass full of water and is able to imagine the water being poured out and the glass now empty. Because threads on a warping frame look so different from the way they will look on a loom, the weaver must mentally transform

Figure 2.29. Rosy, age seven, daughter of Maruch Chentik and Telex Pavlu, in her toy loom. Nabenchauk, 1995. Photograph by Patricia Greenfield.

Figure 2.30. Nine-year-old Paxku' Pavlu winds a warp on a komen, or warping frame, while holding her younger sister, Xunka, the baby of the family. (Xunka was the Pavlu baby who was baptized in chapter 1.) Nabenchauk, 1991. ©Lauren Greenfield/VII.

them to imagine how they should be arranged on the loom.

Let me illustrate this point with two photographs (figs. 2.31 and 2.32). The first shows a weaver winding white thread on a komen (lower right) as the thread comes off a spooling device (lower left). The threads are wound in a **U** shape on the komen, with the open ends of the **U** looped around the wooden rod at the left side of the komen. Threads forming the closed end of the **U** go around the right side of the komen, although the closed end of the **U** is not visible in the photograph. But this is not how the threads will look on the loom. The **U** shape will be

straightened out, as it is in figure 2.32. The threads on one side of the rod (see fig. 2.31) will end up at one end of the loom—either top or bottom (see fig. 2.32)—and the threads on the other side of the rod will end up at the other end. In order to understand what she is doing, the weaver must be able mentally to connect the image of threads on a warping frame

with the image of threads on a loom. To do so, she must be able to understand how to transform the configuration of threads on the warping frame into the configuration of threads on the loom. This is where mental transformation, the hallmark of Piaget's stage of concrete operations, comes into play. (The transformation is the "operation" in "concrete operations.")

Figure 2.31. Maruch Chentik, Rosy and Paxku's mother, is winding her white warp on a komen. Note a rod at the left of the frame holding the looped threads in place. The threads on the left side of this rod will be attached to one end of the loom, and the threads on the right side will go to the other end. Nabenchauk, 1991. ©Lauren Greenfield/VII.

Figure 2.32. This loom, set up with a white warp wound on a komen, shows the configuration of threads after they have been straightened out and transferred to a loom. ©Lauren Greenfield/VII.

In contrast, this sort of mental transformation is not necessary to set up a play loom. Because of the extra supporting ropes on the sides, the weaver can wind the warp directly on the loom. A sequence of two photographs illustrates this process. In figure 2.33, a young girl has just started winding a warp directly on her toy loom, which is already set up. The top and bottom end-sticks (bottom end-stick in photo) are held in place by white string that connects the sticks; one of the two side strings is shown clearly at the top of figs. 2.33 and 2.34. In figure 2.34, the girl continues winding the warp between the end-sticks in what will be its final position. She does not need to mentally imagine a transformation in order to connect the winding process to the completed setup on the loom. In Piaget's theory of development, a younger child, in the preoperational stage, can manage this more direct sort of thinking. (In Piagetian theory, preoperations are what the child can do before operations, that is, before mental transformations.)

The important conclusion from this analysis is that Zinacantecs' implicit theory of development corresponds to Piagetian

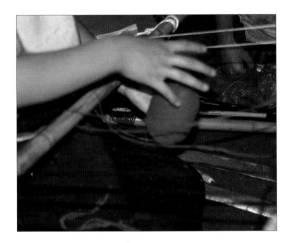

Figure 2.33. A young girl has begun winding the warp of her toy loom. Nabenchauk, 1995. Photograph by Patricia Greenfield.

Figure 2.34. The girl continues winding the warp. Nabenchauk, 1995. Photograph by Patricia Greenfield.

theory. Whereas Zinacantec girls start on the toy loom from about age three, they generally do not set up a real loom before age seven, the stage of concrete operations as described by Piaget. What is most interesting is that a developmental theory is implicitly (but not explicitly) built into the progression of Zinacantec weaving tools. This implicit theory describes the child's abilities at each stage, and tools are then matched to those abilities. The progression of tools reveals an implicit cultural theory of instruction as well as an implicit theory of development. The tools show us specific cultural expressions of universal stages of development while simultaneous-

ly showing us the Zinacantecs' implicit conceptions of these stages. They reveal that a theory of cognitive development and a developmental theory of instruction are built into the culture.

When Ashley Maynard, at the time a twenty-three-year-old graduate student at UCLA, learned to weave, our friend Paxku' Pavlu, then thirteen, displayed this same pedagogical theory of weaving apprenticeship. She started Ashley on a toy loom, then moved her to a play weaving on a real loom. Finally, she let her wind the warp for a small bag on a warping frame, with considerable help. Sequencing—learning one process before

attempting another—became verbally explicit in a conversation between the two. Ashley asked Paxku' why they were winding on the warping frame when previously they had wound the warp on the loom. Paxku' replied, "You know well already," referring to Ashley's experience in using the toy loom. Apparently this sequence was based on cognitive development rather than manual dexterity. Ashley later noted in her master's thesis that although winding on the toy loom was cognitively simpler than winding on the warping frame, it was manually more complex.[19]

If this pedagogical theory corresponds to actual cognitive development, then young girls who show competence in winding a warp on a toy loom should make errors when winding a warp on the warping frame, or komen. I had the opportunity to watch seven-year-old Rosy Xulubte' wind a warp on both a toy loom and a komen. She successfully wound on the toy loom but got confused and made errors on the komen, even with help from her mother. The Zinacantecs' implicit theory of cognitive development, Piaget's explicit theory, and my developmental theory of the tools were all supported by the differences in Rosy's performances in winding a warp on a toy loom and on a komen.

In 2000 Ashley and I carried out a

study to confirm this sequence of cognitive development in an experimentally rigorous way and to test its universality.[20] Ashley gave children in Nabenchauk and Los Angeles a series of tasks in which they had to figure out how different warps, on either a toy loom or a warping frame, would turn out after they were woven. Examples of these tasks are shown in figures 2.35, 2.36, and 2.37. In the case of the toy loom, the correct piece of cloth matches the color (fig. 2.35)or the length and configuration of stripes (fig. 2.36) of the warp. In contrast, to understand how a warp wound on a warping frame will turn out (see fig. 2.37), one must mentally unfold the warp to figure out the correct answer— the cloth that is approximately twice as long as the folded lengths on the frame.

As predicted from our theory, the youngest children in the study, age four, understood in many instances how a warp on a toy loom would turn out once woven. However, they generally failed to understand how a warp wound on a warping frame would turn out. Even more interesting were their errors. They generally made the choice that one would expect if they were simply matching the size of the frame to the size of the cloth—that is, using the preoperational strategy of visual matching instead of the concrete opera-

Figure 2.35. Ashley Maynard prepares the experiment in Nabenchauk, 2000. Which piece of cloth can be produced from the warp on the loom? Solving this problem requires simple color matching. Photograph © by Keith Dannemiller.

tional strategy of visual transformation. By age six, the beginning of Piaget's concrete operational period, a few children were able to make the correct choice when

looking at the warping frame. By age ten, the overwhelming majority could do it. Although children in the United States, unfamiliar with backstrap loom weaving,

Figure 2.37. Which piece of cloth can be produced from the warp on the frame? The correct answer is the second piece from the right. Its length is what the warp on the frame will be when unfolded from its U shape. Photograph by Ashley Maynard.

lagged in this task, they showed the same sequence of development, upholding Piaget's conclusion that the cognitive stages in question are universal. The most interesting conclusion for my purpose here is that the Zinacantecs' theory of weaving apprenticeship, normally implicit, reflects and is sensitive to actual cognitive development in weaving learners.

This analysis notwithstanding, cognitive development is not necessarily important to Zinacantecs in the way it is to North Americans or Europeans. Whereas it is possible to imagine a mother in the United States taking her daughter to a weaving class if she thought it would

Figure 2.36. Which piece of cloth can be produced from the warp on the loom? The warp rests on a white cloth in front of the child. In Los Angeles, four-year-old Darby Anne Tarlow is tested on this item. The correct answer is the second piece of cloth from the loom—the piece that is the closest match in pattern and size. Photograph by Patricia Greenfield.

advance the child's cognitive development, this is not the case in Zinacantán. Later, when I discuss the Maya theory of knowledge, it will become clear that cognitive development is not the type of knowledge valued in Zinacantán. At most, cognitive development would be seen as a means to enable a socially useful skill to be performed.

LEARNING TO WEAVE ON THE REAL LOOM
The Next Developmental Stage

Although people in the United States or Europe would not think of weaving as a stage of development, the Zinacantec theory of child development very much defines development in terms of work. Each stage is characterized by what work a child is able to do.[21] According to Leslie Haviland Devereaux's informal conversations in Nabenchauk, the Zinacantec theory is that parents can and should influence children's learning to work. Further, Leslie was told that a girl will start to weave when she has enough "soul" or "spirit" (ch'ulel). Leslie's friends in Nabenchauk told her that spirit was necessary because weaving is so hard: frustrating, taxing, time-consuming, and intellectually demanding. With the spirit, Leslie was told, a girl will weave of her own volition. If parents ask a girl to weave before she is

developmentally ready, in the sense of having ch'ulel, she will "mess up."

When does spirit typically arrive? Under exceptional circumstances, a first "real" weaving on a "real" loom could take place when a girl is as young as five years. More typically, girls start weaving on an adult loom at age eight or nine.[22] The average age has not changed since 1970. By mid-adolescence, Zinacantec girls are usually skilled weavers.

We cannot understand the Zinacantec theory of development, what it means to be a skilled weaver, or, indeed, the longevity and cultural stability of Maya weaving without first understanding the Maya theory of knowledge. Research by the anthropologist Isabel Zambrano in Mitontik, another Tzotzil-speaking Maya community in highland Chiapas, provides a key.[23] The Tzotzil word na' can be glossed as "know" in English. But as Zambrano points out, the kind of knowledge central to the word na' differs from that indexed by the English word "know." Na' includes knowledge of the soul or heart; "know" refers to knowledge of the mind. The central meaning of na' is knowledge of practice that is both habitual and characteristic of a given person. In contrast, the English "know" refers centrally to factual knowledge (as in "I know the population

of Mexico City"), to theoretical understanding ("I know this concept"), to the solution of novel problems ("I know the answer"), and to skills ("I know how to add" or "I know how to ski"). Habit and character are not implied.

Of all of these connotations of "know," probably the last meaning—knowledge as skills—is closest to the central connotation of na'. Even so, the two words are not an exact match, because the habitual aspect of na' is missing from "know." When someone says, "I know how to add" or "I know how to ski," the person is not saying "I add habitually" or "I ski all the time." At the edges of "know" and na' there is overlap of meaning: na' includes, for example, thinking, calculating, and remembering.[24] Yet the central concepts differ. To say "I know how to weave" in Tzotzil is to assert far more than skill development; it is to say that I am in the habit of weaving, and weaving is a part of my identity, of who I am. It is knowledge of the heart, not just of the mind.

The Zinacantec method of weaving apprenticeship, in its broadest sense, follows from this emphasis on knowledge of the heart and habitual practice. Zinacantecs believe that a girl's socialization as a weaver should start at birth and be constantly reinforced by everyday activities and motives, long before weaving itself begins. It also follows that, in being habitual, characteristic, and part of the heart or soul, weaving knowledge allows the weaver to overcome frustration and distraction while meeting weaving's intellectual demands. Finally, it follows from this definition of knowledge that learning to weave cannot be imposed from outside. Instead, knowing how to weave must be part of a girl's definition of herself.

Studying the Learning Process

In 1970 Carla Childs and I conducted a video study of fourteen Zinacantec girls at various stages of learning to weave.[25] Videotaping is a wonderful method for combining naturalistic observation with rigorous analysis or, in our case, microanalysis. Our equipment was the first Sony portable, black-and-white, reel-to-reel videotape recorder, with an external microphone set up under the loom. This was the first video field study of cultural apprenticeship that had ever been done. By recording behavior in its natural context, videotaping can elucidate questions of adaptation to the natural environment, and we tried to keep the environment as natural as possible.

There is always concern about how "natural" a naturalistic videotape is. We felt this concern especially keenly because of the Zinacantecs' ambivalence toward visual images. It was reassuring, therefore, that Petu' Cruz de la Cruz, a Zinacantec living in San Cristóbal de las Casas whom I hired to help transcribe tapes, believed our video scenes were very natural and that neither we nor the camera had affected the weaving apprenticeship. When I asked Petu' about the tapes in which large numbers of people were present, she replied that that was what happened whenever people came to visit.

Weaving videotapes were made, by appointment, in each family's courtyard, or occasionally in the house, if it rained. Our assistant, Xun Pavlu, accompanied us to virtually every taping session and introduced us to the families. Families were told that we wanted to see girls learning to weave. Most arrangements were made with the mother. Afterward, we showed the participants parts of their tapes and took a Polaroid photograph of each girl, which we gave her as a gift. Weaving learners were also paid for their participation. We repeated this general procedure for the next generation of weaving learners when we studied them in 1991 and 1993.

For the quantitative analyses that I summarize in this book, we analyzed two techniques: the way the learner attached the warp threads to one of the loom's two end-sticks and the way she inserted the first two weft, or horizontal, threads into the warp, or vertical, threads. These were two of the more difficult parts of the process, in which teaching or help was most likely to be observed. During the videotaping, both we and the participants spoke in Tzotzil. In 1970 Carla talked with all of the learners and mothers, while I handled the video recording. In 1991 we repeated this division of labor for most of our participants. When Carla was no longer available, I was assisted by Leslie Devereaux, who talked to the participants, and by Lauren Greenfield and Hannah Carlson, who made the videos. In the last two cases, I talked with the participants.

Carla Childs extensively coded the videotapes. That is, she measured how much time was spent in each of several well-defined categories of activities or interactions; we then used these time measures as variables in our quantitative analyses. Our categories all related to weaving apprenticeship—to various techniques of learning and teaching that had emerged from our video observations, such as learners' observation of the teacher weaving, collaborative weaving between learner and teacher (fig. 2.38), and verbal instruction by the teacher. The term *teacher* here does not refer to a formal role, but rather to the person who informally guides or helps the learner. Carla's knowledge of backstrap loom weaving, Tzotzil, and the Zinacantec families contributed to the validity of her coding.[26] In addition to the videotapes, we had several sources of fairly elaborate demographic data: interviews by our research team conducted in both 1970 and 1991–93 and a Stanford Medical School survey of the community done in the summer of 1991.

We used the coded video records to describe and quantify apprenticeship processes in 1970 and in the 1990s. We used the demographic data to identify the nature of sociocultural change over two decades and how much it had affected the participants and their families. We also used the video records to carry out qualitative analyses of the use of the body in weaving, the subject to which I turn next.

Figure 2.38. The mother of three-year-old Rosy Xulubte' gives Rosy collaborative help by lifting up the heddle so that Rosy has a shed, or space, in which to place her beater stick. Nabenchauk, 1991. ©Lauren Greenfield/VII.

Use of the Body in Learning to Weave

An important feature of the habitual aspect of learning to weave in Zinacantán is the tremendous amount of practice girls receive over many years in the relevant body positions.[27] Unlike their American counterparts—for example, adult students in a backstrap loom class I observed in Cambridge, Massachusetts—Zinacantec

girls need very little instruction in body techniques when learning to weave. Following the Zinacantec definition of knowledge, these techniques are already habitual and characteristic of the learners. Nonetheless, we observed a developmental progression in the teaching and learning of body techniques, with younger girls needing more instruction than older girls.

Our videotape analysis indicated that by the age of six or seven, first-time weavers on a real loom needed little instruction, if any, in body techniques.

Octaviana Xulubte', age five in 1991, was our second-youngest first-time weaver on a real loom. Her weaving (fig. 2.39) was a bit larger than her three-year-old niece Rosy's (fig. 2.18). Octaviana was given quite a bit of body instruction. Like her niece, Octaviana was told to lean back several times. She was also shown how to hold the beater correctly. She demonstrated her awareness of body techniques, however, when, after waiting patiently in a sitting position while her sister set up the loom, she moved into a kneeling position on her own initiative as soon as it was time for the weaving to begin. She then maintained the position for nearly an hour.

Unlike her younger niece Rosy, Octaviana demonstrated her knowledge of body technique when she rose up and leaned forward or backward at appropriate times during her first weaving lesson. She also took the initiative to adjust her back-strap downward, so that it would lie on the correct part of her back (fig. 2.40). It was hard for us to imagine an American five-year-old behaving this way, in terms of either body techniques or technical knowledge.

As Zinacantec girls mature, they may no longer need any instruction in body techniques. Loxa 203, age seven, was seen on video expertly demonstrating her knowledge of body techniques—for example, leaning back into the backstrap as she wove. Although she had some difficulty with the more complex part of the weaving process—simultaneously leaning, lifting

the heddle, and rotating the beater and spacer—it was only because her hands were too small to grasp the two sticks and hold them parallel. She had no difficulty coordinating the three activities. Her mother, who sat near her during the entire hour-long weaving session, did not once tell Loxa to lean back, sit down, or rise up. Loxa was able to modulate all the body techniques in her very first weaving session. Her mother also proudly told us that Loxa herself had wound the warp on a komen.

Another young learner in our sample, Menencia Xulubte', age seven in 1991, though not as proficient as Loxa in the movement of her body for the complex part of the weaving process, was able to lean back steadily and keep the loom taut during an hour-long weaving session. But the need for instruction is variable among the young weaving learners. Unlike Loxa, Menencia required instruction to lift the heddle in order to create a shed, the opening through which to pass the beater and the bobbin. Markarita Xulubte', the instructing sister, whispered an imperative to Menencia (trucks were rumbling by, so her words cannot be heard on the video-tape) and then demonstrated how to lift herself up on her knees. Menencia complied. Later, however, Menencia stayed

down, and Markarita ignored her, yanking her forward a bit with the belt in order to create the shed herself.

Maruch 228, an eight-year-old weaver working on her first piece of cloth, also got some body instruction. Again, her error was a matter of degree. Her actions were perfectly coordinated, but her lean-ing forward was insufficient to create a space for the beater to enter. In another example, the mother of Loxa 204, a nine-year-old weaver working on her second piece of cloth, twice gently placed her hand on her daughter's back when she needed to lean farther forward to make a shed. But this Loxa had already initiated the gracefully combined leaning of the body, lifting of the heddle, and rotating of the beater and spacer.

Even the youngest learners, then, demonstrated a degree of knowledge of the body techniques important for weav-ing. This knowledge increased with age. Because of their innate characteristics of motor stillness and long visual attention span, reinforced by culturally mandated experiences, such as practice in kneeling, balance, and movement, Zinacantec girls were at an advantage for weaving. For all but the very youngest girls, weaving instruc-tion focused primarily on the manual and cognitive skills required, rather than on body techniques. Only occasionally were Zinacantec learners older than five given instruction in basic body techniques. Skill in using the body as part of the weaving frame was, for the most part, a given. It was the foundation upon which manual and cognitive skill could be based.

A non-native learner, on the other hand, must be explicitly instructed about what to do with her body while weaving and may have difficulty with motor requirements such as balance, kneeling, coordination, and keeping movement restricted. Ashley Maynard and I, as non-native learners of weaving in Nabenchauk, received quite different instruction from that given to the Maya learners we video-taped. Our teachers placed much more emphasis, both verbal and nonverbal, on body techniques than was necessary for their much younger Zinacantec learners.

Ashley, a first-time weaver at twenty-three, was instructed in weaving during two months of fieldwork in Nabenchauk in 1995. She encountered problems because she was unable to kneel for long periods of time. Kneeling was very painful for her, and she resorted to sitting cross-legged, much to the derision of the Zinacantec teachers and other women who observed her. Often, while she was weaving, a girl or woman would enter the

Figure 2.39. Octaviana Xulubte's weaving, still on the loom. The weaving is 10 inches long and 1 7/8 inches wide. Photograph by Don Cole.

*Figure 2.40. Octaviana Xulubte', age five, adjusting her backstrap as an older helper steadies the loom. Nabenchauk, 1991.
©Lauren Greenfield/VII.*

had more trouble leaning forward and backward with the proper tension and at the proper times during weaving, and we required extensive instruction in these body techniques. Unlike the native learners, Ashley had to be told many times to "Lean back!" or "Come closer!" Often the teacher, a thirteen-year-old girl, physically manipulated Ashley's body by pushing her forward or backward, a teaching technique seen only occasionally with native learners. Even after extensive weaving instruction, Ashley required assistance in lifting the heddle for long and wide pieces of cloth. She lacked the coordination required to do this by herself and would need more practice to be able to weave a large piece of cloth, such as a shawl, alone.

I became a first-time weaver in 1970, at the age of thirty. In a videotaped learning session, I, too, required repeated assistance. I was told to lean back many times, and during the most difficult part of the weaving—lifting the heddle—I, like Ashley, was told what to do with my body to make the process easier.

Indeed, my status as a non-native learner was demonstrated most clearly when I attempted to lift the heddle. My body position was awkward, bent far forward over the loom (fig. 2.41). This was something we did not see in even the

house or courtyard and say, "Kneel! It's better, easier!" She could only reply that it hurt, causing much laughter among those present. Because of her sitting position, she had difficulty lifting the heddle stick, which, as we have seen, demands a complex body technique (see fig. 2.7). It is much easier to lift the heddle while on one's knees. Ashley's changing from her sitting position to rise up on her knees

often caused the sticks to fall out of the loom. Even taking great care to maintain the sticks' position in the loom, she found it difficult and time-consuming to shift from sitting to kneeling within the backstrap. In using the sitting position, Ashley departed dramatically from Zinacantec body techniques, cultural techniques that she had not mastered.

As non-native learners, Ashley and I

youngest native learners. Compare my body position with that of the nine-year-old Zinacantec weaver who is lifting the heddle in figure 2.7. She has risen quite straight up on her knees. Native learners' unconscious attention to the body technique of maintaining enough tension on the loom to keep it in balance prevents them from ever leaning so far forward. This unconscious attention to body position had been lacking in the adult backstrap weaving class I had observed in Cambridge, Massachusetts, as well.

Although I made no actual weaving error, my body "accent" was quite foreign. It shows up again in figure 2.42, where I lean far to my right to see inside the space I have created for the beater. Just as a skilled user of a language relies on many cues for complete understanding of meaning and nuance, a skilled weaver can rely on many different cues to tell her whether the space has been correctly made. I, however, could rely only on direct visual observation, and so I leaned out to the side, jeopardizing the tension and balance of the loom. A skilled Zinacantec weaver's understanding of the weaving process would prevent her from moving in such a way. A beginning Zinacantec weaver might also have to look into the space, but she would not bend as far forward as I do in figure 2.42.

Figure 2.41. The author lifts the heddle. Note the nearly horizontal body position, very different from that of Zinacantec weavers (compare fig. 2.7). Nabenchauk, 1970. Video frame by Carla Childs.

Figure 2.42. The author leans over to look inside the shed she has just created. Nabenchauk, 1970. Video frame by Carla Childs.

To what extent does the native use of body techniques depend on starting to weave at a young age? To what extent does it depend on the innate foundation and general cultural reinforcement I described earlier? In other words, are there "sensitive" periods—developmental windows—in which people are neurologically primed to learn weaving more easily, as is the case for language learning? Or are innate temperament and experience the keys? In order to examine this question, we analyzed the videotapes of our three oldest first-time Zinacantec weavers. Most girls in Nabenchauk begin learning to weave by the age of eight or nine. Three girls in our sample, however, did not learn to weave until they were teenagers, when they had their first weaving session in front of our camera.

The oldest late learner, Paxku' 221, was fifteen in 1991. Unlike her mother, whom we had videotaped learning to weave in 1970, Paxku' had not learned to weave as a young girl because she was a wageworker, a new phenomenon in Nabenchauk. She wound thread for wages because her mother was a widow, without a husband to support the family. The other two older first-time weavers were Loxa 222 and Katal 230, each thirteen at the time of her first independent weaving project. Loxa had not woven previously because she, too, was working in a thread business, winding and selling. She indicated that she would learn to weave when she quit working for wages. Katal had not woven before because she had a mild learning disability. Instead, she had wound thread on spools for the family shop.

These three weavers were therefore natural subjects for an experiment—albeit an imperfect one—on the role of age in native learning of body techniques. Would their body movements, positions, and balance look more like Ashley's and mine because these girls were learning later than others in Nabenchauk? Or would their body techniques look more like those of young Zinacantec girls who learned to weave earlier in their development?

The answer was the latter. In many respects, all three girls were indistinguishable from the young native learners. They displayed restrained movement and "native" body positions. They were all good at movements that were reinforced in other culturally valued skills, such as making tortillas and carrying wood. That is, they were good at kneeling, leaning forward, and balancing.

Two of these later learners demonstrated skill at balancing the loom. Loxa held the loom taut and level with one hand

while retying her backstrap with the other. When she needed to reach across her loom to pick up a new stick, she did so without leaning forward and losing tension on the loom. Paxku' also had to reach across her loom to receive a new beater that a boy brought to her. She reached only as far as she could while maintaining the balance of the loom and then held her hand gracefully poised over her head, demanding that the boy bring the stick closer.

This comparison shows that being born into and growing up in Zinacantec culture provides certain basic body skills fundamental to weaving on a backstrap loom: restrained movement, the ability to kneel comfortably for long periods, and the ability to maintain one's balance while leaning easily forward or backward. Earlier experience with play weaving and opportunities to observe skilled weavers might also have enhanced the weaving-specific body skills of the first-time learners. These earlier experiences, especially play weaving, might have occurred during a sensitive period when they could stimulate the neural development required for the later acquisition of weaving skills—at whatever age that acquisition took place.[28]

Alternatively, because this was not a perfect experiment, there could exist a

decrement in body skills correlated with beginning to weave after age fifteen, the age of our oldest Zinacantec first-time weaver, despite play weaving and other priming experiences. A comparison of an adult Zinacantec learner would reveal the presence or absence of such an age-related decrement.

WEAVING APPRENTICESHIP
Developmental Sensitivity and Systematic Teaching

Upon this foundation of body techniques is built the manual and cognitive knowledge necessary to weave. Contrary to the conventional wisdom in anthropology, which holds that learning and teaching are fairly casual and unsystematic in nonindustrial societies, our 1970 video study revealed a highly systematic form of weaving apprenticeship in Nabenchauk, one very much in line with the Maya theory of knowledge. I believe our findings differed from received wisdom in anthropology because we carried out the first video microanalysis of naturally occurring apprenticeship and because we took a developmental approach, sampling girls who were at different stages of learning to weave.[29]

As we have seen, little girls had ample opportunity to watch weaving before they themselves began to do "real" weaving. In 1970, an average of one girl under six (usually too young to do real weaving) was present near each weaver as we made our fourteen videotapes. When we videotaped first-time learners in 1970, more than half of each weaving session was spent not in weaving but in observing the informal teacher (usually the mother) working on the loom. During the two most difficult parts of the process that we videotaped—attaching the warp threads to an end-stick and placing the first two weft threads across the warp—beginners spent 53 percent of the time observing rather than weaving (fig. 2.43).[30]

But there is another side to observation. In order for the learner to observe the teacher weaving, the teacher must take over the loom from the learner. So while the teacher is providing a model for the learner to observe, she is also helping the learner accomplish a part of the weaving process that may be too difficult for her.

Most importantly for our understanding of the apprenticeship process, weaving teachers showed sensitivity to the learner's developmental level. To the extent that learners had more weaving experience, teachers removed themselves from the weaving process. Consequently, learners with more prior weaving experience—

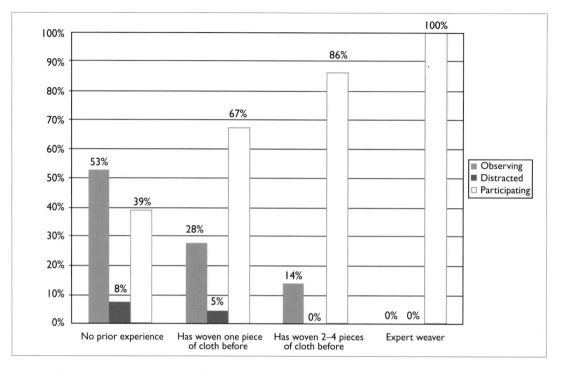

Figure 2.43. Percentage of time learners at different stages of weaving experience in 1970 spent observing the teacher, distracted from weaving, or participating in the weaving. The percentages are based on time spent during two tasks: attaching the warp threads to an end-stick and placing the first two weft threads across the warp. (Childs and Greenfield, 1980)

measured in number of items woven before our video session—watched less and participated more in the weaving process (fig. 2.43). This sensitivity to the learner's skill level is an important component of systematic teaching or apprenticeship.

The data in figure 2.43 make another interesting point. Note how attentive the learners were to the teachers' models. Even the first-time weavers were distracted from the teacher's model only 8 percent of the time. By the time a girl had woven two to four prior items, she was attentive to the teacher's model 100 percent of the time. We see developmental continuity from early newborn attentiveness to attentiveness to the teacher's model as girls begin to do real weaving.

The theory of informal education includes a concept called "scaffolding" that is important here.[31] In construction, a scaffold is a tool used to enable a worker to reach heights that would not otherwise be possible. When it is not needed, the scaffold is withdrawn. In informal education, a teacher can provide a scaffold of help and then gradually withdraw it as it is no longer needed. We can think of the teacher as taking over the weaving at hard parts and serving as both a model and a scaffold for the beginning learner. Teachers' gradual withdrawal from their scaffolding role is also seen in figure 2.43, as learners participate more and more with increasing experience.[32]

Our 1970 weaving teachers actually had several ways of helping learners. On the nonverbal level, they could either take over the weaving, providing help and a model for the learner, or they could help her by working cooperatively with her on a particular task. Taking over does not allow the learner to participate, but working collaboratively does: the teacher simply helps the learner. We saw this kind of help again in 1991. For example, the mother of Rosy Xulubte' inserted the bobbin (fig. 2.22) and lifted the heddle (fig. 2.38) for Rosy when she wove for the first time on a real loom, but Rosy still did her part, for example sticking in the beater (fig. 2.38).

If teachers are sensitive to the learner's level of developmental skill, they should take over the weaving more often with less skilled weavers but work collaboratively more often with relatively skilled learners. That was exactly what happened in 1970. For the entirely inexperienced learners, teacher intervention was cooperative 36 percent of the time. For those who had woven one piece of cloth before, the proportion was 47 percent, and for those who had previously woven two to four items, the proportion was 76 percent. Correlatively teachers took over less often as learners gained increasing weaving skill.

This sensitivity to level of developmental skill came out in a related finding as well. We expected that if teachers possessed such sensitivity, then learners would spend more time weaving independently—without any help—as they became more experienced. This, too, was the case. During the two hardest parts of the weaving process that we taped, attaching the warp threads to the end-stick and inserting the first two weft threads, first-time weavers worked on their own only 7 percent of the time. In contrast, girls who had completed one previous weaving worked independently on these tasks 52 percent of the time, and the percentage went up slightly, to 58 percent, for girls who had woven two to four prior articles. The most expert weaver

wove independently 100 percent of the time. To the extent that learners were more skilled, as reflected by their prior weaving experience, teachers backed off, letting the learners become increasingly independent in their weaving. Systematic scaffolding had occurred: the scaffold of help was used most intensively where it was needed most—by the beginners—and was gradually withdrawn as learners gained weaving experience.

Another way in which teachers could guide the apprenticeship process was through verbal communication. Although the conventional wisdom in anthropology holds that cultural learning is nonverbal,[33] we found that verbal guidance was very important in weaving apprenticeship in Nabenchauk. It, too, was geared to the learner's skill level, as well as to the difficulty of a particular component of the weaving. Most verbal communications were requests in the imperative mode—"Lean back," or "Don't put it in like that." As the learner's skill improved or she moved to a less difficult part of the process, commands became fewer and the rate of statements (for example, "It's finished") greatly increased. Questions ("Where is the bobbin?" "Like this?") also increased slightly, whereas explanations remained rare.[34]

One of our most interesting findings about communication during weaving apprenticeship in Nabenchauk had to do with the role of multiple modes of communication, in which verbal and nonverbal interventions are combined. Nonverbal interventions included the teacher's participating in the weaving, guiding the learner's body, and pointing. Multiple modes have the advantage of redundancy and should therefore be helpful for beginners. They also relate language directly to the concrete context—in this case, weaving. Indeed, for the least experienced learners in 1970, we found that the majority of teacher-initiated interactions (68 percent) combined verbal and nonverbal elements. This proportion declined steadily for learners of increasing experience. For the most experienced weavers, only 34 percent of interventions combined language and nonverbal information. Perhaps most striking was how sensitive the communications of teachers were to the informational needs and skill levels of the learners. Thus, language proved to be an important part of weaving apprenticeship, contrary to the notion that language is not central to processes of cultural learning. Nonetheless, the infrequency of outright explanation points to one type of verbal communication that was not part of

this apprenticeship process, although it is central to school-based learning.[35]

Developmental sensitivity to the learner's abilities came out in another way. In both 1970 and the 1990s, less experienced learners were given smaller items to weave —things such as baby garments, tortilla covers, and servilletas. The inexperienced girls were often, though not always, the youngest and smallest in our study sample. But even when first-time weavers were older, they began with small items, notably tortilla covers. One small first weaving, for example, measured 4 by 12 inches (fig. 2.44). Because the size of a weaving is determined by the length and width of the warp setup, it is interesting that in our 1990s sample the warp was sometimes wound by a more experienced weaver and sometimes by the first-time weaver herself. Clearly, both teachers and learners adapted the size of the first real weaving to the developmental capabilities of the learner.

When Ashley Maynard learned to weave in 1995, all of the foregoing features of weaving apprenticeship were in evidence. Paxku' Pavlu, her weaving teacher, asked Ashley to watch her weave at the beginning and helped her more actively in the early stages of learning, when she was less skilled. Paxku' also decided exactly what Ashley would weave, grading the items

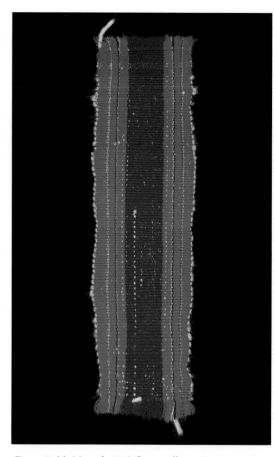

Figure 2.44. Maruch 201's first small weaving, woven in Nabenchauk, 1991. Photograph by Don Cole.

from small to large, and what parts of the overall weaving Ashley was ready to do, beginning with the easiest. Paxku' used language in a contextualized manner, focusing on instructions accompanied by pointing at the relevant part of the weaving

Figure 2.45. One-on-one interaction between teacher and learner in weaving apprenticeship. Nabenchauk, 1993. Photograph by Patricia Greenfield.

or weaving tools. Clearly, the implicit mental model of how to transmit a cultural skill was general enough to permit the teaching of an adult gringa.[36]

By learning to make tortillas and carry wood, Ashley also tested the generality of the Zinacantec apprenticeship model across different tasks. Her teacher used the same principles in teaching Ashley these other skills. Observation was consistently important: "Paxku' told me to watch her in my earliest lessons of doing each of the tasks. I would sit with her and watch while she did the activity. This was how I was expected to learn."[37] In each task,

Paxku' always adjusted the level of instruction to Ashley's level of learning. She also decided which component of the task should be learned first—for example, pressing a tortilla preceded putting it on the grill to cook. Across all three tasks, there was very little talking. "When Paxku' did speak, she always accompanied her words with the action she was describing. For example, she would place a ball of tortilla dough on the press, close the press, press down, and say, 'Like this' in Tzotzil. In chopping wood, she would chop wood and say, 'Like this.'" She used no theoretical language about making tortillas or carrying firewood, nor did her verbal instructions reach beyond the task context. Explanations were rare. In short, the Zinacantec method of transmitting weaving knowledge is a true cultural model that Zinacantec teachers generalize across domains. Ashley's dissertation research showed that Zinacantec children begin learning this model very young, as they care for their younger siblings.[38]

WEAVING APPRENTICESHIP VERSUS SCHOOL LEARNING

In Nabenchauk, where only a minority of girls went to school in the 1990s, weaving and schooling were seen as alternatives. They represent two instructional styles

that researchers from the United States and Europe widely categorize as informal (or apprenticeship-style) education and formal education, respectively.[39] Weaving apprenticeship is characterized, first, by a one-on-one relationship between teacher and learner (fig. 2.45). Sometimes a single learner can even have more than one teacher. This high ratio of teachers to learners contrasts with the one-to-many relationship between teacher and learners in school, and it creates a much more personal relationship between teacher and learner than is possible in the classroom.

In addition, most of the focus in the informal learning situation is on the learner rather than on the teacher. In school, the paradigmatic situation is for the learners to look at the teacher; in weaving, it is for the teacher to look at the learner (fig. 2.46). Indeed, Ashley Maynard identified the teacher's focus on the learner as one of the key features of the Zinacantec model of teaching, across all three tasks that she studied.[40]

Teacher characteristics also differ drastically in the two instructional systems. In weaving apprenticeship, the teacher is typically a mother, sister, aunt, or cousin. In school in Nabenchauk and other Zinacantec hamlets, the teacher is typically a stranger—often a male from a different ethnic group who does not even speak Tzotzil. Unlike some other Tzotzil- and Tzeltal-speaking communities in highland Chiapas, such as Mitontik,[41] Nabenchauk does not have bilingual schooling with indigenous teachers. It has Spanish-only schools with monolingual Spanish teachers, something that has acted to keep the school separate from the community.

Another way in which the two instructional modes differ is in the desired learning outcome. In apprenticeship learning, the desired outcome is a concrete and immediate product. In weaving apprenticeship in Zinacantán, girls begin to produce useful textiles at around age nine. Play weaving is put aside, and real weaving begins as the typical weaving apprentice learns, in most cases, by producing functional textiles.

In school learning, by contrast, skill development itself is one of the most immediately desired outcomes. The skills explicitly targeted in the early years of schooling include literacy, numeracy, and acquisition of the Spanish language. Among the skills students are implicitly expected to master are classroom protocols of space and time allocation, institutional hierarchy, and other institutional practices.

The difference in the learning outcomes projected by the two systems results in

Figure 2.46. Serving as her daughter's weaving teacher, a mother watches as the child learns to weave. Nabenchauk, 1991. Videotape frame by Patricia Greenfield.

different styles of learner-teacher interaction. In the apprenticeship instructional form, the importance of a successfully completed product increases the cost of errors and makes help from the expert more likely. In our 1970 study, the "expert" generally offered whatever help the apprentice needed to complete a weaving.[42] Even in 1993 we saw this happen in many instances. In contrast, school offers an

ideology of independent learning. In figure 2.47, for example, three Nabenchauk schoolgirls work at a blackboard. They are not helping each other, nor is the teacher helping any of them. Instead, each works independently.

On the basis of her pioneering comparison of education at home and school in highland Chiapas in the 1960s, Nancy Modiano offers another point of

Figure 2.47. Three Nabenchauk girls work independently at the school blackboard. Nabenchauk, 1991. ©Lauren Greenfield/VII.

comparison: "When a young child fails to obey his parents' orders he is considered too young to understand; a schoolchild who fails to understand his teacher is considered too stupid. The teacher or a system that offers virtually all instruction in a foreign language is rarely blamed. The teachers too reflect this view."[43]

Last, and probably most importantly, schooling transmits a different set of values. Maya parents want their children to learn Spanish, but at the same time they regret the loss of values such as courtesy and a sense of social responsibility. They complain that their children are becoming individualists. Whereas the development of Maya children is defined in terms of work, school allows plenty of time for play, a situation that is sometimes perceived as a conflict of values. On the

pragmatic level, parents cannot afford the loss of children's economic contribution and often keep them home to do chores.[44] The contrast between school values and home values was well expressed in some of Xun Pavlu's comments during a 1969 interview. He told me that the older children would not be sent to school if they were needed at home to draw water, get wood, or look after sheep. Therefore, the youngest were most often sent to school. When I asked Xun whether parents ever sent their smartest children to school, he replied, "The stupid ones go to school so the teacher can make them smart." Parents bring up their smart children themselves.

Whereas schooling is organized to transmit knowledge of the head (know), weaving apprenticeship is arranged to transmit knowledge of the soul (ch'ulel) or

heart (na'). Long-established mechanisms of transmission, both direct and indirect, have fostered the survival of backstrap-loom weaving for more than a thousand years. Yet changes have taken place in weaving transmission that have allowed apprenticeship both to adapt to and reflect a changing economic milieu. Up until now, these changes have overlain the bedrock of constancy that has been the focus of this chapter. But this is not necessarily a prediction for the future. Developments are taking place in the highlands of Chiapas that could potentially undermine the universality and centrality of backstrap-loom weaving for girls growing up in Nabenchauk. I take up these developments in chapter 3.

Figure 2.48. Day of the Dead, an important symbol of intergenerational continuity. Nabenchauk, 1991. ©Lauren Greenfield/VII.

Figure 3.0. A Zinacantec girl weaves indoors by electric light.

CHAPTER THREE

Apprenticeship Transformed

Despite the endurance of tradition, Zinacantec weaving apprenticeship is not static. It adapts to, reflects, and supports changing social and economic conditions. ❖

Socialization is future oriented—it prepares children for an adulthood that has not yet arrived. It follows that changing socialization patterns should be a key component of psychological adaptation to social change. An important question is this: Under conditions of change, do parents merely re-create the socializing process they underwent as children? Or do people possess a capacity to develop new methods and processes as societal conditions—in this case, economic conditions—change? My major theoretical idea is that not only do cultures change over historical time, but so do the very processes of cultural learning and cultural transmission. More specifically, a somewhat different set of learning processes is highlighted when cultures are relatively stable—that is, when they are substantially oriented toward conserving tradition—than when they are in a more dynamic state, oriented more toward innovation.[1]

LEARNING TO WEAVE IN A WORLD SUSTAINED BY AGRICULTURE: 1970

In 1970, Carla Childs and I perceived three main themes in the Zinacantec social world. One was respect for Zinacantec tradition—*baz'i,* or the "true" way.[2] For example, we once saw some Zinacantecs by the road who were not wearing Zinacantec clothing. I asked a group of girls why those people were dressed that way. The answer, in Tzotzil, was, "They don't know how to dress." The Tzotzil language itself was (and is) called *baz'i k'op,* the "true language." In weaving, baz'i was reflected in the fact that Zinacantecs had a stock of only four patterns. To learn to weave was to learn to reproduce those patterns. Leslie Haviland Devereaux, in her 1978 dissertation, eloquently described the other side of the coin: "Each utensil, each object possesses a known, discrete and finite set of uses, which is

observed by everyone. Inappropriate use of objects, even if it is without practical consequence, causes consternation and embarrassment."[3] In other words, to create a new use for an object was to act inappropriately.

A second theme was the interdependence of family and community members. Examples of interdependence abounded in everyday life. Women prepared all meals for their husbands and families; the men provided corn and beans, which they grew. Children were responsible for caring for younger siblings. Women and girls wove clothing for the family. Families lived together in a one-room house; no one slept alone.

A third theme was the age-graded flow of authority from older to younger persons. Evon Vogt, in his comprehensive ethnography of Zinacantán, wrote about the relationship between younger brother and older brother as exemplifying the central relationship in the culture. Respect of the younger for the older was the key to this relationship.[4]

Each of these themes, for which many other examples could be given, was apparent in the microcosm of weaving apprenticeship in 1970. Viewing our videotapes from that year, we saw an apprenticeship process well adapted to maintaining respect for tradition in the domain of weaving. The expert weaver, usually the mother, stepped in to help any time the learner did not know what to do. Each learner was thus guided to weave in exactly the same manner practiced by her predecessors. There was no opportunity for trial-and-error experimentation, which might have led to innovation in textiles.

Weaving apprenticeship was also strongly interdependent. Many segments in our videotapes strongly depicted this interdependence. Figure 3.1, for example, shows two bodies, those of XK and her daughter K1, working as one at the loom. Figure 3.2 shows their four hands on the loom together. In figure 3.3, a mother and older sister from another family help a first-time learner with her weaving.

The age-graded flow of authority was also clear: In virtually all cases, the primary teacher was a member of the older generation. In one case, family 146, where there

Figure 3.1. Two bodies working as one: A mother helps her daughter. Nabenchauk, 1970. Videotape frame by Patricia Greenfield.

Figure 3.2. Four hands on the loom: A mother helps her daughter. Nabenchauk, 1970. Videotape frame by Patricia Greenfield.

were two teachers, the mother and an older sister, the age-graded line of authority was particularly salient. In the video, the mother, standing near the loom, tells the older daughter what to do; the older daughter, seated at the loom with her younger sister, the learner, in turn demonstrates what to do, while the young learner watches attentively.[5] (Fig. 3.3, right-hand frame)

Even tools follow a path from oldest to youngest. In the same sequence, the mother prepares a stick for weaving, then hands it to the older daughter, who in turn demonstrates its use for her younger sister (see fig. 3.3). Although the youngest is learning from the older sister, it is clear from the recorded dialogue that the older sister is also learning from the mother.[6]

Another aspect of the authority relation was the use of directives, usually imperatives, in the teaching process. In 1970, directives such as "Lean back" or "Lift it up" were teachers' most frequent utterances, particularly in the early stages of instruction. Learners uniformly complied with the teachers' directives. This observation accords with an observation made by Marida Blanco and Nancy Chodorow in 1972 that a Zinacantec parent's highest praise for a child is, "He obeys well, he works well."[7]

In sum, weaving apprenticeship in 1970 was a vehicle for the social reproduction of three important cultural themes: the notion of a single "true" way, the interdependence of family members, and

Figure 3.3. Mother and older sister help Katal 146, a first-time weaver. Left: *Mother prepares a stick for weaving.* Middle: *She hands it to her older daughter.* Right: *The older daughter demonstrates its use for her younger sister. Nabenchauk, 1970. Videotape frames by Patricia Greenfield.*

the age-graded flow of authority from older to younger. Because weaving apprenticeship was intergenerational, it functioned as a microcosm in which these values could be transmitted to the next generation. The transmission of value took place through practice: it was implicit rather than explicit.

LEARNING TO WEAVE IN AN ENTREPRENEURIAL WORLD: THE 1990S

Change in Zinacantán has always been cyclical. The Zinacantecs have a long tradition of commerce, dating back to pre-Columbian times, when Zinacantán was an outpost for trade with the Aztecs. In 1970, however, the time of our first study

of weaving apprenticeship, the Zinacantecs were probably at their height of agricultural self-sufficiency. Even so, indigenous commerce had begun to develop. The first local store had appeared in the late 1950s, withstanding the anticompetitive value orientation that was, at the time, an important component of the culture. Such stores, selling Coca-Cola, liquor, cigarettes, and other small items, quickly multiplied and spread from hamlet to hamlet.[8]

The establishment of stores illustrates the important point that, in looking at historical change, one must recognize that the beginning and end points of the study period are arbitrary. Change does not begin when one starts the study or end when one finishes it. When Carla Childs

and I arrived in Zinacantán in 1969, an economic shift from subsistence agriculture toward money and commerce had already begun. For example, Zinacantec farmers were not just growing crops for their own families; they were also renting land in "hot country," at lower elevations, in order to grow corn and beans for cash.

Similarly, signs of movement toward textile commerce were beginning to appear. A few families were selling their "mistakes"—poor-quality weavings—to stores in the neighboring city of San Cristóbal de las Casas. Leslie Haviland Devereaux noted that in 1976, "the entire domain [of textile production] was undergoing change in both technology and economic organization."[9] In 1991, when we returned to study the next generation, I saw that this trend toward money and commerce had continued at an accelerated pace since our last visit.

Indeed, a quantum leap in commercial development had taken place. According to a taxi driver whom I interviewed on these matters, the government had helped launch the indigenous transportation business around 1976 or 1977. Its purpose was to transport people and their produce. In the early 1980s, the ruling party, the PRI, gave some Volkswagen vans (for community transport) and trucks (for transporting produce) to Zinacantán. But it gave them to individuals, not to communities. According to a Tzotzil-speaking deputy to the National Assembly whom I had the opportunity to interview in 1997, the PRI gave the vehicles to individuals in order to gain political control. It identified leaders (caciques) who could deliver people and their votes to the party.

In a community where land was held in common, privately owned trucks and vans constituted the first form in which Zinacantecs had known substantial individual ownership of capital goods. The individually owned vehicles made commercial entrepreneurship a feasible means of earning a living. Not only could someone sell his own produce, but he could also buy goods in one location and sell them in another.[10] I found that men had become not only innovators in their commercial activity but also individualistic entrepreneurs. The economic conditions for individual initiative had been born.

Innovation and individual initiative contrast in a fundamental way with respect for tradition, a dominant value theme during our first wave of research. Individual ownership also implied greater economic independence for each nuclear family; this shift weakened the second value, that of interdependence, that had formerly been so important. With their involvement in various facets of commerce, sons now had their own sources of income and no longer depended on the older generation for land.[11] Sons also had the necessary technical skills, such as the ability to drive, that their fathers did not possess. This state of affairs served to reduce the age-graded flow of authority, the third core Zinacantec value.

The rise of commerce brought with it consumerism, which has further contributed to a decline in the values and practices of interdependence. Whereas earlier forms of commerce relied on barter, money has become an increasingly important medium of exchange in the recent surge of commercial development. Money has brought with it a movement toward a strong consumer economy, featuring goods such as radios, audiotape and videotape players, and televisions—goods that were absent in earlier waves of Zinacantec commerce. Television itself heightens people's motivation to acquire still other consumer goods by displaying them on the screen.

Consumer goods heighten the importance of money and its accumulation, and this new valuation in turn lessens people's motivation to contribute resources to the community. An illustration of this trend is found in the decline of the religious cargo system during the 1990s. A cargo is an office in the religious hierarchy, which is indigenous with an overlay of Catholicism. The duties of the office require extensive contributions of time, food, and money to the community. The decline of the cargo system reflects Zinacantecs' decreasing willingness to make these communal contributions.[12]

Interdependent practices have similarly declined at the level of the family. Husbands who are commercial entrepreneurs no longer automatically spend their money on their families. They now choose between that option and the option of investing in their businesses (for example, in trucks or goods to sell) or spending money for their own pleasure.[13]

Many of these changes have accelerated even further since the enactment of the North American Free Trade Agreement (NAFTA) and the Zapatista rebellion of January 1994. Indeed, soon after the rebellion, at least one man in Nabenchauk was rewarded for his loyalty to the PRI with a Volkswagen van, which he used to become a commercial entrepreneur. As an example of change following the mandated demise of corn price supports by NAFTA, at least one family in Nabenchauk had, by 1997, begun to buy subsistence corn and beans rather than grow them.

At the same time, a group of entrepreneurs in Nabenchauk bought individual taxis and began a private taxi service between the village and San Cristóbal de las Casas. Before the Zapatista uprising, taxis, like many other forms of commerce, had been the prerogative of non-Indian Mexicans, or Ladinos. Individual taxis increased the independence of both drivers and passengers, who could now travel in private rather than group vehicles.

What effects had these economic and social changes had on weaving practices? In 1970 we had been struck by the way first-time weavers in our study looked like professionals. Clearly, some of their expertise owed itself to the developmental preparation the girls had already experi-

enced, as I described in chapter 2. But some of it had to do with the value placed on doing things according to baz'i, the true way. This value led to careful guidance by the teacher and a relatively errorless kind of learning for the apprentice. After I returned home from my 1970 fieldwork, I had the opportunity to attend a backstrap loom weaving class in Cambridge, Massachusetts. It was the class's second session. I was astonished: the women kept leaning forward and collapsing the loom! I had never seen anything like that in Zinacantán and never have since. The Cambridge teacher, moreover, seemed not to know what backstrap loom weaving was supposed to look like. I had a sudden insight: this was trial-and-error learning, and it was what we in the United States favored. We wanted children to learn to do things for themselves, to experiment and make new discoveries. That was not what Zinacantecs wanted at all. They wanted children to grow up knowing the one "true" (read Zinacantec or traditional) way of doing everything.

But as we have seen, economic change between 1970 and the 1990s was transforming the Zinacantec economic system in a more entrepreneurial direction. I wondered whether entrepreneurship would bring a new emphasis on innova-

tion in weaving and independence in weaving apprenticeship.[14] Had changes in the economic macrocosm affected the microcosms of weaving apprenticeship and textile production?

I began to study the transformation of weaving in 1991, when Carla Childs and I returned to videotape the next generation of weavers in the families we had met in 1970. Because we were able to trace and find our original families, we had a well-controlled natural experiment. Everything, including the age of the study participants, was held constant; the only variable was historical period. The study's weakness was that in having skipped twenty-one years of life in Nabenchauk, we could not observe the processes of change as they had taken place in the intervening years. Consequently, although our research design was extremely well suited to detecting effects of historical change, it was less well suited to re-creating the precise historical processes by which those effects had come about. Still, the unevenness of social and economic changes across families enabled us to reconstruct something of this process of historical change.

Studying two generations of girls learning to weave across two decades revealed transformations in the cultural themes of respect for tradition, family interdependence, and age-graded authority. With the change to an entrepreneurial economy came lessened respect for tradition and the baz'i way, and increased interest in innovation. Because entrepreneurs must continually solve new problems and find new ways of making their commerce profitable, they value innovation. The entrepreneurs we observed in Nabenchauk were continually coming up with new sources and markets for their commodities—deciding what to buy where and where to sell it. In chapter 1, we saw that innovation had hit weaving and embroidery as well. In textile production, as in the economy as a whole, respect for tradition had been significantly transformed. A more detailed analysis of changes in the textiles themselves are the subject of chapter 4. In the rest of this chapter, I want to describe the ways in which the economic transformation of Zinacantán has altered the themes of interdependence and age-related authority in weaving apprenticeship.

MODERATING INTERDEPENDENCE WITH INDEPENDENCE

Changes in the economy in Zinacantán have been both reflected in and supported by changes in the informal education process that is weaving apprenticeship.

This transformation in the mechanisms of cultural apprenticeship was illustrated by K1, the apprentice weaver we met in figures 3.1 and 3.2, as she matured and taught her own daughters to weave. For comparative purposes, I focus on L201, one of K1's daughters, whom we videotaped in 1991 at age nine, about the same age her mother had been when we videotaped her in 1970 (figs. 3.1 and 3.2). L201 was one of fifty-eight weaving learners from the next generation who participated in our video study in 1991 and 1993.[15]

We found that whereas K1's mother had anticipated her need for help as she learned to weave, her daughter L201 had to take the initiative to summon a teacher to help her. Compare the images of K1 learning to weave in 1970 (see figs. 3.1 and 3.2) with that of L201 learning to weave in 1991 (fig. 3.4). Note the greater physical distance between learner and teacher—older sister X201—in 1991. This distance, a mark of the increasing independence of learner and teacher, is yet another link between weaving apprenticeship and the economic system. It is paralleled by the physical distance between people in commercial transactions—for example, the distance enforced by barriers such as counters and stands. In this and

Figure 3.4. In 1991, L201, a daughter of K1, the learner shown in figures 3.1 and 3.2, learns to weave. She is assisted by her older sister, X201. Nabenchauk, 1991. Videotape frame by Patricia Greenfield.

other ways, commerce removes the personal element from human relationships. At the same time, money makes a plurality of economic relationships possible. The sociologist George Simmel sees this combination as the most favorable situation for bringing about inner independence: "The feeling of individual self-sufficiency rests on the interchangeability of persons."[16]

Another mark of the historical change toward greater independence of learner and teacher is to be seen in the fact that in 1991, the teacher, an older sister, pays no attention to the learner: note the direction of the older sister's gaze in figure 3.4. In 1970, the teacher, K1's own mother, was

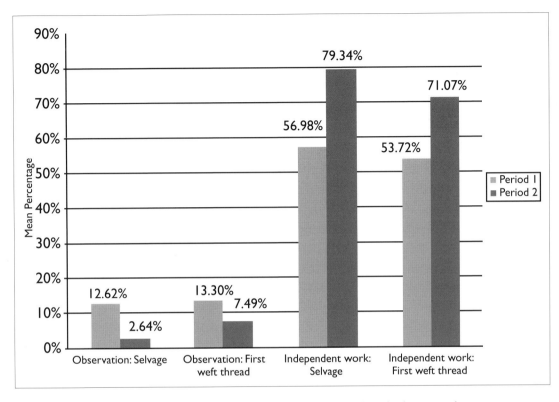

Figure 3.5. Percentage of time learners spent observing a model and working independently, 1970 and 1990s.

highly involved with the learner (see figs. 3.1 and 3.2). The decline of time spent observing other weavers in the 1990s corresponds to the decline of a single true (baz'i) way and the erosion of age-graded authority, a topic to be discussed in the next section. Moreover, in the 1991 video frame, it is unclear how much L201's older sister even knows about weaving herself. Most likely, she had only woven

and sold servilletas and had attached an end-stick for her younger sister's first weaving. The relative inexperience of such a teacher would have enhanced the trial-and-error nature of the learning process for her younger sisters.

This longitudinal comparison within one family was substantiated by the quantitative analysis of our full sample of seventy-two from the two generations of

weaving learners—our fourteen weavers from 1970 plus the fifty-eight girls from the next generation. Fifteen of these fifty-eight learners were daughters of the 1970 learners. Three 1970 weaving learners each had one daughter in the new sample, four had two each, and one had four daughters at various stages in learning to weave. There were also seventeen nieces, one younger sister, and twelve cousins of previous weavers in the sample of fifty-eight. We were truly fortunate in being able to find and recruit the next generation of weaving learners two decades later.

In line with the historical case study of K1 and L201, we found a significant increase from one generation to the next in the amount of time learners spent working independently—that is, without help from a teacher—in two of the harder parts of the process that we had studied: attaching the warp threads to one of the loom's two end-sticks to form the selvage edge and inserting the first weft thread (statistical analyses are presented in the endnotes).[17] Significantly more emphasis was placed on learning by experience—that is, less time was spent observing a model—in the generation learning to weave in 1991. Thus, although observation has been highlighted as a feature of cultural learning, it is not a static process but is adapted to ecological conditions. Figure 3.5 shows how the percentage of time learners spent observing a model decreased from one historical period to the next and how, simultaneously, the percentage of time spent weaving independently went up.[18]

This objective analysis was confirmed by our participants' subjective recollections when we interviewed the second generation of weaving learners and their mothers, some of whom had been in our original sample in 1970. Whereas only one (5 percent) of the nineteen mothers interviewed said that she had learned to weave by herself, ten (22 percent) of the forty-five girls mentioned learning to weave completely or partly on their own. Part of the reason might be that acrylic fibers, which had seen universal adoption by 1991, are easier to learn on than cotton or wool.[19] Ease of learning, however, cannot have been a major factor, because the highly complex new technology of brocade weaving was associated with an even stronger sense of independence: 49 percent of thirty-nine girls said they had learned to weave the fancy brocade borders of ponchos by themselves. In sum, the subjective construction of increasing independence clearly mirrored the objective facts.

The movement from interdependence to independence showed up in other facets of Zinacantec socialization as well. For example, in Tzotzil a babysitter is called a baby "holder." This metaphor reflects a Zinacantec philosophy of infant care totally different from that in the United States or Europe. For Zinacantecs, a baby should remain in constant bodily contact with another human being. Indeed, the belief that human beings should not be alone is strong in Zinacantán, extending from newborn to adult. In 1991 the thought of my spending a single night alone in my house in San Cristóbal was so worrisome to our assistant and friend Maruch Chentik that she asked her daughter Paxku' to accompany me to San Cristóbal and spend the night there. Paxku' willingly complied. Accustomed to a one-room Zinacantec house, however, Paxku' could not stand the thought of sleeping alone in her own bedroom and asked if she might sleep on the sofa near the foot of my bed. Recall from chapter 1 that a man is not permitted to live alone without a woman to pat his tortillas. The one-person household is neither permitted nor understood in Zinacantán.

The Zinacantec philosophy of togetherness was still strong in 1991, yet infant care practices were moving slowly toward greater fostering of independence. Beds arrived in Nabenchauk between 1970 and our return in 1991, replacing the dirt floor or wooden platform of earlier years and providing a safe, warm place in which to put a baby down. Putting a sleeping baby on a bed alone during the day increased the separation of baby and mother, in comparison with earlier days. A baby still never slept alone at night, and infant care practices that expressed and fostered interdependence were still more striking than those that fostered and expressed independence. Yet a movement toward increased separation of infant and caregiver had begun.

Besides the use of beds, there were in 1991 other signs of increasing socialization for independence from infancy onward. Looking back at figure 2.0, for example, note that the baby is in a crate that is being used as a crib. This new technology is creating bodily separation between the baby and its caregiver during the child's waking hours. Although the caregiver is nearby, this is still greater separation than one would have found a generation earlier. In 1993 a boy asked me to buy a *scaro nene* (literally, "baby car") for his baby brother; he seemed to be talking about a walker. Walkers promote even greater physical independence than do cribs, by enabling babies to move around before they are able to walk by themselves. In 1993 I also noticed that the only activity

Slok'ol 3.6. Chjal jtos sp'as tey sk'elobil ta vun. Nabenchauk, 1991. © Lauren Greenfield/INSTITUTE.

of dangers that I attempted to explain) was that this way she could leave the baby in the care of her oldest daughter while she went to San Cristóbal. What is striking here is the mother's assertion of her own independence.

THE EROSION OF AGE-GRADED AUTHORITY

Part of the erosion of authority in Zinacantán stems from older people's lack of knowledge of new technologies. A critical new technology in weaving and embroidery, for example, is the printed pattern (fig. 3.6). Compared with their mothers, significantly more girls in 1991 knew how to use paper patterns for weaving or sewing.[21] Often, it was the younger women and teenage girls, not their mothers, who knew how to weave the complex brocaded geometric and figurative designs such as flowers, deer, birds, and numerals that had become obligatory on the borders of men's ponchos (for example, see figs. 1.13 and 4.15) and all over baby blouses (figs. 3.7 and 3.8 show the brocade weaving from a baby girl's baptismal blouse). An older weaver might have her daughter weave the fancy border, or she might farm it out to a younger girl to do for payment. Weaving, like driving, has become a domain in which the older generation has

Zinacantec children did alone was going to school. This observation agrees with a research tradition that sees school as an individualizer in Chiapas, elsewhere in Mexico, and all over the world.[20]

Perhaps most notable as a sign of increasing socialization for independence was the baby bottle, which I first saw in Nabenchauk in 1993. People were filling bottles with soda, not milk, so they were adjuncts to nursing, with its body-to-body contact, and not substitutes for it. In 1996 I saw bottles being used for milk. A mother who was using the bottle for milk for the first time with her sixth child told me that one motive to continue it (in the face fewer skills than the younger, upsetting the lines of respect and obedience that traditionally flowed from younger to older.

To my surprise, part of the reason for this generational difference lay in increased school attendance by girls. By 1991 about one-third of Nabenchauk's girls had attended school at some time. In 1970 the figure was 10 percent. A survey of Zinacantec men carried out some ten years before our first study revealed that community resistance to schooling centered around cultural loss. Men felt that a girl who knew how to read would no longer be Zinacantec and would neglect her women's work—making tortillas, tending sheep, carrying wood, and so forth.[22] In 1969 Xun Pavlu made the same point in more pragmatic terms: older children needed for chores are not sent to school; therefore, the youngest go to school. In 1991 two of the girls we were closest to told us that that they had wanted to go to school but could not because they had to take care of a younger sibling (literally, hold the baby).

In 1991, moreover, many girls were leaving school in order to learn to weave. Weaving was and is the major subject in a Zinacantec girl's traditional education. Yet schoolteachers, it was said, had introduced

Figure 3.7. Sleeve detail of brocade weaving from a baby's blouse. Nabenchauk, 1991. © Lauren Greenfield/VII.

printed patterns, the source of most of the figurative designs being used in brocade weaving and embroidery. In Tzotzil, *school* is literally translated as "learning paper"; the term for reading translates as "looking at paper." When a weaver uses a paper pattern, she says she is "looking at paper." One mother of a beginning weaver told us that only girls who had been to school

used printed patterns, for only they were used to "looking at paper." In this way, formal schooling is another force that disturbs the authority relationship between older and younger.

Also pertinent to intergenerational relations in weaving apprenticeship is the historical movement away from "senior" weaving teachers such as mothers, aunts,

Figure 3.8. Detail of brocade weaving from a baby girl's baptismal blouse. Nabenchauk, 1991. © Lauren Greenfield/VII.

Our quantitative analysis allowed us to generalize from this one family. From the complete sample, we selected those girls who were weaving their very first item before our video camera or had woven only one kind of item before, most often a small cloth such as a servilleta. These were the least experienced learners in the sample, and those most in need of a weaving teacher. It was in this group that the generational shift toward younger weaving teachers was most striking. Indeed, statistical analysis revealed a significant historical shift toward younger weaving teachers or helpers for these less experienced learners.[23]

Interviews with the second generation of weaving learners and their mothers dramatically confirmed what the videos showed. Whereas eighteen (95 percent) of nineteen mothers said they had learned to weave from their mothers, only twenty-nine (64 percent) of the forty-five girls interviewed said the same thing. Not one mother mentioned having learned to weave from a member of her peer generation, but five girls (11 percent) did. The peer generation included older sisters, an older teenage aunt, or other peers. In this way, the shift over time from interdependence to independence was complemented by a movement from older to younger teachers.

and even grandmothers. In the 1990s the weaving teacher more often came from the same age cohort as the learner—for example, an older sister or a very young aunt.

This historical trend is exemplified by the case of K1's daughter L201 (see fig. 3.4), whose weaving teacher was her thirteen-year-old sister, rather than her mother. The older sister was also a learner in our video study, so she offered an interesting example of the use of young helpers. When the same older sister wove before our video camera, one of her younger sisters, a rank beginner, served as her helper. The older sister had no teacher with greater expertise than her own.

The erosion of maternal authority was even greater for fancy brocade weaving. We asked thirty-nine girls how they had learned to weave brocaded poncho borders, and only 26 percent answered that they had learned from their mothers. The majority (53 percent) said they had learned by themselves, a response indicating their growing independence.

OTHER SIGNS OF CHANGE
Trial and Error, Initiative, and Playful Experimentation

Learning to weave in Nabenchauk involved more trial and error, more self-initiative, and more playful experimentation in 1991 than it had in 1970. During the earlier study, we had seen not one major error, even for first-time weavers. Yet in our first nine weaving videotapes in 1991, three of the learners made such serious mistakes that they had to redo major parts of their weaving. The girl L201 again provides a good example. When she learned to weave in 1991, her teacher, an older sister, did not hover over her, ready to prevent errors before they happened. Indeed, the role of the teacher in preventing errors was nonexistent in this video. Instead, L201's role in preventing her own errors was much greater than we had seen when her mother learned to weave in

1970. In 1991, L201's teacher limited her role to correcting errors after they happened, which led to an increase in trial-and-error learning and experimentation relative to the mother's apprenticeship twenty-one years earlier. The trial-and-error process went so far that after we turned off our camera, the older sister unraveled the younger sister's weaving, because it had turned out so poorly.

This is the camera's perspective on change, a view from the outside. We were also interested in the inside view, the participant's own perspective. L201's mother, K1, told us in a 1991 interview that L201, like her other daughters, had begun to weave on her own initiative—she had started while her mother was away on a day trip to San Cristóbal. Interestingly, the actual weaving was a scaffolded sibling collaboration: the older sisters had done some of the harder parts. Older sister X201 had attached the end-stick and helped generally, and middle sister M201 removed the weaving from the loom. L201 had done the weaving proper.

When we asked K1 whether that was how she had begun to weave when she was little, she said no, her mother had said to her, "Weave!" Thus, K1's perception was that the initiative to begin learning to weave had been transferred in

one generation from teacher to learner. Her perception was confirmed by the rest of the 1990s sample. Whereas in 1993 most mothers (67 percent) recalled their mothers having started them on backstrap loom weaving with an imperative ("Weave!"), most girls (61 percent) recalled starting to weave through their own volition ("I weave").[24] One pragmatic condition that supports girls' initiative to begin is that the materials are now readily at hand, and the early stages of weaving are easier with acrylic yarn than they used to be with cotton and wool.[25]

We do not know exactly how mothers feel about this change. It fits, however, with the Zinacantec notion of readiness. Girls are not supposed to weave until they get enough soul, a developmental stage. Soul is intimately tied up with apprenticeship; it implies that a child can listen to instructions, follow instructions, do what is needed, and tolerate frustration.[26] The importance of readiness implies that it could also be important for the novice to take some initiative in beginning the learning process. On the other hand, respect for authority is also part of the baz'i way of life. Under the traditional worldview, more people would have supported the imperative approach to weaving instruction.

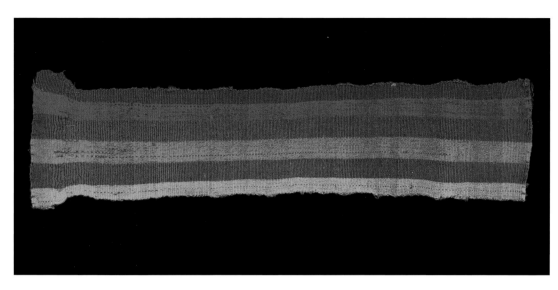

Figure 3.9. L201's "little nothing" (second weaving), woven by the learner shown in Fig. 3.4, aided by her two sisters, M201 and X201. The weaving is 16 inches long, 3 3/4 inches wide. Nabenchauk, 1991. Photograph by Don Cole.

In contrast to our 1970 sample, first-time weavers in 1991 were making nonutilitarian items, playful things that had significance only as learning tools. For example, with the help of her sisters, the learner shown in figure 3.4 made a "little nothing" (literally, *yech no'ox*, like that only) (fig. 3.9). Her sister M201, too, had made a "little nothing" (refer to fig. 2.44) for her first weaving, sometime before we arrived to do our study. These small items were a sign of an increase in playful experimentation in 1991. Beginning weavers in 1970 had, in contrast, limited themselves to weaving utilitarian items, albeit small ones,

such as baby garments and tortilla bags.

By 1991, then, more frequent learner initiation of weaving was one way in which learners were more independent of their teachers. Trial-and-error learning and playful experimentation constituted still other facets of independent learning. Both trial and error and playful experimentation are discovery-oriented learning processes, well suited for innovation.

THE DYNAMICS OF CHANGE

In my theory, I had tied changes in Zinacantec weaving apprenticeship to changes in the economic system. But

what proof was there that economic participation was the causative factor? My colleagues and I decided to do statistical analyses to find out. These analyses indicated that the movement away from an interdependent style of apprenticeship to a more independent one was not uniform in Nabenchauk but was instead concentrated among the most commercially active families.[27] Specifically, the newer modes of learning and teaching were found most frequently in families in which mother and daughter were most actively engaged in textile-related commerce or paid work. We counted a number of ways in which girls and their mothers could participate in textile commerce: they could sell their weavings; they could sell thread in a retail thread store in their home; and they could weave or embroider on order for other Zinacantecs. Girls could also wind thread for pay. Although weaving on order has a venerable history in Nabenchauk, the other forms of textile commerce had greatly expanded since our departure in 1970.[28]

Our analysis indicated that the more of these activities in which girls and their mothers were involved, the more independent their style of weaving apprenticeship was likely to be. Interestingly, formal schooling of women and girls, which had increased from the earlier to the later historical period, was statistically unrelated to the shift in apprenticeship style.

A case study illustrates these dynamics. One of our first-time weavers in 1991 was older than any we had studied in 1970. Her mother never came near her while she was weaving and left the house before the daughter had finished. This girl received less help and guidance than any other first-time weaver or, indeed, any girl of her age in our 1970 sample. In line with the dynamics of change revealed in the statistical analysis, the mother told us that her daughter had not woven before because she had a job winding thread for money.

Because not everyone in Nabenchauk had been equally affected by recent economic developments—some people still followed a subsistence agricultural way of life—we might have anticipated tension between the old and new ways. I found such tension in a little drama that occurred around play weaving on a toy loom. Maruch Chentik's daughter Rosy had spontaneously set up a toy loom in the family's courtyard. Upon discovering her, I came to watch. A teenage girl next door saw Rosy working and decided that what she was doing was not good, so she came over and unraveled the entire warp. In figure 3.10, she is in the middle of taking out Rosy's warp threads. Clearly,

Figure 3.10. Rosy Pavlu's teenage neighbor undoes her play weaving. Nabenchauk, 1991. Photograph by Patricia Greenfield.

the teenage neighbor felt that Rosy should not make her own mistakes. About Rosy's warp, she made the evaluative comment, "Bad."

This incident offered evidence of tension between two cultural models of learning. It turned out that Rosy's mother had another model in mind: independent learning. "Let her do it herself," said Maruch. "She doesn't know how," replied the self-appointed teenage teacher. This reply reflected the older model of carefully guided, relatively errorless learning, in sharp contrast to the mother's model. Later, Maruch elaborated her model even more explicitly. She told me that it was better for Rosy to learn by herself, as her older sister had done. She had neither helped nor talked to Rosy's older sister, Maruch said.

Rosy's family was much more heavily involved in commerce than was the neighbor's family, so the conflicting models also represented the two ecologies—the ecology of agriculture and subsistence versus that of commerce and money. Later I asked Rosy about her own model of learning: Did she want to weave by herself or with help? She replied, "By myself." Upon further questioning, she added that it was "worse" to have the girl help. So Rosy, like her mother but unlike her self-styled teacher, had in mind the newer model of more independent learning and apprenticeship.

The case of older sister X201 serving as nine-year-old L201's weaving teacher, which I described earlier, indicates one mechanism at play in the historical transformation of apprenticeship style. In 1991, K1, the 1970 weaving learner pictured in figures 3.1 and 3.2, assigned her daughter, thirteen-year-old X201, to help nine-year-old L201 with her weaving during the video session. While L201 worked on her weaving under X201's not-so-watchful eye, K1 was embroidering a blouse that I had ordered from her. When she finished the blouse, I was to buy it at an agreed-upon price.

This incident suggests one mechanism by which the change to peer teachers might take place. In assigning X201 to help her younger sister with her weaving, K1 might simply have been adapting to the fact that she had an alternative income-producing activity available: embroidering a blouse on order. Still other cases exemplified economic adaptation as an important mechanism. For instance, some 1991 mothers were not present when their daughters were videotaped learning to weave because they were away selling at markets in distant cities.

In these cases, the greater use of peer teachers or the greater independence of the learner would not constitute a conscious change in pedagogical philosophy or goals but simply an unconscious adaptation to a new economic reality. The driving force behind the change would be mothers' adaptations more than daughters' preferences. Indeed, we saw absolutely no sign of daughters rebelling against maternal authority. The philosophy of teaching of the commercially involved mothers seemed to be following changes in their pedagogical practices. Heavily involved in textile commerce, Rosy's mother, Maruch, made it clear that she thought her daughters should learn to weave by means of independent experimentation. Economic

conditions, then, may influence apprenticeship practice, which in turn may influence apprenticeship values. I have never thought that the changes in weaving apprenticeship resulted from conscious changes in pedagogical philosophy; it makes much more sense to think of them as unconscious adaptations that might ultimately lead to changes in conscious values.

The links between weaving commerce and the value of women's independence became clearer over time. In the summer of 1997, I discovered that one of the weaving learners in our 1991 video sample was now weaving in an older style for a museum in Zinacantán Center, a tourist magnet as well as the traditional ritual center of Zinacantán. She was then twenty, and I asked her, jokingly, why she was not yet married. She answered with a question: "How old was Lauren when she got married?" "Twenty-five," I replied. "That's a good age for me, too," she said. Would she have wanted to wait so long if she had not been earning money by weaving? I think not. Moreover, this type of weaving commerce would not have been possible without the development of an indigenous transportation system, including local van drivers who spoke Tzotzil, which made it feasible for women to travel to markets on their own.[29]

In September 1997 a friend in Nabenchauk asked me to lend her three thousand pesos—prefacing her request in the newly traditional way, with a liter-and-a-half bottle of Fanta orange soda. She wanted the money to start her own textile business. She said she would buy thread and weave servilletas to sell on the high-way above the village and in Zinacantán Center. She was not going to tell her husband and asked me not to tell, either. I inferred that she wanted to be financially independent of her husband, who had been taking all the household money and using it to repair his van, which he had crashed three times in one summer. I lent her the money without telling her husband. By 2000 her daughter had pur-chased a sewing machine and was using it to embroider for money. Both had used weaving commerce to gain independence from an erratically alcoholic husband and father.[30]

One of the important trends in the commercialization of weaving in highland Chiapas in recent decades is the formation of weaving cooperatives such as Sna Jolobil, or House of the Loom. Sna Jolobil began in 1978 with fifty members and $100 in capital. At that time, according

to Maya textile authority Walter Morris, "few tourists bought weavings. Twelve years later, the association included 800 Maya women and sold $120,000 worth of traditional textiles. Sna Jolobil created a market for thousands of women in the Chiapas Highlands who supplement their family income through sales of handwoven fabrics."[31]

Because no member of our sample belonged to a weaving co-op (there was only one member of Sna Jolobil in all of Nabenchauk), we could not study the influence of this particular form of textile commerce. However, Tsuh-Yin Chen, another member of our team, established a field site in San Pedro Chenalho, a more isolated Maya community in highland Chiapas. There she initiated a comparison between mothers who wove mainly for family use and those who belonged to weaving cooperatives and wove for profit. Chen expected that mothers who wove for family use would teach their daughters in the carefully guided manner of our 1970 sample, and that co-op weavers would allow their daughters more independent trial-and-error learning. In addition to the value of independence for the creation of novelty, the co-op mothers themselves "had experienced experimentation and adaptation when they joined the coopera-

tives. They had to learn to use cotton and wool when before they used only acrylic. They also learned to make articles never woven before."[32]

Chen used systematic observation and interview techniques to document the modes of apprenticeship experienced by daughters who were learning to weave. In line with the hypothesis that mothers' textile-related commerce led to more independent learning, she found that the daughters of co-op members were receiving less guidance and less intervention in their learning processes than were the daughters of women who did not belong to the co-op. This finding begins to indicate the generality of our findings concerning relations between economic development and processes of cultural transmission.[33]

Another aspect of cooperatives is their influence on what is woven. In a certain ironic sense, they create novelty in textiles in that members are encouraged to go back to ancient designs that are distinctly different from those dictated by today's cultural norms. Similarly, whereas the norm for materials today is chemically dyed acrylic yarn, cooperatives such as Sna Jolobil and another in Tenejapa insist on natural materials and dyes. Weaving cooperatives serve to reconstruct a past that is no longer a part of everyday life.

Figure 3.11. "Learning paper" at school in Nabenchauk, 1991. © Lauren Greenfield/VII.

HOW FAR CAN CHANGE GO?

In some highland Maya communities, such as Chenalho and Mitontik, weaving is no longer universal among girls. These are communities in which schooling has come to be seen as a credentialing process that provides entrée to jobs, particularly teaching jobs.[34] These are also communities that offer bilingual schooling, Spanish-Tzotzil or Spanish-Tzeltal, with indigenous schoolteachers. At the time of our study in Nabenchauk, all schoolteachers in Nabenchauk were from the outside, Spanish-speaking, Ladino world, and there was no bilingual education; all schooling took place in Spanish.

In Nabenchauk, schooling was considered an economic tool—people learned Spanish and arithmetic for commercial transactions—and not a credentialing process. Absent bilingual schooling, and absent a view of schools as offering career development, the rate of female schooling was much lower in Nabenchauk than in Mitontik or Chenalho. In Mitontik some 90 percent of girls were going to school between 1981 and 1990; in Chenalho the rate was 100 percent in Chen's 1991 sample.[35] In sharp contrast, the figure in Nabenchauk was about 30 percent for our early 1990s sample of weaving learners age seven and older.

Corresponding to this high rate of schooling in Chenalho, very few women and girls there still wove, although the Maya backstrap tradition existed there as in Zinacantán. Chen was obliged to visit seven hamlets, each with a population of between 50 and 120 families, in order to find 20 families for her study. She discovered that most women who wove also belonged to cooperatives. "A common response to why girls were not weaving was: school. Girls do not have time to weave because they go to school. However, when the girls were asked directly why they did not weave, they all answered that they did not like weaving and that they would prefer to find a job so they could buy their clothing."[36] One mechanism by which schooling may have such an impact is by creating two separate authorities, school and home. Because one can differentiate oneself from either, schooling is a force for individuation, a trend that is visible in textiles themselves.[37]

This is very different from the situation in Nabenchauk, where girls generally said they wanted to weave because weaving was "good." In Nabenchauk, weaving as a near universal seems to have maintained itself quite stably. Leslie Devereaux's 1976 survey of 225 households in Nabenchauk showed that only three Zinacantec women had never learned to weave.[38] We did not do a comparable survey in the 1990s, but George Collier provided me with data from his 1993 census of the neighboring Zinacantec hamlet of Apas. There, 259 out of 287 women reported currently weaving for themselves, and 22 out of the 28 who did not were over sixty-five, presumably a bit old to weave. In other words, 1 percent of women were nonweavers in Nabenchauk in 1976, and 2 percent of women were nonweavers in Apas in 1993—virtually no change had taken place at all.[39] Backstrap loom weaving had remained a constant in the Zinacantec world. What factors have kept the rate of weaving so much higher in Zinacantec hamlets such as Nabenchauk than in Mitontik and Chenalho?[40]

Because the Tzotzil-speaking Zinacantec mothers of Nabenchauk cannot communicate with their children's Spanish-speaking teachers, they are able to distance the culturally foreign schools from home and community life. In the words of a bilingual Maya teacher, Elias Pérez Pérez, "Monolingual teachers don't penetrate the world of students and their families."[41]

Moreover, in Nabenchauk and other Zinacantec hamlets, the ethnic difference between Ladino teachers and Zinacantec families keeps teachers from becoming role models for their students. A number of young weavers in Nabenchauk told us that they had quit school in order to weave, thus following in the footsteps of their mothers rather than their teachers.

If bilingual schooling with indigenous teachers, particularly women teachers, ever comes to Nabenchauk, I predict that some girls will follow the lead of their indigenous teachers, continuing their education to the level of teacher training. This development will, I expect, begin to displace the socializing experiences described in chapter 2. Ultimately, I believe, bilingual schooling and Tzotzil-speaking teachers have the power to break the chain of virtually universal transmission of backstrap loom weaving in Nabenchauk.

This has not happened yet. In 1997 one Nabenchauk father expressed a wish for bilingual schooling to come to the village, reasoning that children advance more rapidly with bilingual education. That same year, Nabenchauk for the first time became the residence of two Zinacantec teachers. Both taught in Chenalho and were bachelors. If they were to marry and become fathers, a new socialization pattern, with a strong emphasis on school-based credentials, would be likely for their children. Ultimately, this pattern could undermine the universality of learning to weave in Nabenchauk. Although the historical change in apprenticeship style described in this chapter has so far been associated with an efflorescence of weaving, bilingual schooling and indigenous teachers may eventually undercut weaving's important role in the education of Zinacantec girls.

Figure 4.0. Brocade weaving. Nabenchauk, 1991. © Lauren Greenfield/VII.

CHAPTER FOUR

Relaxing the Textile Rules

Implicit rules have long existed for constructing Zinacantec textiles. With the rise of commerce and money has come a relaxation of the rules and greater individual creativity. ❖

I begin with the archaeological history of Zinacantec textiles to show the ancient origins of at least one of the stable textile "rules." A very few woven textiles dating from around the time of the Spanish conquest have been found in Chiapas, in a cave near the modern city of Comitán.[1] The most interesting thing about them, in relation to modern Zinacantec weaving, is their basket weave pattern. It is significant because basket weave is one of the two weaves Zinacantec weavers have used in modern times.

A basket weave is a plain weave in which adjacent weft threads are grouped together, as are adjacent warp threads.[2] Compare the ancient basket weave (fig. 4.1) with a modern one (fig. 4.2). In the body of the ancient textile, weft threads are grouped pairs, and in its selvage, warp threads are grouped in fours. In the modern example, weft threads appear to be grouped

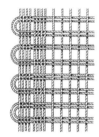

Figure 4.1. Schematic representation of an ancient basket weave found in a cave near Finca Chiptic in the vicinity of Comitán, Chiapas. The body of the fabric is done in semi–basket weave (threads grouped in one direction only), with doubled weft thread; the selvage is done in complete basket weave, with weft thread doubled and warp threads grouped in fours. Reproduced from Johnson, "Chiptic Cave Textiles from Chiapas," fig. 13, with permission of the Journal de la Société des Américanistes, Paris.

Figure 4.2. Modern basket weave shawl done in Zinacantán, 1962. Photograph courtesy of Frank Cancian.

Figure 4.3. Woman depicted on Bonampak Stela 2, circa 790 C.E. She is wearing a huipil *with overworked embroidered seams and decorated arm openings. Reproduced from Altman and West,* Threads of Identity, *with permission from the Fowler Museum of Cultural History, UCLA.*

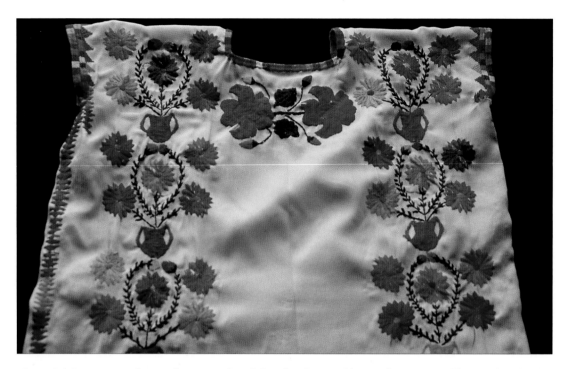

Figure 4.4. Decorative stitching on the seams and armhole embroidery are obligatory for Zinacantec blouses such as this one, embroidered by Loxa Xulubte'. Nabenchauk, 1993. Photograph by Patricia Greenfield.

in pairs, and warp threads in threes.

The basket weave has long been the foundation of one of the common types of women's shawls in Zinacantán. Although, as I show later in this chapter, the decoration of such shawls has changed remarkably in recent years, the use of the basket weave remains a stable "rule" for this item of clothing.

Even earlier evidence exists for the decoration of women's blouses. A stela at the Maya site of Bonampak in Chiapas, dating to around 790 C.E., shows two basic articles of Zinacantec female clothing: the *huipil,* or rectangular blouse, and the skirt (fig. 4.3).[3] Note that the seam of the huipil is overworked with decorative stitches, and the arm opening is embroidered, exactly as on a contemporary Zinacantec huipil (fig. 4.4). Two informants in Nabenchauk agreed that there was a relationship between the clothing depicted on this stela and Zinacantec huipiles.[4] Other elaborately decorated garments are seen in depictions of rulers on preconquest friezes in the major Maya temples, such as the frieze on lintels 25 and 26 at Yaxchilan (fig. 4.5), where Lady Xoc is clearly wearing a huipil with decorated arm openings in the image on the right.

In a book finished in 1541, Fray Toribio de Motolinía spoke of the way the Indians of New Spain used feathers to weave mantles. Today, women still weave chicken feathers into wedding huipiles in Nabenchauk (fig. 4.6). The *Florentine*

Figure 4.5. Two images of Lady Xoc of Yaxchilan. Left: *Lintel 26.* Right: *Lintel 25. In the image on the right, she is clearly wearing a huipil with decorated arm openings and seams. Photograph by Jeffrey Jay Foxx,* Living Maya. *Reproduced with permission from Harry N. Abrams.*

Figure 4.6. *Wedding huipil with feathers, woven by Xunka Tulan and her daughter, Nabenchauk. The huipil, commissioned by Gene Stuart in 1976, took about a year to complete. Courtesy of the Fowler Museum of Cultural History, UCLA. Photograph by Don Cole.*

Figure 4.7. *Chicle chewer wearing a huipil. Reproduced from de Sahagún,* Florentine Codex, *Book 10, plate 139, by permission of the School of American Research.*

Codex shows a huipil (fig. 4.7) that is very similar in design to the wedding huipil. The codex is Aztec in origin, but it is known that Aztecs and Zinacantecs traded with each other in the Postclassic period and that Aztecs who settled in San Cristóbal de las Casas "left permanent traces in the costumes of Zinacantán."[5] In any case, embroidered and brocaded textiles and headdresses made with quetzal plumes and other precious feathers were depicted in Maya murals at Bonampak in lowland Chiapas about 800 C.E.[6]

Donald Cordry and Dorothy Cordry, in their monumental study *Mexican Indian Costumes,* wrote that "the Indian woman's costume worn today seems to be that of the upper-class pre-Hispanic woman."[7] If this is the case, there could well be a connection between what ruling-class women such as Lady Xoc wear in the temple friezes and the popular dress of the present. Today, like Lady Xoc, all Zinacantec women and girls, along with other Maya women, wear highly decorated huipiles. But whereas the rectangular

shape—a product of backstrap loom technology—has been a constant of Zinacantec huipiles for many years, the kind of decoration seen on both male and female garments in the classical friezes and today has not. When I first went to Zinacantán in 1969, its textiles and clothing were very plain. Given the preconquest origins of decoration, what needs to be explained is the period of lapsed decoration, rather than its presence in the 1990s. I will try to do so by testing my economic hypothesis.

HISTORICAL TRANSFORMATION

My notion was that commercial activity, whenever it occurred, would be associated with innovation and individuation. It is safe to say that the Mayas of the Classic period had both active commerce and highly individuated clothing. Lady Xoc, for example, is seen in figure 4.5 wearing two outfits, each with a different pattern. The Zinacantecs in particular have an ancient tradition of commerce. In preconquest times, Zinacantán, among all the communities of highland Chiapas, was a trading outpost for the Aztecs of northern Mexico.[8] When the major Maya cities fell after 900 C.E., Zinacantán became a thriving market, gaining impressive control over the trade in precious feathers, salt, and amber. Despite perpetual warfare with the lowland Chiapanecs, Zinacantec merchants maintained a far-flung network of trade relations.

According to Robert Laughlin and Carol Karasik, "at the time of the Conquest the fame of the merchants of Zinacantán was so great that simply to be a native of that town was deemed an honor.... Until the early nineteenth century Zinacantecs engaged in extensive trade, carrying cacao and coffee from Guatemala to Tabasco, and tobacco to the Pacific slopes. But

tropical diseases and dispossession of their goods by the Ladinos severely curtailed their traditional occupation. Economic exploitation by landowners, political officials, even priests, was the order of the day."[9]

At that point—the early nineteenth century—agriculture began to predominate in the economic life of highland Chiapas. Following a new land law in 1867, Tzotzil- and Tzeltal-speaking Indians often became "laborers bound by debts on land owned by Ladinos."[10] Through commercial activities, Zinacantecs appear to have escaped the worse excesses of this period. "They were popularly known as independent muleteers and petty traders in the region before the twentieth century, as well as salt sellers. They ran strings of up to twenty mules, carrying agricultural goods to the towns and manufactured goods to the villages, food and money and gunpowder to the contending armies of the revolution, and even mail. Some residents of Nabenchauk today remember carrying on this activity well into the 1930s."[11]

According to my hypothesis, the commercial periods in Zinacantec history should feature more innovative, individuated, and variable textiles, and the agricultural periods should display more

conservative, uniform textiles. In pre-Columbian times, according to the archaeological record, lively commerce was indeed associated with highly individuated clothing for the upper classes. Unfortunately, no record of the clothing of ordinary folk survives.

After the conquest, weaving remained important. Throughout New Spain, Spaniards encouraged weaving and exacted woven textiles, in addition to men's labor, as tax and tribute.[12] In Guatemala, however—of which Chiapas was then a part—a sixteenth-century Spanish royal warrant banned brocaded figures in cloth, along with Maya hieroglyphic books.[13] Clearly, political factors must be added to economic ones if we are to understand the complete history of postconquest Maya textile design. Data from the mid-twentieth century help us to investigate whether agriculture is associated with plain, uniform designs, and commerce with complex, varied ones.

INNOVATION IN THE CONTEXT OF STABLE DESIGN RULES

To look at the relationship between economic mode and textile design in the modern era, I begin in 1940, the first year for which I have been able to find infor-

Figure 4.8. Zinacantec men dressed in handwoven clothing in 1940. The three men on the left wear red-and-white-striped wool ponchos (which appear to be all white), cotton shirts, and cotton shorts. Photograph reproduced from Cordry and Cordry, Mexican Indian Costumes, *345, with permission of the University of Texas Press.*

mation about both the Zinacantec economy and Zinacantec clothing. Before 1940, Zinacantec men were mostly traders, although they had been gradually making a transition to farming since about the 1930s. The anthropologist Robert Wasserstrom, a former member of the Harvard Chiapas Project, tells us that in 1940 Zinacantán was granted the right to expropriate land, and so began the period in which agriculture dominated the Zinacantec economy.[14]

The 1960s saw the consolidation of the shift to corn farming. In that year, 96 percent of the men in one Zinacantec community, Nachih, had cornfields of some kind. The dominance of corn farming continued into the 1970s. By 1983, however, the diversity of Zinacantec occupations had greatly increased. In the hamlet of Nachih, the growing number of niches in the domain of trade was particularly notable. Because of Nachih's location right on the Pan-American Highway, its economic transformation was probably a few years ahead of that in other Zinacantec hamlets.[15]

According to my economic theory, we should find comparative stability in Zinacantec clothing between 1940 and the 1970s, the agricultural period. After 1983, with the increase in commercial occupations, we would expect an increase in the rate of change—that is, in innovation. And indeed, this is what the existing data show.

In 1940 Donald and Dorothy Cordry, students of Mexican costume, visited highland Chiapas and photographed Zinacantec clothing.[16] They found men wearing red-and-white-striped, woven, woolen or cotton ponchos *(pok' k'u'ul)* with woven white shirts underneath and woven white shorts (fig. 4.8). A high ratio of white to red in the stripes gave the impression that the ponchos were white. Because they were made out of two identical pieces of cloth joined in the middle, with armholes and seams on

Figure 4.10. Man's cotton poncho in 1954. Courtesy of the UCLA Fowler Museum of Cultural History. Photograph by Don Cole.

Figure 4.9. Man's wool poncho, cotton shirt, and cotton shorts in 1954. The close-up of the poncho makes the red-and-white stripe visible. Very narrow bands can be seen at the sides of the poncho. Courtesy of the UCLA Fowler Museum of Cultural History. Photograph by Don Cole.

either side, the ponchos had mirror-image symmetry, a point that becomes important later in poncho history.

Jumping ahead a few years to 1954, we can look more closely at the man's poncho, shirt, and shorts, this time a set in the collection of the Fowler Museum of Cultural History at UCLA (figs. 4.9 and 4.10). The outfit is essentially identical to that worn in 1940. In figures 4.9 and 4.10, the red-and-white background stripe of the poncho is more visible than in figure 4.8, but white still predominates over red. The balance of the two colors changed drastically over the next forty-three years. A border at the bottom of the wool poncho also appeared in a rudimentary form about this time (fig. 4.9). This feature expanded and was important for ponchos over the next sixty years.

In 1962 Frank Cancian took a photograph in Nabenchauk (fig. 4.11) that shows that the man's poncho, shirt, and shorts were still very much the same, including the symmetry of the poncho. Like the 1954 poncho (fig 4.9), it has a narrow border at the bottom of the poncho. A woven side border has also become visible. Frank's 1962 close-up of a cotton poncho (fig. 4.12) highlights the omnipresent background stripe, constructed in the warp-winding process. Continuity still prevailed in 1969, though a thin brocade border—brocade means that supplementary

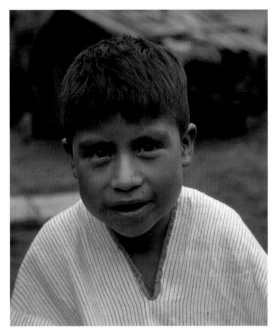

Figure 4.13. Man's poncho from Nabenchauk, 1969, with a very thin brocade border. This photograph also shows the omnipresent red-and-white background stripe. ©Lauren Greenfield/VII.

Figure 4.11. Boy wearing a wool poncho, cotton shirt, and cotton shorts in Nabenchauk, 1962. Although the poncho looks pink, it is actually woven in alternating, narrow red and broad white stripes. Note the narrow, weft-woven border at the bottom of the poncho. Photograph courtesy of Frank Cancian.

Figure 4.12. Close-up of a cotton poncho, with its background stripe. Nabenchauk, 1962. Photograph courtesy of Frank Cancian.

wefts have been placed on the top layer of the weaving—had appeared at the bottoms of ponchos (fig. 4.13).[17] Change was continuing at a snail's pace. From 1940 and into the 1990s, the man's poncho was defined as being made from two pieces of red-and-white-striped woven cloth. The sides were held together by tassels run through embroidered holes (see fig. 4.14).

In 1969 and 1970, when we first studied how Zinacantec girls learned to weave, we found that their main goal was to replicate existing modes of production and design. Although Leslie Haviland Devereaux noticed that new styles had been valued since her arrival in the late sixties, the changes were tiny and were generally shared among the whole community. Girls and women were definitely interested in minor individual differences between weavers and weavings, but the latitude for variation was small.[18] Individual touches existed mainly in the narrow woven edges of men's ponchos and women's shawls, in the thin line of brocade at the bottoms of ponchos, and in the small patches of embroidery around buttonholes on shawls (look ahead to fig. 4.41 and 4.42). Small innovations were (and still are) concentrated among teenage girls. Because weaving was and is considered the pinnacle of Zinacantec womanhood and an important attribute in attracting a husband, teenage girls had the motivation to sew and weave. Even so, in 1969 and 1970, we never witnessed the birth of a new mode of clothing production in the village, let alone a weaver who expressed pride in innovation.

Around 1976 and 1977, the government helped launch the indigenous transport business to carry people and their crops to market. People said that it was also around this time that change began. Before this time, I was told, things were much more static. By 1991 the pace of change was accelerating, and the pace of innovation in textile design reflected this timetable. The first sightings of exuberant floral designs on ponchos date to the late 1970s.[19] A photograph from 1982 (fig. 4.14) shows a young man wearing a poncho with a triangle design done in brocade weaving at the bottom. Store-bought trousers have replaced woven shorts; a store-bought shirt and sweater have replaced the woven shirt.

Strikingly, the proportions of red and white in the poncho in figure 4.14 have been reversed. This change probably indicates the beginning of the shift from cotton to acrylic thread, a petrochemical by-product of the Mexican oil boom. Across Chiapas and Guatemala, Mayas have traditionally favored the color red.

Since ancient times it has been extracted from cochineal, a scalar insect, and has been quite expensive. Even when commercial cotton thread first came into use, red was more expensive than white. With acrylic thread, red for the first time cost no more than white, so red could be added freely to the striped pattern.

By 1991 woven shirts had become rare in Nabenchauk, and woven shorts nonexistent except for ritual purposes. Yet the pattern of continuity as well as change in the poncho was revealing. The poncho shown in figure 4.15 follows the same form as earlier ones. It is made of two symmetrical pieces of whole cloth; its sides are fastened by two sets of macraméd cords with tassels, which are inserted through embroidered holes; and it features a red-and-white-striped background. It also follows what might be considered the most important "rule" of Zinacantec weaving: do not cut the cloth. (The one traditional exception is the neck hole of men's shirts.) Indeed, Zinacantecs, unlike some other Maya groups, never cut their weaving off the loom in such a way as to require a hem. They either weave a piece to the end of the warp loops (a difficult process) or leave dangling warp threads as a fringe (as in the poncho and the servilleta). Owing to this stricture against

cutting cloth, all garments and household textiles are square or rectangular. Form, symmetry, embroidered holes, tassels, and background stripe are the stable design rules for the man's poncho. As we will see, however, stability is relative, not absolute.[20]

I use the term "rule" rather than "convention" for two important reasons. I see the ensemble of conventions for a particular Zinacantec garment as making up a "grammar" of interrelated parts. This idea became particularly clear as the designs became more complex in recent years. I do not think this notion of interrelated design features is well captured by the term "convention." And although I believe these rules are inaccessible by verbal interview, I believe they would be accessible if one showed Zinacantec informants garments that broke a basic rule and asked them, "What is wrong here?" The notion of right and wrong is also better captured by "rule" than by "convention." The rules might also be considered to be generative, analogous to the way in which a small number of grammatical rules can generate an infinite variety of sentences. As the variety of Zinacantec designs increased over time, the design rules for different textile items did seem to generate a potentially infinite number of variations of the same item—not least the man's poncho.[21]

Figure 4.14. Man's cotton poncho in 1982. The poncho is now predominately red and has a narrow band of brocade weaving along the bottom edge, done in commercially produced, chemically dyed thread. Photograph courtesy of Frank Cancian.

Figure 4.15. Man's poncho, Nabenchauk, 1991. © Lauren Greenfield/VII.

FROM COMMUNITY CREATIVITY TO INDIVIDUAL CREATIVITY

The design rules for the poncho are emblematic of a community model of creativity. The community model is conservative. Its ideal is to maintain traditions that identify a group of people as a community. The poncho as I have described it was the identifying mark of a Zinacantec male. Its color and its form, tightly linked to backstrap loom technology and to the tradition of not cutting woven cloth, remained essentially unchanged for a long time. In contrast, rapid change and individuation are emblematic of individual creativity, the Western model of the creative ideal. Since the late 1970s, Zinacantecs have been moving toward this model, as can again be seen in the man's poncho.[22]

Within the framework of poncho

Figure 4.16. Poncho woven by Lupa 235 for her son in October 1992. Collected in Nabenchauk in 1993. Photograph by Don Cole.

Figure 4.17. Poncho woven by Xunka Xulubte' and embroidered by her sister Maruch in June 1994. It was made for Maruch's husband, Chepil. Photographed in Nabenchauk in August 1995 by Patricia Greenfield.

Figure 4.18. The author purchased this poncho from Chepil 1, whose wife wove it for him in 1997. It was one of the first in Nabenchauk with no white in the red body. The weaver had seen a few such ponchos before. After weaving it, she paid to have it machine-embroidered in Nabenchauk. Collected in Nabenchauk, August 1997. Photograph by Don Cole.

design rules, many changes had taken place by the early 1990s. Materials for weaving were predominantly acrylic rather than wool, which had become scarce, or cotton, which had become prohibitively expensive. As acrylic yarn spread, so did the prevalence of chemical dyes. In the 1990s, the ratio of red to white in the striped pattern continued to increase. But most noticeable was the expansion and elaboration of the brocaded bottom borders of ponchos and their embroidered tassel holes. In the poncho shown in figure 4.15, both border and tassel holes have sprouted flowers. Nevertheless, the flowers

are simply elaborations of the older notion of the embroidered hole; they respect the traditional concept, including its mirror-image symmetry, while at the same time building on it. Similarly, the brocaded border is an expansion of the simple weft-woven border that had begun in the poncho at least thirty-seven years earlier.

But the crucial test of an increased rate of change comes when we compare the 1991 poncho (see fig. 4.15) with ponchos from 1992, 1994, 1997, 1998, and 2002–3 (figs. 4.16–4.20). Beginning in 1992, the design rules for the Zinacantec poncho,

which had been very strict, began to be broken. In figure 4.16, note first that the decorative designs—both in the brocaded border and especially in the embroidered area above it—have lost their symmetry. Designs on the left and right side of the poncho are no longer mirror images of each other, as they were in 1991. Second, the embroidered designs on the top have broken loose from the anchors of the embroidered tassel holes. They have spread away from the edges of the poncho to

Figure 4.19. Man's poncho, circa 1998, hand-embroidered in imitation of machine embroidery. Collected in 2000. Photograph by Don Cole.

Figure 4.20. Machine-embroidered poncho woven by Maruch Xulubte' and machine-embroidered by her sister Loxa. It was made at the end of 2002 for Maruch's son for the New Year fiesta, 2003. Photograph by Don Cole.

embroidered by machine in Nabenchauk. By 1998 machine embroidery had become a valued aesthetic. This change is highlighted in a poncho (see fig. 4.19) that has been hand embroidered to resemble machine stitchery. In seven short years then—from 1991 to 1998—the pace of change greatly exceeded anything that had happened during the agricultural period of 1940 to 1970 or even 1982.

The notion of an accelerating rate of change manifested itself dramatically in 2003. By then, the background stripe, bilateral symmetry, and even the color red had completely disappeared from the poncho. Machine embroidery had become standard. In figure 4.20 we see a dark woven poncho with no background stripe but with all-over machine embroidery. Its peacock design crosses the center line, destroying the last vestige of bilateral symmetry. There has indeed, as expected on theoretical grounds, been an increase in the rate of textile change in Nabenchauk during the commercial period.[23]

A PARALLEL HISTORY IN RITUAL CLOTHS

The acceleration of change during the recent commercial period can be seen not only in men's ponchos but also in a kind of ritual cloth called a tovalya (fig. 4.21).

become nearly an all-over design, rather than a side-border design. The pace of change has accelerated.

The same trends were manifest in 1994 (see fig. 4.17), along with some new additions. The side borders of the poncho have been extended so far toward the center that the red-and-white-striped pattern no longer predominates. The basic rule of the poncho as a red-and-white-striped garment has been stretched almost to the breaking point. In addition, the striped borders have changed color from predominantly pink to predominantly purple, another innovation. The use of

silver thread as a background color for the brocade band is novel, as are the peacock and parrot images.

The 1997 poncho (see fig. 4.18) introduces a completely new element: machine embroidery substituting for both the brocade-woven band along the bottom and the hand embroidery on the top. A second new element is that the body of the poncho is solid red instead of the conventional red-and-white stripe. A woman wove this poncho for her husband, Chepil 1, one of the most financially successful entrepreneurs in the hamlet. She then paid 380 pesos (at 6 to the dollar) to have it

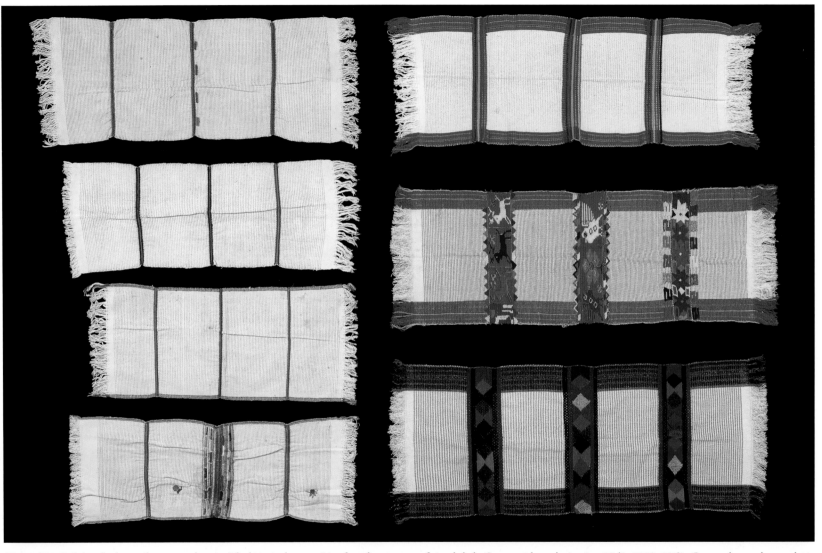

Figure 4.21. Left-hand column, from top to bottom: The historical progression of tovalyas—a type of ritual cloth. Cotton with synthetic trim, 1943, 1958, 1968. Cotton plus wool or synthetic trim, 1973. Right-hand column, from top down. Cotton plus acrylic, 1983. All up to this point were in the Petul Vásquez family collection, acquired by the author in 1993. Tovalya, cotton and acrylic, woven in 1992 and collected in 1993. This piece was woven by Loxa Hernandes Paresvan to use in discharging the responsibilities of a future cargo or religious office. The author purchased it for 460 pesos. Tovalya, acrylic, woven by Maruch Chentik for her husband Telex's cargo, Paxion Primero, in Zinacantán Center, February 2002. It was collected in Nabenchauk in 2003. Photograph by Don Cole.

Figure 4.22. Two Zinacantec boys dressed in virtually identical ponchos in 1962. Photograph courtesy of Frank Cancian.

Figure 4.23. Three Zinacantec boys, all first cousins, dressed in different ponchos in 1991. © Lauren Greenfield/VII.

Tovalyas are used to cover tortillas both in the church for communion and during the ritual meals that are part of a cargo, or lay religious office. The earliest tovalya illustrated here is from about 1943; the latest was made in Nabenchauk in 2002 (see fig. 4.21). Note the acceleration of change between 1983 and 2002, including a change in the basic color scheme in 2002. Indeed, the concept of "new colors" had arrived. The color scheme in the 2002 tovalya is basically the same as that in the latest poncho (see fig. 4.20).

Nevertheless, some basic tovalya "rules"

have remained constant. All the examples, back to 1943, have a white warp (the lengthwise threads) and the same striped background design in the weft (the crosswise threads). Each tovalya has three broad weft stripes across its interior. Compared with the poncho, this ritual cloth is more conservative, probably conforming to a general rule concerning ritual items. Consider the Western wedding dress, which still reflects styles of the Middle Ages, and the Zinacantec wedding huipil, which seems to antedate Spanish contact. Interestingly, the tovalya seems to have served as the

inspiration for the servilleta, which is made exclusively for the non-Zinacantec market.

Yet within this framework of convention or rules, change is indeed taking place, and at an accelerating pace. From 1943 to 1968 —twenty-five years—the basic tovalya design remained the same. Over the next fifteen years (1968–83), the only real change was a widening of the weft bands. Ten years later (1992), we see much greater change (see fig. 4.21). Figurative and geometric designs have been added to the weft stripes through brocade weaving. Each of the three design bands uses a different repeating figure: deer, birds, and geometric flowers. After another ten years, the basic color scheme has changed, bringing it into harmony with the "new" colors of the times. Although the basic layout and background stripe have not changed, novelty has supplemented tradition as a value.

INDIVIDUATION

The increase in the rate of change in both ritual cloths and ponchos stems from an even more important change that has taken place during the latest commercial period in Zinacantán: increased individuation of designs. Whereas in the earlier, agricultural period, each clothing item had a restricted range of variation, this is

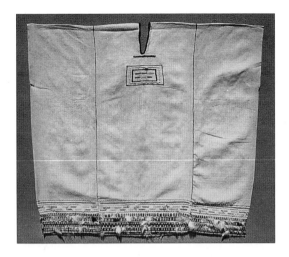

Figure 4.24. A Zinacantec wedding huipil from 1940. Feathers have been spun into the thread in the lower border. The huipil also features a preconquest type of rectangular design below the neck opening. Reproduced with permission from Cordry and Cordry, Mexican Indian Costumes, 344.

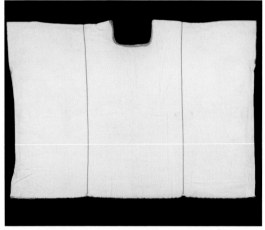

Figure 4.25. Zinacantec huipil, or blouse, 1948. From the Petul Vásquez family. Photograph by Don Cole.

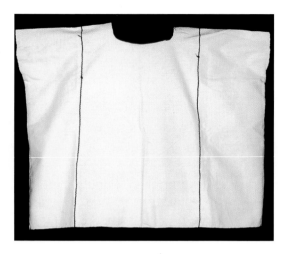

Figure 4.26. Zinacantec blouse, 1960. Photograph courtesy of the San Diego Museum of Man.

no longer the case. Take ponchos: in 1962 they all looked alike (fig. 4.22). I was fortunate to have the opportunity to analyze the individuation of everyday clothing as seen in Frank Cancian's archive of Zinacantec family photographs that he took in 1961 and 1962. I studied a total of sixty-one family photographs; clothes were visible in all of them. I found absolutely no variability in men's and boys' shirts, shorts, and wool ponchos, women's and girls' shawls and blouses, and girls' baby blouses. The poncho was almost standard from photograph to photograph; the only

dimension of variability was in a narrow woven band at the bottom, which appeared in some photographs but not others.

In sharp contrast, uniformity was not the case in 1991 (fig. 4.23). Basic poncho norms were still in effect: the rectangular shape, the construction with whole cloth, the background stripe, and the basic positioning of woven and embroidered decoration. But now we see variation and individuation in motifs and details of design placement. As I show in chapter 6, the variation is greater between families than within families, but even within a single family, weavers are creating great variability in designs. Individuation

happens against a background of both constancy and the loosening of poncho "rules" over time.

The same type of accelerated change and individuation has taken place in other items of clothing. A good example is women's blouses, or huipiles. To see the basic blouse rules, it is interesting to look at a Zinacantec wedding huipil from 1940 (fig. 4.24) and one from 1976–77, very similar (see fig. 4.6). A gauge of the conservatism of this style is a huipil shown in the *Florentine Codex,* dating from the time of the Spanish conquest (see fig. 4.7). Although the huipil in the codex was an Aztec production, its shape, color, and

RELAXING THE TEXTILE RULES

Figure 4.27. A Zinacantec girl from Nabenchauk wearing a white blouse, 1966. Photograph courtesy of Frank Cancian.

Figure 4.28. Blouses. Zinacantán Center, 1971. Photograph by Frank Cancian from Another Place, *repro-duced courtesy of Frank Cancian.*

design below the neck, involving two con-centric rectangles, echo across four hundred years to modern Zinacantán.[24]

The wedding huipil also illustrates the rules that define a Zinacantec blouse and the ancient origins of those rules. Persisting through change, the rules reflect the con-servative model of creativity, emphasizing conformity and community identity. The square shape derives from Maya weaving traditions, in which one avoids cutting woven cloth. The huipil shown in figure 4.24 was woven in three pieces. Note the thin vertical lines of embroidery joining the pieces down each side, as well as the neck embroidery and decoration. Elements that were conserved over hundreds of years include the square shape, the neck embroidery, the vertical embroidery, and the white background color. Indeed, according to anthropologist Sylvanus Morley, "white cotton cloth, said to date from just before the Spanish Conquest, is reported from a small cave near Tenam in the highlands of Eastern Chiapas."[25]

Look now at Zinacantec huipiles made in 1948, 1960, 1966, and 1971 respectively (figs. 4.25–4.28). Note that all of the basic design features have been conserved. Each blouse is plain white with a narrow band of embroidery down the two sides and around the neck. Like the wedding huipil, everyday blouses used to be woven in three pieces and then sewn together. By 1960 (see fig. 4.26), the stitching down the front was no longer needed to join three pieces of material, because blouses were now made from one piece of store-bought material. The embroidery down the front is merely a reference to an earlier time when blouses were woven in three pieces.[26] From a structural perspective, the

Figure 4.29. A Zinacantec woman wears a white blouse with bands of multicolored embroidery down the front and back. Photograph taken between 1977 and 1982 by Jeffrey Jay Foxx. From Living Maya. Photograph reproduced with permission of Harry N. Abrams.

two columns of stitching have become merely decorative—but they preserve one of the rules defining a Zinacantec blouse. In this case, the tradition of community identity maintains a form even when it loses its function.

From 1948 (and undoubtedly much earlier) to 1971, then, the Zinacantec

blouse remained essentially unchanged. Sometime between 1977 and 1982, it began to be transformed. Just at the time when commerce began to develop, the thin vertical bands of embroidery began to expand (fig. 4.29). By 1991 commercial activity was in full swing, and the Zinacantec blouse had both accelerated its rate of

Figure 4.30. Detail of woman's blouse embroidered with deer. Nabenchauk, 1991. © Lauren Greenfield/VII.

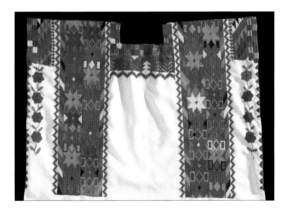

Figure 4.31. Woman's blouse embroidered with geometric flowers. Nabenchauk, 1991. © Lauren Greenfield/VII.

Figure 4.32. Blouse embroidered with fields of diamonds. Nabenchauk, 1991. © Lauren Greenfield/VII.

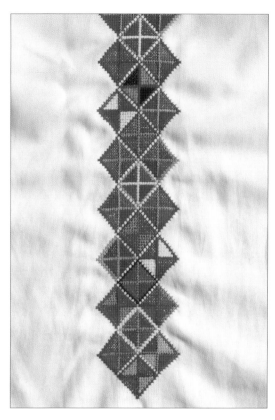

Figure 4.33. Detail of blouse embroidered with fields of diamonds. Nabenchauk, 1991. © Lauren Greenfield/VII.

change and become greatly individuated. The lines of embroidery had expanded into figures such as deer (fig. 4.30), geometric flowers (fig. 4.31), and fields of diamonds (figs. 4.32 and 4.33). The basic

rules seen in the earlier periods were generally still in effect: the shape of the blouse and the positioning of the embroidery were the same. But the individuation expressed within that framework had greatly increased. The practice of individual creativity had begun, but it was still manifested within the context of commu-

nity creativity—that is, according to the basic rules defining a Zinacantec huipil.

During the 1990s, the rate of change accelerated to a pace incomparably greater than anything observed from 1954 through 1970 or even 1980. As early as 1991, Zinacantecs were starting to break the rules for huipiles. Flowers began to

Figure 4.35. Petu' 238's blouse, completed in August 1993, the month of her interview. Photograph by Patricia Greenfield.

Figure 4.34. In the author's 1993 textile elicitation/interview study, Loxa Xulubte' identified this blouse as both her best and most original embroidery. She created it in 1991. Photograph by Patricia Greenfield.

Figure 4.36. Rosy Xulubte' embroidered this blouse on a sewing machine in November 2002, when she was fifteen. She embroidered it for her mother for All Saints' Day (K'in Santo). Photograph by Don Cole.

escape from the straight lines of embroidery on either side of the front and back of a blouse. A huipil made by Loxa Xulubte' in 1991 (fig. 4.34) shows the beginning of this trend. In a blouse by Petu' 238, completed in August 1993, the lines of embroidery down the front and back are completely gone (fig. 4.35). The blouse is no longer really identifiable as Zinacantec. Indeed, a few weeks earlier, we had seen a girl wearing a similar blouse that she had purchased in Comitán, where she worked with her father in the market. Her sister had used it as a model for still another blouse. Ten years later, this style had become commonplace.

Figure 4.37. Xunka 205 wove this blouse in May 1993 out of cotton called baz'i no *(real thread). The cut neck hole and one-piece construction show the influence of purchased blouses. Photograph by Patricia Greenfield.*

Considering what we have already seen in ponchos, it should not be surprising that machine embroidery has begun to replace hand embroidery in blouses, too (fig. 4.36). Most shocking of all in the blouse shown in figure 4.36 is its blue color, which has replaced the long-standing white. The notion of "color coordinates" has arrived; the turquoise color scheme seen here utilizes the "new" colors and forms an ensemble with shawls made in a similar color scheme.

Another development of the 1990s was the reappearance of the handwoven blouse (fig. 4.37), which we had not seen in 1969 and 1970. This development stands apart because of its "retro" nature. Unlike the much older woven blouses, this one is made in a single piece, and the vertical stripes are now woven into the material

itself. I see the resurrection of handwoven blouses, although they were still relatively rare in the 1990s, as part and parcel of innovation in design. They are innovative in another respect as well: they depart from the current standard of store-bought material. Certainly, because they coexist with all the other kinds of blouses made during the 1990s, they add greatly to the individuation and variability that are important facets of design innovation.

One factor facilitating the renaissance of the handwoven blouse may have been the greater amount of time available for weaving in the 1990s as women's other tasks became less arduous. Running water, for example, eliminated the chore of drawing and carrying water. Presses for making tortillas eliminated the need to pat them by hand, and electric mills became available for grinding corn. Because merchant husbands were often traveling in their work, wives were losing the culturally central role of making tortillas for their husbands. A weaving renaissance might therefore have revalidated women's domestic roles.[27]

Another type of handwoven blouse, the small girl's baptismal blouse, or *xela k'u'ul,* again shows the increase in complexity shared by ponchos, tovalyas, and huipiles. Like these other items, baptismal blouses illustrate the individuation of design in

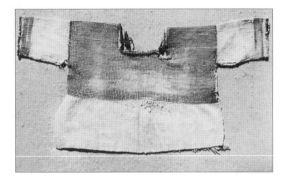

Figure 4.38. Girl's baptismal blouse (xela k'u'ul) from 1940 or earlier. Such blouses were customarily presented to a goddaughter. Reproduced by permission of University of Texas Press from Cordry and Cordry, Mexican Indian Costumes.

the 1990s and, most dramatically, the accelerating pace of change. The baptismal blouse was traditionally a gift from a child's godparents.[28] After the baptism the girl wore it on other occasions and even for everyday use.

Comparing a baptismal blouse from 1940 (fig. 4.38) with one from 1969 (fig. 4.39 top), we see that the two are similar. But comparing the 1969 blouse with one from 1991 (fig. 4.39, bottom), we see a great difference in the complexity of the woven design. The 1940 and 1969 blouses utilized a very simple kind of brocading in lines and stripes. In contrast, the 1991 model involves brocade weaving of complex geometric designs. Individuation of

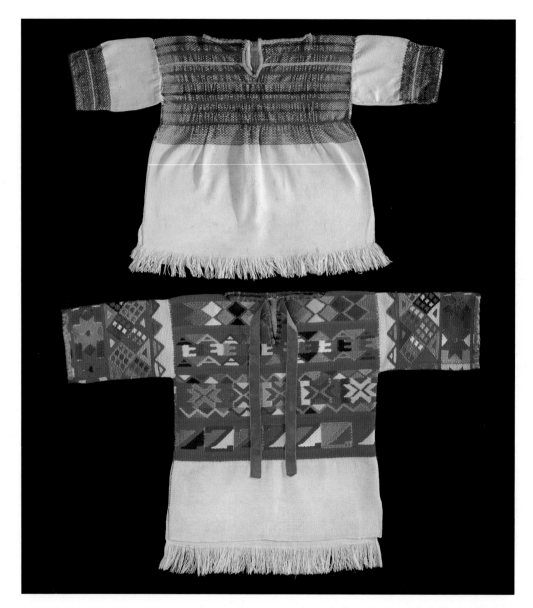

Figure 4.39. Baptismal blouses from 1969 (top) and 1991 (bottom). The 1969 version was worn by Lauren Greenfield at ages three and four. The older one is of cotton and wool; the newer one is of cotton and acrylic. ©Lauren Greenfield/VII.

Figure 4.40. Flowered baptismal blouse, cotton and acrylic. Nabenchauk, 1991. Photograph by Don Cole.

design can be seen by comparing the geometric-patterned blouse from 1991 with a flowered blouse made in the same year (fig. 4.40). Although equally complex, their brocaded designs are quite different.

In the domain of blouses, like that of ponchos, the practice of individual creativity, including innovation and individuation, seemed to be growing stronger in the 1990s. Moreover, a part of the loosening of Zinacantec design rules

Figure 4.41. Cotton pok mochebal, *or red-and-white striped shawl, 1963. From the Petul Vásquez family, Nabenchauk. Photograph by Don Cole.*

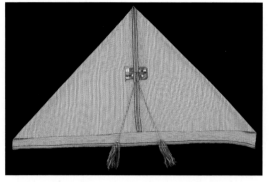

Figure 4.42. Cotton pok mochebal, *or red-and-white striped shawl. Nabenchauk, 1969. Photograph by Don Cole.*

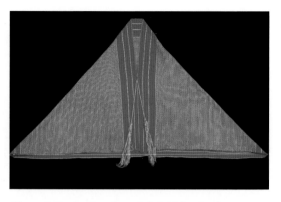

Figure 4.43. Acrylic pok mochebal. *Nabenchauk, 1991. Photograph by Don Cole.*

seemed to be interethnic influences that came directly from new forms of commercial activity. I return to interethnic influences later in this chapter. But first I want to generalize the argument to a third item of clothing, the shawl.

A PARALLEL HISTORY IN SHAWLS

In 1963 a woman's shawl known as the *pok mochebal* was red-and-white-striped cotton (figs. 4.41 and 4.44). In 1969 it remained largely the same in design (fig. 4.42; see fig. 1.1), but by 1991 the decendents of the earlier shawls had become almost solid red (fig. 4.43), the outcome of a historical competition among weavers over who could produce the reddest shawl while maintaining the traditional configu-

ration of red-and-white stripes. Baby carriers, woven in the same configuration of stripes, showed the same movement over time toward broader red stripes and narrower white ones (figs. 4.44 and 4.45).[29]

By 2000 the white had completely disappeared from the red-and-white-striped design in women's shawls, leaving them solid red (fig. 4.46). The borders (blue striped in fig. 4.46) had grown, and large embroidered flowers had expanded beyond the tie-hole embroidery. Most astonishing, one of the firmest "rules" was broken in a shawl I purchased in January 2003: the red had completely disappeared and was replaced by purple, one of the "new" colors (fig. 4.47). Another interesting aspect of this shawl is that its hand embroidery resembles machine embroi-

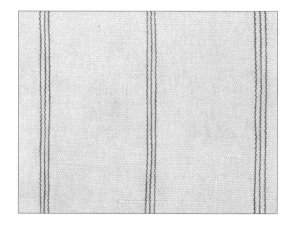

Figure 4.44. Cotton baby carrier pattern, 1943. The pattern is the same as that of the pok mochebal. *From the Petul Vásquez collection. Photograph by Don Cole.*

dery, which had become very popular.

Another traditional Zinacantec woman's shawl was the *pirik mochebal*. This warmer, wool and cotton shawl was woven in the

Figure 4.45. Xunka Pavlu, daughter of Telex and Maruch, in an acrylic baby carrier with the same red-and-white stripe as that seen in women's shawls. Note the complex stripe pattern and high ratio of red to white. Nabenchauk, 1991. © Lauren Greenfield/VII.

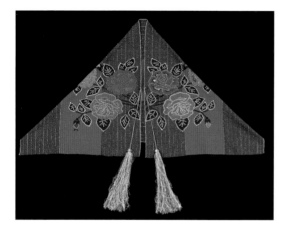

Figure 4.46. Example of a 2000 model pok mochebal from Nabenchauk. Photograph by Don Cole.

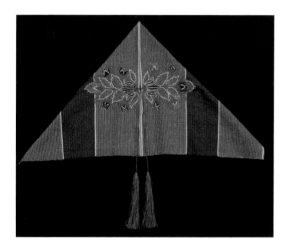

Figure 4.47. Pok mochebal purchased in Nabenchauk in January 2003. This shawl was made by Luch, goddaughter of Paxku Vásquez. Although the hand embroidery resembles machine embroidery, Luch said that hand embroidery was better because machine embroidery was thicker. Photograph by Don Cole.

Figure 4.48. A Zinacantec basket weave shawl (pirik mochebal), 1961. Photograph courtesy of Frank Cancian.

Figure 4.49. Two versions of the pirik mochebal, the basket weave shawl: left, 1969; right, 1991. The shawl on the left is made of natural wool and cotton; the one on the right is made of acrylic yarn. © Lauren Greenfield/VII.

modern basket weave (see fig. 4.2). Change came slowly to basket weave shawls between 1961 (fig. 4.48) and 1969 (fig. 4.49, left); it lay mainly in a little embroidery around the tie-holes, as seen in the 1969 version. By 1991 the basket weave shawl was often woven from acrylic thread in neon colors (fig. 4.49, right). The striped border had grown enormously, and the tie-holes now sported large, ornate, hand-embroidered flowers. Interestingly, even before the tie-hole embroidery turned into true flowers, it was called *nichim,* which means both

"flower" and "embellishment."[30]

By 2000 the flowers were larger yet, and the color scheme was bolder (fig. 4.50). Basket weave shawls not only displayed elaborate, individuated embroidery but also came in a rainbow of colors (see frontispiece). Individual uniqueness and creativity had entered the scene in an immediately visible way.

In contrast to the red-and-white-striped shawl (pok mochebal), which women wore to fiestas, the pirik mochebal was their choice for everyday activities in Zinacantán in 1991, whether working in the cornfields (fig. 4.51), picking fruit (fig. 4.52), tending sheep (figs. 4.53 and 4.54), or going to school (see figs. 3.11 and 6.23). Because the basket weave shawl was usually woven

For example, wool, a popular clothing material two decades earlier, had originally been introduced by the Spaniards. The use of wool in textiles, however, had declined greatly since the beginning of the twentieth century. By the mid-1970s, fewer than twenty women in Nabenchauk knew how to weave in wool. The modern settlement pattern made it difficult for every household to keep sheep. By 1991 the human population explosion in Nabenchauk (a doubling in two decades to about three thousand persons) had reduced the available grazing land and made sheep few and far between (fig. 4.53). It had also become difficult to buy wool from the neighboring Chamulas, who had traditionally sold it at Nabenchauk's Saturday market, perhaps because the Chamulas now found it more profitable to make the wool into tourist items. In using acrylic yarn to weave both their pok mochebal and their pirik mochebal shawls, Zinacantecs were following a centuries-old custom of using materials from outside their community to define a distinctively Zinacantec way of dressing.[31]

ANCIENT AND NEW DESIGN SOURCES

Accelerating change and individuation in Zinacantán have sometimes incorporated the conscious reclaiming of ancient history

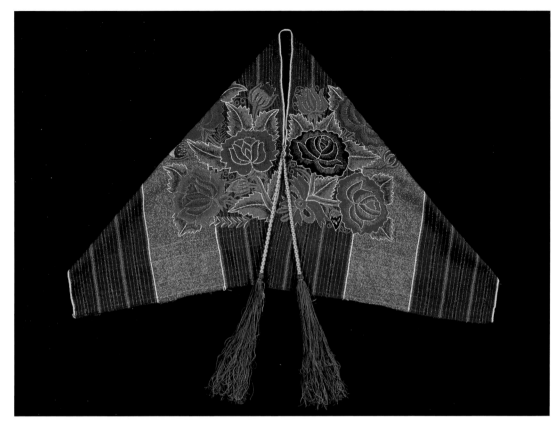

Figure 4.50. A 2000 model of the basket weave shawl. Photograph by Don Cole.

from acrylic thread, there was no longer necessarily a difference in warmth between it and the pok mochebal, although a warmer version of the basket weave shawl was occasionally woven out of wool and acrylic. Although wearing a shawl to pick fruit or work in a cornfield may appear awkward, shawls are still de rigueur if a girl or woman leaves her household compound. As a result, few outsiders are aware of the elaborate blouses that Zinacantec women have been creating to wear underneath.

At first glance, it seemed to us in 1991 as though traditional Maya textiles had been invaded by the modern world. But Zinacantec tradition has never been static.

Figure 4.51. A Zinacantec girl wears a basket weave shawl (pirik mochebal) as she works in a cornfield. Nabenchauk, 1991. © Lauren Greenfield/VII.

Figure 4.52. Three women wear basket weave shawls as they pick fruit. Nabenchauk, 1991. © Lauren Greenfield/VII.

and religion.[32] As in the development of commerce, what appears new is occasionally very old. For example, a pattern of filled-in triangular zigzags that weavers were using in the 1990s (fig. 4.55) has its source in ancient Maya beliefs. Every weaver labeled these zigzags "mountains." A large, triangular mountain rising above the valley of Nabenchauk is worshiped as sacred; ancestral gods are thought to live in it and other sacred mountains in Zinacantán, and many rituals are performed for them. These gods provide models for human behavior in Zinacantán.[33]

Many anthropologists believe that pyramids in Mesoamerica symbolize and re-create the religious and ceremonial functions of sacred mountains.[34] In weaving, we can see this association reflected in a ceremonial Zinacantec belt, now decades old, that was probably used to dress a saint. It contains brocaded triangles with trees next them. The triangles, which are truncated at the top, like pyramids, are called the "ancient house," or pyramid, design (fig. 4.56).[35] During a recent field session in Nabenchauk, in January 2003,

Paxku', daughter of Maruch Chentik and Telex Pavlu, told me that this pyramid design was "like a mountain." She saw the similarity between the woven mountain design shown in figure 4.55 and the ancient house or pyramid design in figure 4.56.

Other design sources are brand new. Although current designs often come from pattern books printed in Mexico City, the predominance of Spanish flower patterns also has real meaning in terms of present-

Figure 4.53. Herding sheep. Nabenchauk, 1991. © Lauren Greenfield/VII.

Figure 4.54. A Zinacantec woman wears a basket weave shawl while shearing a sheep. Nabenchauk, 1991. © Lauren Greenfield/VII.

day economic life. Growing flowers for sale with the aid of chemical fertilizers had become a major source of Zinacantec livelihood by 1991 (fig 4.57), replacing corn in the fields. In 1997 a guide in a women's museum in Zinacantán Center said that Zinacantec clothes now had embroidered and brocaded flowers on them "because we used to grow corn and beans and now we grow flowers."[36]

LABOR ISSUES AND INNOVATION

As textiles became increasingly complex, they required correspondingly greater time to make. In 1991 women and girls actually enjoyed more time to devote to weaving and embroidery than they had in 1970. As I mentioned earlier, this was because domestic work, including weaving, had become less onerous in both time and effort. For example, acrylic thread, unlike wool, does not need to be spun.[37]

On the other side of the balance, the amount of time required for elaborate brocade weaving and embroidery is great. This means that women who are busy with young babies might need to ask a teenage relative or friend to do the brocade work or the fancy embroidery on a piece. In 1991 such work was more often done for money than had previously been the case. As I talked to women and girls, I found nearly unanimous agreement that the fancy embroidery and woven designs were superior to the plainer textiles that had preceded them. People

Figure 4.55. "Mountain" pattern brocaded into the border of a man's poncho. Nabenchauk, 1991. © Lauren Greenfield/VII.

Figure 4.56. The Zinacantec "ancient house" design. Drawing courtesy of Pedro M. Meza and Harry N. Abrams, Inc., from Living Maya *by W. F. Morris, Jr., p. 213.*

Figure 4.57. A family readies flowers to be taken to market. Nabenchauk, 1991. © Lauren Greenfield/VII.

also agreed that they took much more time and effort than before.[38]

Ratcheting up the amount of time required to make clothing, in conjunction with an increase in the use of money, opened the door to people's developing faster ways of producing clothing and to a greater willingness to buy it. Concerning the latter trend, recall from chapter 1 the Guatemalan blouses occasionally made for Zinacantecs in 1991. In the mid-1990s, blouses hand embroidered in the highland Maya community of San Andrés began to gain popularity in Zinacantán. More dramatic was the disappearance of the xela k'u'ul, the girl's baptismal blouse, several years later. Paxku' Pavlu told me in January 2003 that the xela k'u'ul no longer existed because it took too long to make. People were now buying baptismal clothes in San Cristóbal, she said. She was pregnant with her first baby and planned to do likewise.

Another manifestation of the trend toward saving time by buying clothing is the use of store-bought clothing for everyday wear, so that the occasional production of time-consuming textiles is reserved for special events such as fiestas. One example of this has been the trend stopped wearing short pants and instead wore long cotton pants from the market. Young men and adolescent boys began to prefer colorful store-bought shirts as well. From that time forward, men and boys expressed their Zinacantec identity in their red-and-white-striped ponchos. Many now go hatless or wear plastic cowboy hats in place of the once ubiquitous and distinctive handwoven fiber platters with multicolored streamers that were the pride of adolescence in the last generation.[39]

Since the late 1970s, this trend has accelerated. Men working outside of the village no longer wear ponchos when they work—for example, doing agricultural work in the lowlands (fig. 4.58). As of 2002, one no longer saw young boys wearing ponchos as they played basketball in the central plaza of Nabenchauk. Everyday clothing was simply purchased in stores. Handwoven shirts and shorts were used only for ritual occasions such as the performance of religious cargo ceremonies. Even handwoven ponchos were often reserved for fiesta wear.

Greater willingness to purchase clothing and materials is a component of women's openness to using faster, more expedient modes of production. In 1995, for example, Paxku', then thirteen, made a blouse for me with store-bought fabric and commercial

Figure 4.58. Zinacantec men slaughter an animal while working in the lowlands, or "hot country." © Lauren Greenfield/VII.

away from handmade clothing for men. In the early 1950s, Zinacantecs dressed in clothing that was handwoven in its entirety. Men's outfits of short cotton pants, wool belts, long-sleeved cotton shirts, and red-and-white-striped ponchos of either cotton or wool were all handwoven on backstrap looms by Zinacantec women. Women's garments—long cotton skirts, wool belts, white cotton blouses, and cotton or wool shawls—were similarly handwoven. In those days, only a few items of daily attire were purchased: men's neck scarves, the ribbon edging of their shirts and ponchos, the red wool for the tassels on ponchos, and the ribbon streamers of their hats. Women's blouses were decorated with purchased embroidery thread.

By the late 1970s, the men of Nabenchauk had almost completely

Figure 4.59. Paxku' Pavlu sewed this blouse, made with purchased printed ribbon and cloth, and gave it to the author. Nabenchauk, 1995. Photograph by Don Cole.

Figure 4.60. Blouse from San Andrés, another highland Maya community, made for the Zinacantec market. Nabenchauk, 1993. Photograph by Don Cole.

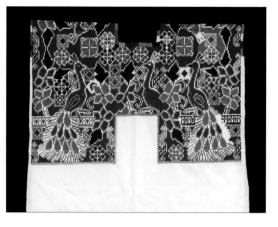

Figure 4.61. The author bought this girl's blouse in 1997 from three women from San Andrés who were selling blouses door-to-door in Nabenchauk. Photograph by Don Cole.

printed ribbon instead of hand-embroidered vertical bands (fig. 4.59). Another attempt to save time can be seen in Zinacantecs' use of the sewing machine to embroider, met first in a poncho in 1997 (see fig. 4.18). By 2002 Zinacantecs also used sewing machines to embroider blouses (fig. 4.36), just as they had known Guatemalans to do, at least since our return to the field in 1991.

In the Zinacantec world of commerce, the sewing machine became important not only to save time but also to make money. People in Nabenchauk first purchased sewing machines sometime between 1997 and 2000. The investment in a machine meant that one could charge 300 pesos (US$30 in 2002) for two to three days' work, say to embroider a poncho. This was much less time than it took to embroider a poncho by hand. A sewing machine became a capital investment. Thus the commercial mentality has grown to the point that people measure time in terms of money. The purchase of hard goods such as trucks and sewing machines was seen as an investment that would bring monetary returns.

As we saw in chapter 1, Zinacantecs also developed for outside use items that could be woven and embroidered quickly and sold for less. New items such as servilletas were developed for the market. In this way, weaving for sale in the wider world beyond Zinacantán entailed innovation and creativity. Yet Zinacantecs maintained their own community identity by never once wearing or using these items.

CREATIVITY THROUGH INTER-INDIAN COMMERCE
Commerce by its very nature requires intercultural communication, beyond the confines of family and community. At the same time, it encourages innovation, because traders are always trying to anticipate the market. Beginning in 1993, I saw people from the highland Maya community of San Andrés selling blouses made

Figure 4.62. San Andrés blouse purchased from Paxku' Pavlu in Nabenchauk, 2000. Photograph by Don Cole.

for the Zinacantec market (figs. 4.60–4.62). This particular commercial relationship appears to be the only one between San Andrés and Zinacantán. Perhaps the central role of San Andrés in the multicultural Zapatista movement encouraged the members of this community to become more cosmopolitan.[40]

San Andrés embroidery is much admired by Zinacantecs. But they do give feedback about what they want in a blouse. In 1993 I heard a Zinacantec girl in Nabenchauk request from a San Andrés seller more embroidery on the sleeve of a blouse. Zinacantecs take themselves seriously as a market force. Note that the huipil example from 1997 (see fig. 4.61) has much more sleeve embroidery than that from 1993 (see fig. 4.60). Even more interestingly, the embroidery on the later blouse, like the Zinacantecs' own embroidery, escapes the confines of narrow lines going down the front. A San Andrés blouse from 2000 goes even further in obliterating the distinction between neckline embroidery and the two bands of embroidery down the front (fig. 4.62).

These blouses illustrate a new willingness to adapt to markets with the recent development of a commercial money economy. They are made in the Zinacantec style, following Zinacantec rules, and not according to the clothing conventions of San Andrés. To see the degree of market adaptation, compare a San Andrés huipil made for internal use (fig. 4.63) with the embroidered Zinacantec-style blouses made by San Andrés women for sale in Zinacantán (see figs. 4.60–4.62).

Whereas in 1993 the San Andrés sales force in Nabenchauk was led by a man, four years later I met an all-female group making door-to-door rounds in Nabenchauk, selling embroidered blouses. Around the same time, San Andrés had become a Zapatista village and therefore had presumably begun the Zapatista program toward gender equality and cooperative work for women. The Zapatista program of "women's liberation" may already have shown results.[41]

One can see this intercultural commerce as a process in which the artisans of San Andrés adapted their embroidery to the Zinacantec model. At the same time, one might interpret the San Andrés blouses as having introduced a new style of embroidery within the general Zinacantec model. This new style was later emulated by Zinacantec girls themselves: my young friend and sometime assistant Paxku' Pavlu herself copied a San Andrés blouse in 1995.

In the early 1990s, the anthropologist June Nash documented the Mexican government's increasing interest in promoting the work of indigenous artisans.[42] In 1999 I found evidence of interaction between this national influence and interethnic relations among the Mayas. At an artisan village run by the Mexican government in Mexico City, I came upon Zinacantec-made servilletas being sold by boys from the Tzeltal-speaking Maya community of Tenejapa in highland Chiapas, who ran the shop. Increased commerce, then, has increased Mayas' interethnic relations and cross-cultural knowledge of other groups. It may also foster a pan-Maya identity.

BEYOND ZINACANTÁN

As predicted from the rise of entrepreneurial commerce in Zinacantán during my research team's absence in the 1970s and 1980s, the production of textiles there reflects a historic change toward greater personal initiative and more individuation in creating textile designs. Designs are becoming more complex and are changing at an accelerating rate. Within the constraints of ever-loosening "rules," the Zinacantecs have moved from a closed system of design to an open one. The end result is much greater design variability, although woven and embroidered clothing still marks Zinacantecs to themselves and to the outside world as clearly as ever.

Figure 4.63. Blouse made to be worn by a member of the San Andrés community. Photograph by Jeffrey Jay Foxx, Living Maya. *Reproduced with permission from Harry N. Abrams.*

To what extent can these conclusions be generalized beyond Zinacantán? A few observations from Tenejapa offer a hint. Tenejapa is less commercial than Zinacantán but nonetheless has seen an increase in commerce. For example, Tenejapa has a weaving cooperative. This commerce, however, is limited to trade between Tenejapa and San Cristóbal de las Casas. Unlike the Zinacantecs, Tenejapans do not trade all over Mexico, nor do they buy goods in one place to sell in another. They sell mainly their own goods— agricultural products and textiles. But considering that there had been some increase in commerce in Tenejapa, I thought it worthwhile to see whether a corresponding increase in design individuation had taken place.

As a case study in Tenejapa, I analyzed skirts made by a twenty-three-year-old and by her fifty-four-year-old aunt. As predicted by my theoretical framework and empirical findings in Zinacantán, the younger woman's skirts showed much more variability than did the older woman's, an indication of increasingly individuated and variable design. The Tenejapa weaving cooperative provided additional evidence of design individuation and variability. In its store were designs and materials from old traditions not seen in current clothing and textiles in the community. The co-op had revived these designs in order to increase the connection to the past and to make money. In essence, the revival of the old in Tenejapa, as in Zinacantán, has not replaced but has added to present-day variability in textile design. In Tenejapa, as in Zinacantán, the rise of commerce has been associated with the rise of individuation, innovation, and variability in the sphere of textile design.

Chamula, a neighboring Tzotzil-speaking community, has been through similar changes, particularly among Protestants expelled from their communities (for being Protestant) who have started new communities, or *colonias,* near San Cristóbal de las Casas. These expelled Chamulas moved more abruptly than the Zinacantecs into a completely cash economy. Women quickly began to sell their handmade textiles. Like Zinacantecs, Chamula girls and women have developed faster methods of producing textiles by reducing size and weaving loosely, thus increasing the monetary value of their labor. At the same time, producing textiles for the market has produced a variety of innovative textiles and techniques.[43]

Can we find evidence in the Maya world even farther from Zinacantán for an increase in the rate of design change in the wake of commercial development? Maya Guatemala, too, with its accelerating change in handwoven textiles, fits this scenario. There, too, it appears that textile commerce reaching even beyond the Maya world, beginning in the 1960s, has gone hand in hand with increasingly rapid changes in the textiles themselves.[44] The cases of Tenejapa, Chamula, and Guatemala indicate that the historical rise in design individuation, alongside a rise in commerce, is not necessarily specific to Zinacantán but may reflect a more general relationship between individual psychology and economic participation. In the coda to this book, I show that these principles reach even beyond the Maya world.

Figure 5.0. Nine-year-old Paxko' Pavlu, daughter of Telex Pavlu and Maruch Chentik, constructs her idea of a beautiful pattern. Nabenchauk, 1991. © Lauren Greenfiled/VII.

CHAPTER FIVE

Inside the Mind

An experiment shows how young Zinacantecs come to "see" basic textile designs and colors and what they consider beautiful. Ways of seeing are not constant but change over time. ❖

A Zinacantec girl sits in front of a wooden frame, a pile of colored sticks next to her. "(Now) you look at the shawl here," Carla Childs says in Tzotzil, pointing to a 1991 shawl in front of the frame. "You look at what it is like," she says, showing the shawl's red-and-white stripes with her hand. "The same as this you stack the sticks on their side." (Here and elsewhere I give a literal English translation of the Tzotzil instructions; the Tzotzil original appears in an endnote.)[1] Figure 5.1 shows how one nine-year-old girl, Paxku' Pavlu, responded to these instructions in 1991. It shows her representation of the striped design of the shawl.

In what sense do I mean "representation"? Human perception is categorical: it lumps together things that human beings are capable of discriminating.[2] Internal, perceived categories can be externalized

Figure 5.1. Paxku' Pavlu, age nine, places sticks in a frame to represent a contemporary pok mochebal, or red-and-white-striped shawl. Nabenchauk, 1991. © Lauren Greenfield/VII.

through representation—that is, by using a medium such as a painting or a diagram to selectively construct or reconstruct things or events. Therefore, researchers should be able to use people's external representations to study their internal perceptions. Carla and I did exactly this in Nabenchauk, first in 1969–70 and again in 1991. In short, the frame and the sticks in our experiment constituted our technique for looking inside Zinacantec children's minds. They offered a way to externalize mental representations into behavior that could be seen and studied.

For example, we studied children's use of sticks to represent a 1969 shawl. Figure 5.2 shows the experimental situation and what the same girl, Paxku' Pavlu, constructed for this older shawl when she was tested in 1991. At age nine, she was able to represent the fact that a stripe of a given color appeared in different widths in the shawl pattern, but she was unable to depict this variability accurately. For example, she represented variability mainly in the width of the red stripes, when in fact it lay entirely in the white stripes (which were narrow within the "red" shawl stripe and broad between red stripes, as the right side of fig. 5.3 shows). Our results indicated that this inaccuracy was mainly a matter of cognitive development. Only teenagers in the

Figure 5.2. Paxku' has completed her representation of a 1969 pok mochebal. Nabenchauk, 1991. © Lauren Greenfield/VII.

study could accurately reproduce complex patterns with multiple components.

Tasks such as these gave us a window into the cognitive processes behind the construction of designs in the weaving process, as well as a window into the perception of cultural artifacts. By testing children of different ages, we could also study the growth and development of

these representations with age.

Human beings perceive the world at least partly in terms of opportunities to act upon it. Because different cultural environments and different stages of development provide different opportunities for action, they should also lead to different perceptions.[3] Therefore, one major theoretical question is, How does

Figure 5.3. Pattern of a man's poncho (pok k'u'ul), above, and a woman's shawl (pok mochebal), right, both 1969. Note that the shawl's wide red stripes are composed of three thin red lines separated by two thin white lines. Photograph © Lauren Greenfield/VII.

goal-directed activity affect perception and representation? In our particular context, this question translated to, How does the activity of weaving affect the perception and representation of woven patterns?

Within cross-cultural and cultural psychology, this question has historical antecedents in classical research on relations between culture and perception. In more current terms, our question is part of the cultural study of everyday cognition. We took inspiration for our 1969 research design from Douglas Price-Williams's experimental study of how membership in a pottery-making family influenced Mexican children's development of concepts of clay quantity and how this experience generalized to related cognitive concepts.[4]

But our pile of colored sticks had other purposes as well. We could, for example, use them to see whether the changes discussed in the preceding chapters had implications for the mind, or, more precisely, for the way people represent their world. Because we had found that innovation and novelty in textile design increased greatly from one historical period to the next, we wondered whether cognitive skill in representing novel patterns had also increased.

METHOD
An Experiment in Four Parts

In order to discover the answers to these questions, we developed an experiment consisting of four parts. We asked children, adolescents, and young adults in Naben-chauk to participate in the experiment in both 1969–70 and 1991. For both the 1969-70 and 1991 participants, part 1 consisted of putting sticks in the frame to represent the 1960s-style red-and-white poncho and shawl patterns shown in figure 5.3. Like Paxku' Pavlu, the other 1991 participants had an opportunity to represent the poncho and shawl—now considered old—after they had finished part 2, which I describe later. For all participants, contemporary patterns were the ones they themselves wore or ones provided by the researchers.[5]

In part 2, the experimenter began five

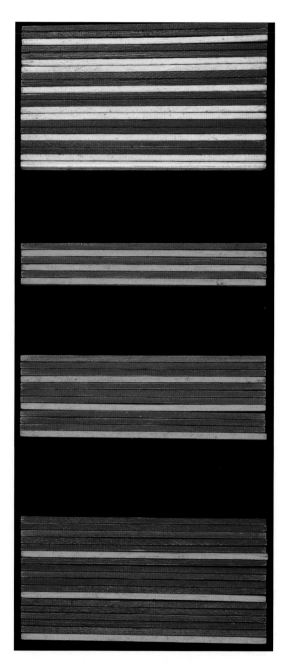

Figure 5.4. Models for continuation of culturally novel patterns. For pattern 5 (top), red, white, pink, and orange sticks were made available; for patterns 6 and 7 (middle two), green, yellow, black, and blue; and for pattern 8 (bottom), red, green, and yellow. (Patterns 1–4, not shown, were the culturally traditional patterns: 1 was the poncho, 2 the shawl, and 3 a simple red-and-white alternation. Pattern 4 was the same as 7, but in red and white instead of green and yellow; we considered it to be a possible poncho pattern.) Photograph by Don Cole.

Figure 5.5. Paxku' studies a culturally novel green-and-yellow striped pattern (pattern 7) that Carla Childs, the experimenter, has started for her to complete. She is to use the sticks immediately to her left. Nabenchauk, 1991. © Lauren Greenfield/VII.

different, culturally novel striped patterns—that is, patterns that did not exist in the Zinacantec environment—and asked the participant to continue them.[6] Figure 5.4 shows patterns 5–8, the first four of the five novel patterns. Before each pattern continuation, the experimenter said, "(Now) I myself am going to stack the sticks on their side. As for you, you watch how I do it." She then created three repetitions of the pattern and said, "Now you stack the sticks on their side the same as this."[7] Figure 5.5 shows one of the novel patterns (six) as it has been started by the experimenter. Paxku' Pavlu is looking at the pattern, getting ready to continue it.

Pattern 9, the last novel pattern and the last item in part 2 of the experiment, was particularly difficult. We called it the "growing" pattern because it started with an alternation of single red sticks and white sticks and then proceeded to alter-

nations of double, triple, and quadruple red and white sticks (figs. 5.6 and 5.7). This pattern also differed from the others because there were three possible "correct" ways to continue it. In European American culture, we have a preference for the "progression" strategy (fig. 5.6, bottom right), which continues to expand the width of the stripes. Indeed, when Carla and I made up this item, we saw no other possible correct answer. The progression strategy was the only one that went beyond the model to create something new, and the cultural value we placed on novelty blinded us from seeing other possibilities.

Our Zinacantec participants, however, created two other legitimately correct strategies: repetition and mirror image (see fig. 5.6 bottom left and center). In line with Zinacantecs' cultural dispositions to re-create the known and to create mirror-image striped patterns in weaving (that is, borders on both sides of woven cloth), participants in the experiment used the repetition and mirror-image strategies to repeat design units from the original model.[8] As I explain later, responses to this pattern revealed changes over historical time in response to culture change.

Eventually we realized that generalization of representational strategies to novel patterns was a form of innovation and therefore a skill that had little value in the agrarian, subsistence world of Zinacantán in 1969 and 1970. When we went back to Nabenchauk in 1991, we expected innovation to be more highly valued, and we thought that preference for novel patterns and skill in representing them might have increased, especially among girls, who now created novel textile patterns and were heavily involved in commerce for the first time. We expected not only to see the new generation do better in representing novel designs but also to see a greater use of the progression strategy. Of all the pattern continuations, this one was particularly interesting because it allowed for so much cultural and aesthetic choice.

The third part of the experiment we called the "creativity" item. Central to our investigation were evolving definitions of creativity in Zinacantán. At the time of our first fieldwork, in 1969 and 1970, weavers had followed an implicit concept of community creativity. A woven pattern represented the distinctiveness of Zinacantán as a community. Within a more general Maya format, garments and cloths were instantly recognizable as Zinacantec. The characteristics of each type of textile were consensually defined and stable with little scope for individual variability within a particular type.

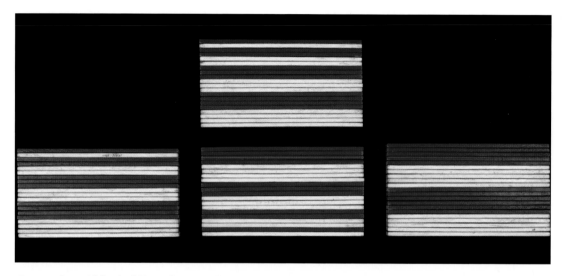

Figure 5.6. Model for the fifth novel pattern, the "growing" pattern, and three possible continuations. The experimenter's model is at the top (pattern 9), and the three possible "correct" responses appear at the bottom: repetition (left), mirror image (center), and progression (right). Thin red and white sticks were available to participants for this task. Photograph by Don Cole.

By 1991 we had observed a shift in the direction of individual creativity. Novel woven and embroidered designs were superimposed on the general Maya and specific Zinacantec textile formats. The rate of change in woven and embroidered textiles had accelerated, as described in chapter 4. Textiles for clothing, home, and ritual use had become individuated, particularly at the level of the family. A new implicit model of individual or at least family creativity appeared to have been accepted (see chapter 6). Creativity as we know it in the West had entered the culture.

We therefore added a more open-ended task to our original experiment when we returned in 1991. The experimenter would say to participants, "With the sticks here, you stack them on their side the way you yourself want. Make it beautiful. The most beautiful you understand—like that you stack them."[9] Participants could use the full array of sticks, which came in eight colors and three widths: narrow, medium, and wide. Red, white, orange, and pink sticks came in all three widths; the other colors—green, yellow, black, and blue—came only in the narrow width.[10]

Figure 5.7. Paxku' works on completing the growing pattern. The experimenter has started the pattern up through the first stripe of four white sticks. Paxku' is completing it using a common error strategy, simplification. She continues to repeat the last two stripes in the model: four red, four white. Nabenchauk, 1991. © Lauren Greenfield/VII.

sticks to give the child an idea of what the task was. When we returned after twenty-one years, this task became our means to study the cultural evolution of color terminology.

We were interested in how color naming practices might affect the use of color in patterns. In Tzotzil, a single word, *z'oh,* covers the English categories red and orange. Another word, *sak,* covers the English categories white and pink. Given that red and orange are treated equivalently in the language, would they also be treated equivalently in the pattern representations? What about white and pink? These questions concerning the influence of language on thought originated in the work of anthropologist Benjamin Lee Whorf.[11] The proposition that language influences or determines thought is known as the Whorfian hypothesis. In order to answer the questions, we provided red, orange, white, and pink sticks that could be used to represent the red-and-white-striped poncho and shawl. They could also be used in the red-and-white pattern continuations.

Our experimental technique served as a tool to compare two generations of Zinacantec children and adolescents living in Nabenchauk. To my knowledge, this was the first time a cognitive experiment

In this part of the experiment, we were most centrally interested in the cultural definition of beauty.

The fourth procedure explored how children of different ages named the colors in which the sticks were painted. We were interested in the relationship between the way colors were labeled and the way they were used in pattern representation. This was a way to explore the relationship between language (color words) and thought (pattern representation) in the aesthetic domain. Subjects were asked to name six colors—green, white, red, pink, orange, and blue (fig. 5.8)—after the researcher named the black and yellow had been repeated years apart in the same population with a view to examining the effects of historical change.[12] As in our study of weaving apprenticeship, second-generation experiment participants in 1991 were mostly the first generation's children, nephews, and nieces. This inter-generational comparison allowed us to explore an important set of issues. To what extent did representations remain constant across historical time? To what extent were they historically and socially contingent? To what extent were they dependent on different kinds of economic participation, technologies, and educational experiences?

In some ways, our experiment stepped outside the Zinacantec cultural definition of knowledge (na') and into the European American cultural definition of knowledge. That is, we gave the participants novel rather than well-practiced, habitual tasks. The children related well to the tasks, however, which involved doing something manually in response to a request made in Tzotzil. Requests for action were an everyday mode of communication between elders and children, and the participants were familiar with it from activities such as weaving apprenticeship and sibling teaching.[13]

Across the two time periods, we recruited 203 children, adolescents, and young adults ranging in age from about three and one-half years to twenty-two years. In all, 97 boys and 106 girls were asked to *laz* ("stack") the sticks in our experiment. It was a series of tasks that all seemed both to take seriously and to enjoy.

The 1969–70 sample numbered ninety participants in all. Of the fifty-one boys, twenty-seven, or 53 percent, had been to school. Of the thirty-nine girls, only four (all between eight and ten years old), or 10 percent, had been to school. The absence of any teenagers in the schooled female sample indicated that girls' schooling was just beginning in Nabenchauk at that time.

The 1991 sample totaled 113 partici-pants. Of the forty-six boys, thirty-four, or 74 percent, had been to school. Of the sixty-seven girls, twenty-three, or 34 percent, had been to school. Only one participant in the entire sample, a boy, had gone as far as secondary school. The village of Nabenchauk offered only ele-mentary schools.

REPRESENTING TEXTILE PATTERNS

In both historical periods, Carla Childs asked participants, in Tzotzil, to place sticks in the frame to make the designs of the man's poncho and the woman's shawl,

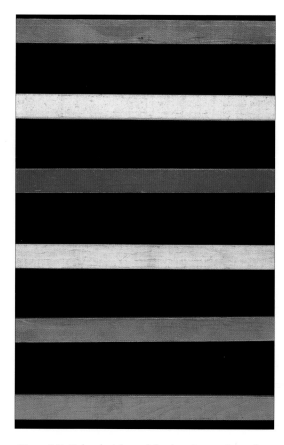

Figure 5.8. Colored sticks used for the color naming task. Top to bottom: olive green, white, red, light pink, orange, and sky blue. Photograph by Don Cole.

for example fig. 5.3.[14] Where possible, their clothes and ours served as stimuli.

Children of different ages displayed different abilities to represent the textile patterns with the sticks. The four- and five-year-olds could successfully place the

Figure 5.9. Old poncho (left) and shawl (right) representation by five-year-old Octaviana 172 in 1991. In both cases, she used the broadest sticks available but placed colors randomly. (Note: From here forward, except where noted, photographs of stick designs are based on reconstructions from the data record.) Photographs by Don Cole.

from the shawl in their representations, for example figure 5.10. They had a single global perception and representational strategy for the two patterns.

By age thirteen, participants could differentiate their representations of the two patterns. Sometimes, as in figure 5.11, this differentiation also involved higher-order integration of pattern elements in the more complex shawl design. That is, two kinds of striped patterns (three thin red stripes separated by two thin white stripes and one broad white stripe) had to be differentiated within the shawl and then integrated into a single striped pattern.

In sum, we found three steps in cognitive development, from a random color strategy to a global representation of the most general pattern features (regular stripes) and finally a representation subtle enough to capture differences between the two patterns and sometimes internal complexity within the shawl pattern.

Indeed, figure 5.11 illustrates only one among a number of representational preferences displayed by our oldest participants. This representational style or strategy has several interesting characteristics. First, it is the product of an accurate analysis of the two design configurations, the simple alternation of red and white that characterizes the poncho and the more complex

sticks in the frame but could not create a pattern. Without exception, they placed the sticks at least partly randomly in response to both the poncho and the shawl. In the response illustrated in figure 5.9, although the child placed the

colors randomly, she did systematically use only the broadest sticks available.

Most eight- to eleven-year-olds were able to make a striped pattern, using both color and width in systematic ways, but they could not differentiate the poncho red-and-white stripe that characterizes the shawl. Second, it is what we called a detailed, or thread-by-thread, representation. That is, the broader stripes are built up out of a number of narrow sticks, just as, in weaving, broad stripes are composed of multiple threads woven side by side.

This thread-by-thread representation contrasts with a style of representation that we never saw in Nabenchauk but found among a group of female college freshmen in the United States after we returned from the field in 1969. We called this an abstract style because it removed the detail that tied the representation to the concrete reality of the woven cloth (fig. 5.12). It was just as accurate as the detailed strategy in analyzing and representing the two configurations, but in using a single broad stick to represent a broad stripe, it simplified and abstracted the design by eliminating the detail.

In 1969 and 1970, accurate, thread-by-thread representation was the dominant strategy among Zinacantec teenage weavers—all girls. It reflected the fact that weavers have to be familiar with the ways in which textile designs are actually constructed. Most of the girls had in fact wound the striped warp designs on the winding board. But even two who had not done so used this strategy; undoubtedly,

Figure 5.10. Chepil 243, age eleven, used the same simple alternation to represent both the old poncho (left) and the old shawl (right) in 1991. Sample textile models for these designs are shown in figure 5.3. Photograph by Don Cole.

like other Zinacantec girls, they had carefully examined the textiles that came into their world. What surprised us in 1969–70 was that thread-by-thread representation was also the preferred strategy of teenage boys who had been to school. Apparently schooling, perhaps because of the visual analysis required to identify letters in reading, had developed in boys the visual skill of pattern analysis.

This representational strategy of the schooled teenage boys contrasted sharply with the strategies of the unschooled teenage boys in 1969 and 1970. Their two most common strategies for differentiating the two patterns were to use color and width of stripe. Using the color strategy, they depicted the poncho as either redder or pinker than the shawl, even though both garments were constructed of exactly the same red and white thread. When a poncho of this type is seen from a dis-

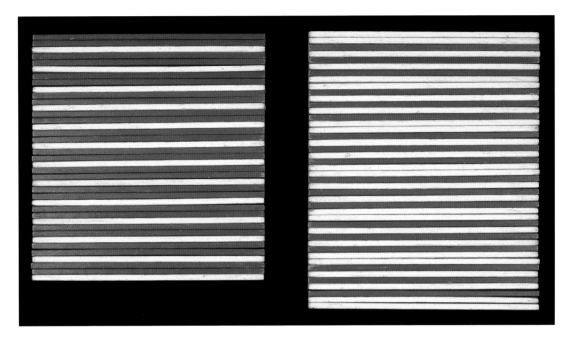

Figure 5.11. Using a detailed, thread-by-thread analysis, thirteen-year-old X201 differentiated the 1991 poncho pattern (left) from the 1991 shawl pattern (right). See figures 4.15 and 4.45 for typical 1991 poncho and shawl designs. Photograph by Don Cole.

The male strategy of using width of stripe to differentiate the two garments persisted into the next generation, tested in 1991, for example figure 5.16.

In part 1 of the experiment, then, we found that across all participants in both historical periods, representational strategies developed according to age from random to global to differentiated. Differentiation included distinguishing between patterns and also, in the striped shawl, between the parts of a single complex pattern. Once basic cognitive capacities had developed, participants' choices of representational strategies reflected their specific experiences and practices, particularly those related to weaving and schooling. Most importantly, as we will see, those experiences turned out to be historically contingent.

tance, it looks solid pink or light red (fig. 5.13), whereas the shawl from a distance reveals its red-and-white stripes, for example figure 5.14. Teenage boys, who neither wove nor closely examined textiles, often focused their representations on how the cloth looked from a distance. This male color strategy persisted into the next generation, tested in 1991 (fig. 5.15).

The other dominant strategy among unschooled teenage boys in 1969 and 1970—using stripe width to differentiate the two patterns—also focused on features that were visible from a distance, without close examination of the textile. If one did not look closely at the complex stripe of the shawl, one could see the garment as being composed of a thick red and a thick white stripe, versus a thin red and a thin white stripe for the poncho (see fig. 5.3). These features were represented in the strategies of a number of teenage boys.

HISTORICAL CHANGE IN REPRESENTING ZINACANTEC TEXTILE PATTERNS

When Carla Childs and I returned to Nabenchauk in 1991 to carry out our experiment with a new generation of participants, we made certain predictions about how changes in weavers' cognition would correlate with the dramatic economic changes we were observing. In part 1 of the experiment, we expected that the shift from subsistence farming to commerce and the use of money would have led to the introduction of the abstract mode of representing woven patterns. Our expectation was confirmed. In 1969 and 1970, all accurate analyses of the shawl design had been detailed, or thread-by-thread. This type of representation occurred in 1991 as well (see fig. 5.11), but abstract analyses of the shawl pattern also appeared in Nabenchauk for the first time.

One example of an abstract strategy for analyzing and representing the two designs was provided by Palas 213, a young man of twenty-two. On the left side of figure 5.17, he has contrasted a narrow red stick, used to represent the narrow red stripe of the 1969 poncho, with a broader white stick to represent its broader white stripe. Similarly, for the red-and-white shawl (see fig. 5.17, right) he used single sticks of three different widths to represent stripes of three different widths. What he did not do was use multiple narrow sticks to represent a single stripe, an approach that would have led to a thread-by-thread representation because, in actual cloth, broad stripes are composed of multiple threads. A major factor in the increase in use of the abstract strategy was schooling. Palas, the only member of the 1991 sam-

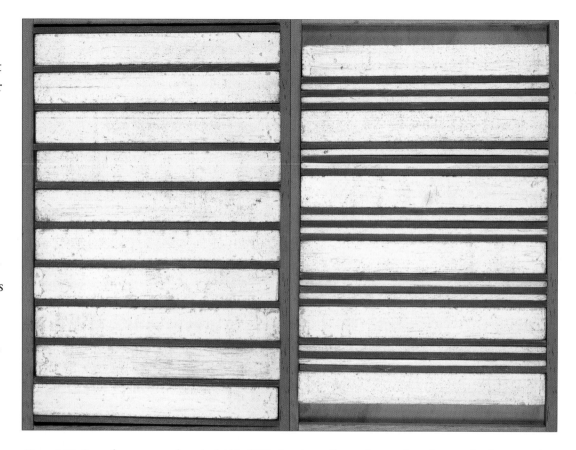

Figure 5.12. Soon after our return from the field in 1969, American college students used an abstract style of representation to differentiate the patterns of the poncho (left) and shawl (right). This example was constructed by Jan 501. Photographs by Don Cole.

ple with a secondary school education, illustrates this relationship.[15]

We also predicted that commercial involvement would be a factor in abstraction. In order to test this hypothesis, we created a quantitative measure of abstraction by counting all the medium and broad sticks used to represent the woven patterns. The assumption behind this measure was that only narrow sticks would be used to represent individual threads and that medium and broad sticks would

Figure 5.14. A red-and-white-striped shawl, when seen from a distance, clearly shows its red stripes. Nabenchauk, 1991. Photograph by Sheldon Greenfield.

Figure 5.13. A red-and-white-striped poncho, when seen from a distance, looks pink. Nabenchauk, 1970. Photograph by Sheldon Greenfield.

generally be used to represent a higher-level, or more abstract, unit, the stripe. We found that participants' commercial involvement—for example, driving a truck, owning a television, working in a local shop, or selling peaches—was causally related to the use of medium and broad sticks (abstraction) in the representation of the poncho and shawl.[16]

Palas 213, who used a large number of medium and broad sticks in his representations of the old (1969) poncho and shawl (see fig. 5.17), again illustrates this relationship. Palas was an agricultural census taker for the government. He was unique in our sample in his reliance on wage work and his use of mathematical abstraction to reduce qualitatively different agricultural items (such as corn, cattle, and land) to abstract numerical values. He was also unique in having to deal with the manifold abstractions of a government bureaucracy. Even in his uniqueness, however, Palas dramatically illustrates the general link between the use of abstraction in everyday life and its use in a task of aesthetic representation.

HISTORICAL CHANGE IN REPRESENTING NOVEL PATTERNS

Turning to our next prediction, recall that in part 2 of our experiment, many of the patterns we asked participants to continue were culturally novel. Because of the development of an entrepreneurial economy in Zinacantán during the 1970s and 1980s, we predicted that skill in representing these novel patterns would increase from one historical period to the next. And that is what we found. Participants in 1991 correctly completed more novel patterns than did those in 1969–70.[17]

In 1969–70 boys had correctly completed more novel patterns than girls. We thought the gender difference would be smaller in 1991, because girls had by then gotten involved in selling textiles and in other aspects of commerce. And indeed, the gender difference had entirely disap-

Figure 5.15. In 1991, Petul 9, a thirteen-year-old boy, used color to differentiate the old poncho (left) and shawl (right) patterns. Using wide sticks, he made the poncho pink and orange, the shawl red and white. Photograph by Don Cole.

peared by 1991. Girls had significantly improved over two decades; boys had not. In essence, by 1991 boys and girls were representing novel patterns with the same level of skill.[18]

Was there a connection, we wondered, between girls' augmented skill in representing novel patterns and the development

we had observed of a trial-and-error style in weaving apprenticeship? Our theory was that a more independent, trial-and-error style of apprenticeship was adapted to an environment in which innovation was valued. More specifically, we thought that an independent style of learning to weave would be well adapted to creating

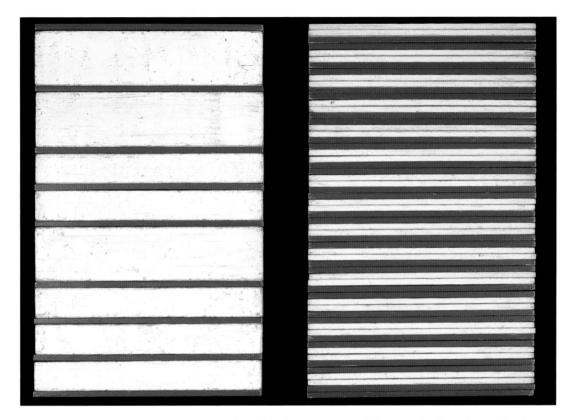

Figure 5.16. In 1991, Xun 218, age sixteen, used a width-of-stripe strategy to differentiate the old poncho and shawl designs. Though he was not totally consistent or accurate, he used wider white stripes for the poncho (left) and wider red stripes for the shawl (right). Photograph by Don Cole.

novel woven patterns. If this theory was correct, then weaving learners who were more independent should also be better at continuing the novel patterns.

To test this idea, we looked at the weaving learners who had also participated in the pattern representation experiment. We correlated learner independence in weaving apprenticeship with number of novel patterns correctly completed in our experiment and found a significant correlation.[19] This correlation offered strong confirmation for our basic theory linking apprenticeship style with traditionalism versus novelty in the artisanal products themselves.

These historical changes in representing novel patterns were set against a general (probably universal) trend toward increasing ability to represent pattern complexity with age. Our five novel pattern models (see figs. 5.4 and 5.6) can be arranged on a scale of complexity involving size of repeating unit and number of subpatterns within a larger repeating unit. Pattern 6 is the simplest: as a simple alternation, it has a repeating unit of two sticks and no subpatterns. Pattern 7 is next in complexity, with a larger repeating unit (four sticks). But it, too, consists of a single repeating unit with no subpatterns. Pattern 8 is the third most complex: it has a larger repeating unit (six sticks) and consists of two subpatterns (red, red, green, and red, red, yellow) within the larger unit. Pattern 5 is slightly more complex, with the same number of subpatterns but a repeating unit of seven sticks. Pattern 9, the "growing" pattern (see fig. 5.6), is by far the most complex: it has the largest repeating unit (twenty sticks) and four subpatterns (red, white is the first; red, red, white, white is the second; and so forth).

This ordering of complexity was also a developmental ordering. The youngest age at which at least half the children correctly extended the simplest patterns, patterns 6 and 7, was seven years. The youngest age at which at least half of them got pattern 8 correct was ten, and pattern 5, twelve. In no group did even half the participants succeed in completing pattern 9 perfectly. In sum, as with textile patterns children were able to represent increasing complexity as they grew older. This developmental pattern held across both historical periods.

In testing for historical changes, as opposed to development stages, pattern 9 served a particularly useful purpose. I have already tracked the efflorescence of innovation in textile design during the 1990s (chapter 4). Pattern 9, the growing pattern, could be used to study the generality of this movement from tradition to innovation. In order to make the pattern grow, one must go beyond the information given and, in a small way, create novelty.[20] The preferred strategies for extending the growing pattern in the earlier period—in line with the cultural preference for imitation as a learning style in 1969–70 and with the devaluation of novelty—were the imitative ones of repetition and mirror image (see fig. 5.6, bottom left and center). Given the conservative zeitgeist in Nabenchauk at that time, it is probably significant that the only two participants to go beyond the information given and "grow" the pattern then were two boys who had been to school, an institution

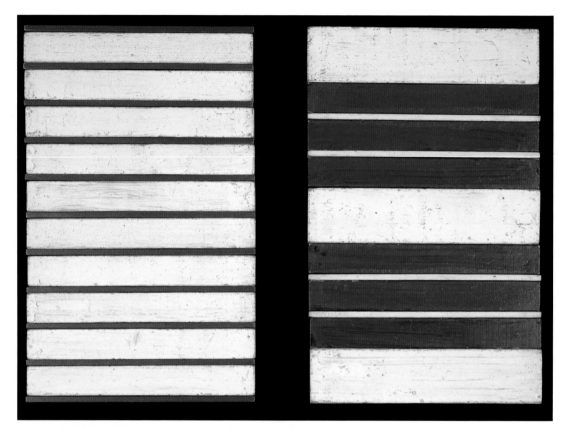

Figure 5.17. In 1991, Palas 213, age twenty-two, used an abstract strategy to differentiate the old poncho (left) from the old shawl (right). Photograph by Don Cole.

that exerted an alien influence on Zinacantec culture.

We predicted that as part of the greater cultural value placed on novelty or innovation in 1991, we would see a shift in favor of the progression, or growing, strategy for pattern 9 (see fig. 5.6, bottom right). This was the strategy in which the participant created something a bit novel, something that went beyond the pattern started by the experimenter. In line with this prediction, we found a dramatic change in the distribution of strategies for correctly completing this pattern. In

Figure 5.18. In response to being asked to make something beautiful in 1991, Mercel 232, age fourteen, created a light-dark pattern resembling the patterns shown in figure 5.21. Photograph by Don Cole.

Figure 5.19. Two small items employing light-dark striped patterns similar in many respects to the light-dark "creativity" response shown in figure 5.20. Top: servilleta made by Petu' 227, age eight, measuring 9 1/4 inches by 19 inches. Bottom: bag made by Loxa 227, age ten, the older sister of Petu'. It measures 10 inches long (including fringe) by 9 inches wide. However, since the cloth is doubled over to make a bag, both pieces are nearly the same size. Both were woven in Nabenchauk in 1991. Photographs by Don Cole.

1969–70 only 18 percent of participants who employed one of the three possible strategies shown in figure 5.6 used the growing strategy to extend pattern 9. In 1991, 62 percent of the participants who employed one of the three correct strategies made the pattern grow.[21] Why did the progression strategy become more common in the second generation than it had been in the first? Schooling, we found, was the major potential motor, with commercial involvement a secondary factor.[22]

A historical increase in pattern innovation had occurred not only in real-world textiles (see chapter 4) but also in Zinacantecs' minds, as a cognitive strategy. This cognitive strategy took the form of skill at representing novel patterns, even to the point of going beyond the information given in the growing pattern. The historical relationship between novelty in the real world (specifically in textile patterns) and novelty in our cognitive experiment provides a clue that this cognitive strategy might have helped make the real-world pattern innovation possible.

WHAT IS BEAUTIFUL?

In part 3 of our experiment in 1991, the creativity task, we asked participants to place the colored sticks in a way that

Figure 5.20. Xunka' 210, age eight, responded to the "make something beautiful" task with an original pattern. Photograph by Patricia Greenfield.

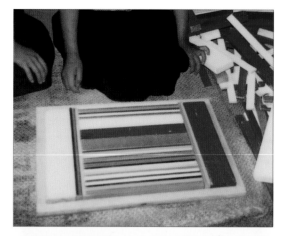

Figure 5.21. Spontaneous constructions by Paxku' Pavlu, age nine. Nabenchauk, 1991. Polaroids by Patricia Greenfield.

would "make something beautiful." Because of our interest in innovation, imitation, and tradition, we classified all the resulting patterns in one of three ways:

as being like one of our patterns from the prior parts of the experiment (the creativity task came after all of the pattern continuations had been completed), as being like

Figure 5.22. Chepil 243, age eleven, responded to the request to "make something beautiful" in 1991 with this original pattern. Photograph by Patricia Greenfield.

Figure 5.23. Lupa 230, age seventeen, responded to the "make something beautiful" task in 1991 with this original design. Lupa also manifested a rather abstract definition of both the design elements—a same-color pair and a pair consisting of a narrow white plus a narrow colored stick. Photograph by Patricia Greenfield.

Participants copied our own patterns only when they resembled an existing Zinacantec textile pattern such as a simple red, white, red, white alternation.

A substantial minority, 36 percent, created original patterns. There was absolutely no relationship between originality and age. The examples of original patterns illustrated here were constructed, respectively, by an eight-year-old (fig. 5.20), a nine-year-old (fig. 5.21), an eleven-year-old (fig. 5.22), and a seventeen-year-old (fig. 5.23).

Indeed, experience rather than age seemed most important; witness the particularly original, spontaneous creations by the nine-year-old Paxku' (fig. 5.21). Because the study occurred in her house, she was familiar with the sticks, watched others participate, and sometimes helped us run the experiment.

Overall, these findings indicate that the dominant criterion for beauty in weaving in 1991 was the Zinacantec norm for striped textile patters. Participants selectively avoided recreating our novel pattern continuations; instead, they re-created traditional Zinacantec pattern types. However, they did not simply imitate the Zinacantec patterns used in the experiment, as figure 5.18 demonstrates. Such a pattern is generated from the participant's

some Zinacantec woven textile pattern, or as being original. Most participants (64 percent) who created recognizable patterns made ones that resembled Zinacantec

woven patterns.[23] For example, they made patterns using an irregular light-dark motif (fig. 5.18) like that used in some small cloth items in Zinacantán (fig. 5.19).

mental model of cultural pattern types

Yet a substantial minority of our experiment participants employed aesthetic criteria involving original patterns. This minority probably represented the direction of change in the future for the community as a whole. As more and more members of the community become increasingly involved in the commercial activities of the surrounding world, both as consumers of commercial items (fig. 5.25) and as entrepreneurs or workers in commercial enterprises, Zinacantecs' respect for novelty and originality—creativity in the Western sense of the word—will undoubtedly rise. Paxku' Pavlu, age nine, who observed and often helped us with the experiment, may indicate the future. Her spontaneous creations broke the implicit rules of Zinacantec striped patterns, our models, and even of our instructions in the case of her tower (see fig. 5.21).

THE ROLE OF COLOR WORDS

As I mentioned earlier, our experiment was designed to address not only Zinacantecs' cognitive representations of patterns but also the relationship between color vocabulary (part 4 of the experiment) and the use of color in pattern representation. Because a fair number of

teenage boys used the contrast between white and pink or between red and orange to differentiate between a poncho and a shawl (see fig. 5.15), we knew that at least some Tzotzil speakers could distinguish red from orange and white from pink, despite the lack of single Tzotzil terms differentiating pink and white, orange and red. Sometimes participants modified Tzotzil terms or used Spanish loan words to distinguish between the colors in each pair. For example, one participant distinguished white from pink by using *sak vilan* for white and *saksaktik* (whitish) for pink. The standard term for white is simply *sak*. Another participant used the Spanish word *rosado* for pink.

But what about participants who did not create or utilize distinctive terminology for white and pink or for red and orange? Perhaps they would see the difference between the colors as less important, particularly earlier in their age-related development. To explore this idea, in both 1969–70 and 1991, we looked to see whether participants who labeled red and orange (or pink and white) with different words or phrases would use colors differently when they continued our patterns, in comparison with participants who used a single term for each pair (or who simply used the wrong term for one of the colors).

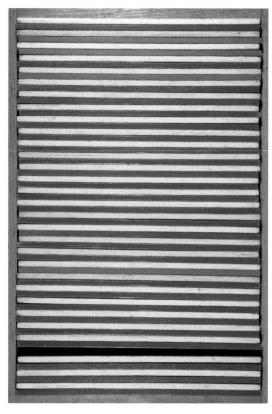

Figure 5.24. In 1991, Maruch 228 continued a red-and-white-striped pattern, randomly substituting pink for white and orange for red. The space in the frame shows where the researcher's model ended and the participant's response began.

We expected to find that when a single term was used for two colors, those colors would be freely substituted for each other when the participant continued the patterns the researcher had started.

We did, in fact, find this type of substitution. For example, Carla might start a pattern by alternating red and white sticks. The participant would respond by constructing an alternating stripe in which orange was occasionally substituted for red and in which pink occasionally replaced white (fig. 5.24). Interestingly, this type of color substitution did not decrease in frequency between the two historical periods.

The big question, though, was whether the linguistic construction of color terminology made a difference in the way Zinacantec participants actually used color in their interpretations of our designs. We found that it made a big difference for the monolingual Tzotzil speakers—those who were old enough to make patterns but had never been exposed to Spanish at school. For example, in 1969–70, 75 percent of unschooled participants between ages eight and eighteen who used the same term to label the white and pink sticks (or an incorrect term for one of the two) also freely substituted pink for white sticks in continuing a design. Only 36 percent of those who employed different terms for

pink and white did so. (We used eight as the lower age limit in order to eliminate children who were too young to construct striped patterns.) Similarly, all of the unschooled participants in this age range who used a single term to label the orange and red sticks freely substituted orange for red in continuing a design. Only 33 percent of those who used different terms for orange and red did so.[24] This link between color terminology and use of color to continue patterns held steady for the 1991 participants as well.

The color substitutions, however, were matters of preference rather than ability. In 1970, eleven of twelve participants who made regular color substitutions in constructing their patterns were able to separate white, pink, orange, and red sticks when explicitly instructed to do so. Our test of the Whorfian hypothesis, then, indicated that language influenced thought in the domain of aesthetic preference but not in the domain of perceptual discrimination. Previous tests of the Whorfian hypothesis that color terminology influences or determines thought had focused on cognitive abilities rather than aesthetic preferences. They often found that language had rather weak effects on thought. Ours was the first test, to our knowledge, of the effects of lan-

guage on aesthetic preferences, something closely tied to cultural norms. It is interesting that in the domain of cultural aesthetics we find a fairly tight connection between language and thought.

Over the years, evidence has accumulated that thought also influences language. This is true in two senses, one of which accounts for language universals, the other for cross-cultural variability. In the first sense, human neural and perceptual equipment creates common thought patterns, which in turn create linguistic universals and universal conceptual prototypes.[25] In the second sense, ecological conditions—particular environmental problems to be addressed—create different habits of thought, which in turn produce different vocabularies. In other words, thought can influence language both in the direction of commonalities and in the direction of differences. Both senses are relevant to color terminology. Our historical study provided a unique opportunity to study this direction of influence, from thought to language.

As Brent Berlin and Paul Kay discovered in the 1960s, languages undergo a universal process of evolution regarding the color terms they encompass. The languages with the fewest color terms are two-term systems; universally, the first two terms are black and white.[26] Red is the next term to be added, followed by green and yellow together and then blue. In line with five-term systems everywhere, Tzotzil has five basic color terms: black, white, red, green, and yellow. The English ten-term system adds blue, orange, purple, pink, and brown to the five basic terms illustrated by Tzotzil. Berlin and Kay, however, made their inferences from cross-sectional or synchronic data—data collected at about the same time across different linguistic populations. They had never followed a given language across time. With our two-generation study, we had an opportunity to do so.

For the first time, we could ask the question, Do systems of color terminology evolve from one system to another? If so, do they do so in the predicted order? What impels people to add color terms? These questions, to my knowledge, had not previously been addressed using a diachronic (longitudinal) study. But cross-cultural variability also needs to be addressed. Why is it that some languages or culture groups have fewer basic color terms than others? Our study was perfectly positioned to answer such questions.

Our historical study allowed us to test for both universals in Zinacantec color terminology and environment-specific influences on it. If color evolution takes a universal course, would an increase in the number of color words follow the pattern described by Berlin and Kay? Particularly interesting in the Zinacantec case was the role of Spanish. To the extent that the evolution of color terminology included Spanish loan words, would these be randomly integrated into Tzotzil or would they follow the universal order predicted by Berlin and Kay? On the side of environmental influences, might changes in the ecology of Zinacantán provide new problems for people to solve that would ultimately change language—that is, color terminology?

Looking at our data from the two time periods, we found evidence for both universals and environmental effects. Unlike the situation in 1969–70, by 1991 manufactured colors were rampant, particularly in the domain of weaving and embroidery. Thread now came in an almost infinite variety of colors. This state of affairs put great stress on the five-term Tzotzil color system, especially when someone went to buy thread and had to ask for a color by name. We therefore expected color terminology to have expanded during the preceding twenty-one years.

We were able to establish that expansion had indeed taken place. In 1969–70 the modal term for blue in our sample was *yox,* the Tzotzil term for green. (The mode is simply the response chosen by the greatest number of people.) Berlin and Kay's evolutionary order predicted that blue would emerge next. By 1991 it had done so: the modal name for the blue stick had shifted from *yox* to *celestre,* the Spanish term for sky blue (which was the blue we had used to paint the blue stick). A new basic color term had been added to the lexicon. As one would expect, green had remained *yox.*

The evolution of basic color terms was orderly and slow: orange and pink had not yet emerged. In 1969–70 the modal term for orange was *k'on,* the Tzotzil word for yellow. It was still the mode in 1991, but *naranja,* the Spanish word for orange, was now a close second. Similarly, the most popular word for pink during both periods was the Tzotzil phrase *sak vilan,* a modification of white *(sak).*[27]

The internally driven conformity to the universal evolutionary pattern is striking. Spanish is not having a uniform influence on Tzotzil color terms. Spanish words are being selectively adopted, exactly in line with the universal sequence described by Berlin and Kay. At the same time, historical change also implies the effect of the environment. Universals in the human apparatus for color vision had driven the order of change in color terminology. Environmental change, and the new problems it created, had driven the change in terminology itself.

If we look at the phenomenon of increasing numbers of color names at the individual level, we find that the average number of color terms used by participants also increased significantly.[28] In 1969–70 participants utilized, on average, four different color terms to name the six differently colored sticks in our experiment. In 1991 they used, on average, five different terms for the same colors. As the demand for color terms expanded in order to fulfill everyday needs, so did individuals' repertoires of color names.

In addition, in line with the theme of increasing individuation over time, we found increasing differences among participants in the color names they used to label a given stick. To use red as an example, our participants together generated four different color terms for the red stick in 1969–70. In 1991 they generated ten different color names for the red stick. Whereas all of the names were in Tzotzil in 1969–70, five were in Spanish in 1991. Nonetheless, in both periods the modal response was *z'oh,* the Tzotzil term for red. This term accounted for virtually the

same proportion of responses in the two periods: 84.4 percent of participants used it in 1969–70 and 85.5 percent in 1991. There was still a common "culture" concerning what to call the red stick, but individual differences were on the rise.

EXPERIMENTAL LESSONS

Our experimental procedure turned out to be a sensitive instrument for detecting cognitive changes that supported and enabled the behavioral changes in apprenticeship described in chapter 3 and the material changes in textile patterns described in chapter 4. Just as Zinacantec textiles revealed a trend toward increasing novelty from one generation to the next, our experiment revealed a corresponding increase in girls' skill at representing novel patterns. Moreover, we found not only an increase in skill at reproducing novelty but also a historical trend toward creating novelty. For example, participants in 1991, but not in 1969–70, went "beyond the information given" to "grow" rather than copy pattern 9.

Presumably, these cognitive skills in reproducing and creating novel patterns both reflected and facilitated the creation of novel designs in weaving and embroidery. Indeed, a substantial minority of our participants, given the opportunity to "make

something beautiful," chose to construct culturally novel designs within our experimental paradigm. All of these historical changes occurred within an envelope of cognitive development: with age, participants became increasingly able to differentiate and represent complex patterns.

Our experimental procedure also proved to be a sensitive instrument for detecting linguistic changes that responded to and supported the new textile designs. The historical increase in the variety of colors used in weaving was mirrored by an increase in the number of color terms used by our Tzotzil-speaking subjects to label a standard set of stimuli. Interestingly, this increase followed a universal pattern in the cultural evolution of color terminology. These findings show how social construction exploits biological potential in response to new conditions.

We had thought that an independent style of apprenticeship would facilitate the creation of novel textile patterns. Combining data from our experiment with data from our video study of weaving apprenticeship, we found that weaving learners who learned in a more independent, trial-and-error fashion were also those who more successfully continued the culturally novel patterns in our experiment. Perhaps they were likely to produce more novel and more original textile patterns as well.

Finally, the movement from subsistence to commerce changed the way some Zinacantecs represented their own woven patterns. Although many participants in 1991 still created a thread-by-thread, or detailed, analysis of the poncho and shawl patterns, for the first time a substantial number of participants analyzed the patterns in a more abstract, less detail-oriented manner. The more schooling participants had received and the more involved in commerce they and their families were, the more abstract their representations were likely to be.

Abstraction is certainly valued in formal education. But why was abstraction associated with commerce? Monetary exchanges reduce all details of goods and services to the single abstract dimension of number.

We believe it is the increased prevalence of abstract monetary exchanges in Zinacantán that has stimulated the development of abstract representation of the woven patterns. The final message of our cognitive experiment is that not only do societies change, but minds change as well. These changes of mind both adapt to and enable changes in culture and in society.

Figure 5.25. Maruch Chentik and her daughters shop for shoes in San Cristóbal de las Casas, a sign of the emerging consumer economy. Until recently, Zinacantec girls and women went barefoot, perhaps because of the ancient Maya belief that they should keep their feet in touch with the earth. © Lauren Greenfield/VII.

Figure 6.0. © Lauren Greenfield/VII.

CHAPTER SIX

The Creative Process

The new creativity in Zinacantán is often collaborative within families. It combines old and new technologies and many sources of designs. ❖

The French anthropologist Claude Lévi-Strauss once remarked that "style is a statement by a culture that it differs from other cultures."[1] Zinacantecs would unanimously agree. For them, weaving and embroidery are, in equal measure, statements of identity and standards of beauty. When I arrived in Nabenchauk in 1969, the standards for Zinacantec weaving had for many years consisted of some three culturally defined striped patterns and one basket weave pattern; the parameters of variability were all but invisible. The concept of creativity as a matter of unique, individual self-expression did not exist in the cultural milieu of Zinacantec clothing and textiles. Creativity was exclusively a matter of community identity and tradition.

In the experiment described in chapter 5, my colleagues and I took a small step toward studying the indigenous aesthetics of Zinacantec weaving. From it, we learned how Zinacantec Maya children of different ages represented their culturally central woven patterns. At the end of the developmental pathway revealed by our pattern representation experiment lay a series of alternative strategies that adolescents used to represent the two most important woven patterns. The particular representational strategy chosen was a function of the activities in which the adolescent was engaged: weaving the cloth, wearing the clothes, going to school. We recognized that these strategies for placing colored sticks in a frame to re-create the striped patterns of textiles were stylistic choices.

But it was only when we returned to Zinacantán in 1991 to find an infinite array of textile patterns that the issues really posed themselves in aesthetic terms.

What Western scholars call creativity—individual uniqueness—had arrived in Zinacantán.[2] What had been assumed to be a universal definition of creativity was proving, in the Zinacantec visual realm, to be historically contingent. In chapters 1, 3, and 4, I explored how and why this happened. In chapter 5, I linked this historical development to individual conceptual development in the context of analyses of novel patterns and representations of beautiful design.

In this chapter, I explore the nature and development of creative processes in textile design as they existed in Nabenchauk in 1993. In the field of creativity research, Howard Gardner has expressed frustration with equating creativity and divergent thinking, the traditional definition of creativity within psychology. Measures of divergent thinking (such as "How many uses can you find for an object?") seem to have little to do, he says, with how people actually create in a particular domain, or even with how creative they are.[3] I therefore tried to use actual textiles to gain a more ecologically valid measure of visual creativity in the domain of textile design.

THE STUDY

My original intent when I returned to Nabenchauk in 1993 was to link design innovation to the apprenticeship processes described in chapters 2 and 3. I thought that girls who learned to weave in a more independent manner would create more innovative designs. To explore this notion, I did a thorough photographic and interview study of textiles and their creation based on almost all the weaving learners studied in 1991 and many of their mothers.[4] But I failed to achieve my original goal. Why?

In contradiction to my assumption—and the assumption behind the whole psychological field of creativity research—the creation of visual design in Zinacantec culture was not an individual process. The goal of designing and producing textiles was not to achieve a unique means of self-expression. Therefore, I could not measure innovation or creativity on an individual level. Although, relative to 1969–70,

novelty and innovation had gone far, innovation in 1993 was still as much a family process as an individual one. The concept of creativity was still linked more to social interaction than to individual inspiration.

Social interaction in Nabenchauk took many forms. Older girls created designs for younger ones to embroider. Girls who had never gone to school copied the textiles of schooled girls who were able to "read" printed pattern books. Mothers and daughters sat and embroidered together, gaining inspiration from each others' designs.

The source of a novel textile design, it turned out, was not solely the mind of the person who made it. Instead, creativity lay in people's conscious arrangement of motifs from multiple sources, both inside and outside of Zinacantec culture. Designs were unique only in their "surface structure." Beneath it, they had a socially shared, underlying "grammar"—that is, they manifested implicit cultural rules for integrating diverse elements into a single "text." The design process sometimes incorporated elements found in ancient Maya culture or in other contemporary Maya communities.

For my interviews in 1993, I went back to girls whom my colleagues and I had

earlier videotaped learning to weave. I first asked to see their best and worst weavings and embroideries, which I photographed.[5] In this way I hoped to discover Zinacantecs' indigenous aesthetic standards of good and bad. But in line with the absence of a concept of individual creativity, the only standards seemed to be those of newness and technical workmanship. In other words, a good weaving was a brand-new one that was evenly and closely woven. In this part of the interview, I also explored the girls' evaluations of the historical changes in textiles. Almost unanimously, they preferred the new textiles.

The second part of the interview was designed to elicit the sources of the component designs of the textiles labeled "best." I expected design sources to include printed patterns, the producer's imagination, and other textiles. What I did not expect, but found, was that girls were inventing their own representational tools—from simple copying to tracing systems—for transferring designs from a printed source to a piece of cloth. Later in the chapter, I present case studies of these inventions.

I was of course interested in intergenerational change in the creative process as Zinacantec society moved from agriculture to commerce. Therefore, in most cases, I

Figure 6.1. In the Zinacantec hamlet of Vochojvo', a woman wears a typical Zinacantec blouse in 1970. Photograph courtesy of Frank Cancian.

carried out the same sort of interview with each girl's mother. I expected that designs of the younger, adolescent generation of textile producers would take images from many sources and combine them in a creative process of integration and transformation. In contrast, I expected the mothers to be more limited in their sources and to show less combinatorial creativity than their daughters.

At the end of the study, I analyzed my interviews and photographs and returned to certain households to purchase some of the most interesting and beautiful (by my standards) textiles I had seen. At this time, armed with the knowledge of a month of interviewing, I was able to ask and understand things that had not been part of my original concepts. I learned much about collaborative creativity and developed the case studies of collaborative creativity that I present later.[6]

In the course of the study, I also learned much about the design rules and accepted ranges of variation that were critical to defining textiles as Zinacantec—to making them markers of identity. A textile is analogous to a written text insofar as it can be "read," or interpreted, by a community of users.[7] Indeed, both English words—*textile* and *text*—come from the Latin root *textus,* meaning "woven." In the Quiché Maya language, the terms for writing hieroglyphics and creating designs by means of weaving utilize the same root, *-tz'iba-*.[8] A literary text can be considered a weaving of words. A given type of Zinacantec clothing is analogous to a literary genre, in that it has its own distinctive rules of expression.

A review of the genre of the Zinacantec blouse, or huipil, recalls the basic rules that govern the production of blouses as both textiles and texts. From an understanding of these basic design rules, we can proceed to understanding the process of design creation of the 1990s. This process utilized the design rules to integrate and connect separate motifs in a unified design. Often, the motifs were "intermedia crossovers"—that is, their design sources drew on non-textile media.[9]

DESIGNS FROM MANY SOURCES

A blouse from 1970 (fig. 6.1) can be used to refresh our memory concerning the genre of the Zinacantec huipil and its probable historical origins. Note the lines of embroidery going down the front of the blouse, the embroidery around its neckline and sleeves, and the embroidery used to join the side seams. The fabric is white. The shape of the blouse is square.

Against this background, let me introduce an especially beautiful blouse made by Lupa Z'us in 1992, when she was seventeen. In this first case study, I explore

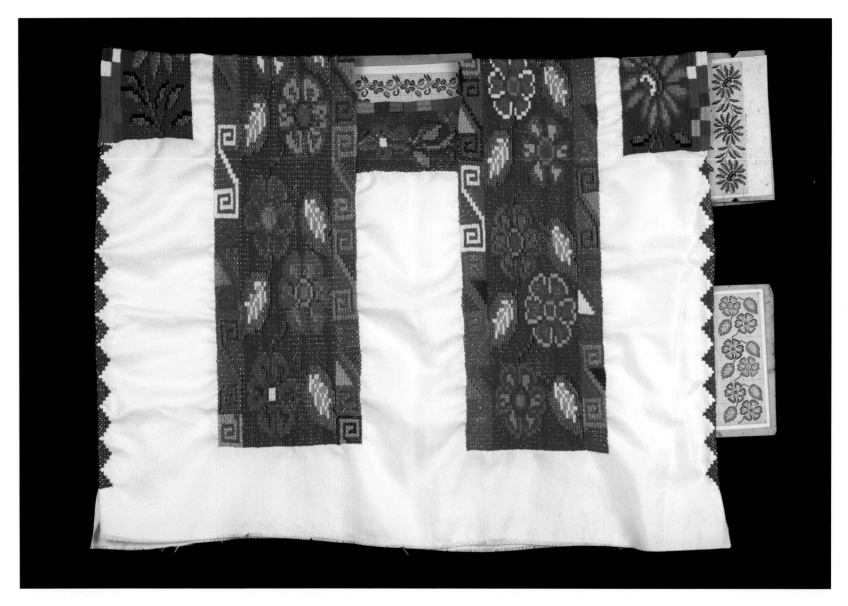

Figure 6.2. Blouse made by Lupa Z'us in 1992, with the three printed patterns used to create it. Photograph by Don Cole.

how images are combined to create designs. I hope to show that the "new" creativity lies in the integration and transformation of source designs within the constraints of Zinacantec rules of textile design.

My interview with Lupa revealed multiple sources for her design motifs. The main sources were three different printed patterns from three pattern books, all published in Mexico City. As can be seen in figure 6.2, one pattern was used for the bands down the front of the blouse, the second for the sleeve embroidery, and the third for the neckline embroidery.

The three patterns certainly do not add up to the blouse in any mechanical way. For one thing, Lupa has transformed the colors of all three patterns. She has also intentionally (by her own statement) elongated the flower pattern used in the front bands. For the pattern on the edges of the vertical bands, Lupa told me that she copied a man's poncho. Finally, for the seams, she did not look at an external source. This zigzag pattern has been identified by other Zinacantec women as representing mountains *(vitz)*. In sum, there were three different kinds of sources for Lupa's blouse: printed patterns from Mexico City, another Zinacantec textile, and her own thought processes.

But at least as interesting as the multiplicity of sources and the transformations they have undergone in Lupa's blouse is the integration of the various design sources. Most importantly, the five design sources (three patterns, a poncho, and Lupa's own thoughts) have been integrated into the traditional blouse design illustrated in figure 6.1. That is, the separate motifs have been arranged in vertical bands going down either side of the front of the blouse and in decorative embroidery at the neckline, around the sleeves, and joining the seams. Note, too, how Lupa has used a single background color, a red purple, to unify the flowers into bands that connote the older bands of embroidery. She has also retained the square shape of the blouse intact. Thus, although this blouse looks, on the surface, very different from the older blouse, its "deep structure" is exactly the same. It conforms to all the norms of Zinacantec blouse structure and is instantly interpretable by a community of users as a Zinacantec blouse.[10] It can serve as a metaphor for the way Zinacantecs in general assimilate, make use of, and transform outside sources into practices and forms that are distinctly Zinacantec.

Lupa's creative process exemplifies what Barbara Tedlock and Dennis Tedlock, referring to Quiché Maya textiles, called "intermedia intertexts" (texts that cross media) and "intercultural intertexts" (those that cross cultures).[11] Lupa, like other Zinacantec women, crossed media by going from paper to cloth designs. Simultaneously, she crossed cultures by integrating designs from Mexico City with Zinacantec blouse norms. The sources of her huipil design provide direct, concrete evidence for processes that the Tedlocks inferred indirectly from the textiles themselves. Their conclusion concerning Quiché creativity and intercultural processes could not be more apt for the Zinacantec case.

According to Tedlock and Tedlock, the intercultural dimension of Quiché intertextuality is not simply the end product of events that took place in the murky colonial past. It is irreducible to an unconscious fusing or blending of elements whose disparate origins have been forgotten—the kind of thing that in anthropology has gone under the name "syncretism." Instead, it results from a continuing creative process that is fully at work in the present day.[12]

Lupa Z'us shows us how original and aesthetically pleasing this mode of creativity can be. She also illustrates the changing value placed on innovation in Zinacantán. Whereas traditionally the word for different, *tos 'o,* had a negative connotation, something like "deviating from a norm," Lupa proudly told me that the blouse she selected as her best embroidery was tos 'o.

She also told me, "It arrived in my head myself. I looked at paper" *(Yul ta hol htuk. Ihkel ta vun).* For Lupa, an external source—the paper pattern she referred to—was not contradictory with the design idea's coming into her head. Clearly, she employed outside sources in the service of an individual, unique design. At the same time, her blouse follows design rules that have their origins in the blouses of an earlier era. The constraints of these rules led to the integration and transformation of motifs that make this blouse so extraordinarily beautiful.

FAMILY CREATIVITY

Lupa's mother, when asked which of her embroideries she considered her best, brought out a blouse embroidered in a geometric design (fig. 6.3). Although it looks quite different from Lupa's huipil, it follows the same design rules. Like the older blouses and Lupa's, it has two vertical bands of embroidery, an embroidered neckline and sleeves, and embroidered side seams. It is made of white fabric and has a square shape.

The mother's source, however, was much different from her daughter's sources. She had made her blouse at the same time Lupa was sewing a similar one (fig. 6.4); the two blouses are almost

Figure 6.3. Blouse embroidered by Lupa's mother with what she considered to be her best embroidery. Nabenchauk, 1993. Photograph by Patricia Greenfield.

identical. To embroider her blouse, the mother had not used paper patterns but simply looked at the way Lupa was embroidering hers. Indeed, Lupa's mother said of her daughter, "She showed me" *(Li y'ak'be kil;* literally, "she gave me to see") how to do the embroidery. Clearly, she felt no shame in copying, and perhaps even felt pride. Lupa was even more explicit: "I

taught my mother" *(Ihchanubtas li hme').* In this case, the traditional flow of authority from older to younger had been not only disrupted, as we saw in chapter 3, but even reversed. Lupa was acting as her mother's teacher in the realm of fancy embroidery.

It was typical in the early 1990s for daughters to have more knowledge of the

Figure 6.4. Blouse embroidered by Lupa Z'us at the same time her mother made the blouse shown in figure 6.3. Nabenchauk, 1993. Photograph by Patricia Greenfield.

new techniques than their mothers did. For example, among girls twelve and older, three-quarters used paper patterns for embroidery, whereas only 10 percent of their mothers did.[13] In this situation, the younger generation were the masters, and the older, the novices. This was a profound shift in the social order from a generation earlier.

Our statistical analyses indicated that in the mothers' generation, before the new methods of designing and producing textiles had diffused among the population, both schooling and television had been important influences on women's use of the new representational tools, paper patterns. Mothers who had gone to school or, even more, had a television at home were much more likely to use paper patterns for either sewing or weaving.[14] Interestingly, television had a closer relationship to the use of paper patterns than did a few years of schooling. Our study results were mirrored by what people told us spontaneously in everyday life. One notion abroad in the village was that all the girls who went to school used paper patterns. Those who had not gone to school simply copied the brocaded or embroidered designs they saw in other people's textiles.

Only one of the mothers in the 1993 sample, Maruch 24, had significant elementary education. Design apprenticeship in her household was interesting because she seemed to have internalized a more pedagogical model from her school experience.[15] Or perhaps schooling had made her better able to provide a culturally modern model for her daughters. She was, for example, skilled in the use of paper patterns. Unlike Lupa's mother, Maruch was able to lead her daughters in design apprenticeship as well as be influenced by them. For example, her daughters Petu' and Loxa, ages eight and ten, had systematically finished the weavings they had begun for our camera in 1991 and carefully saved them. Although both girls had wound their warps in the same striped

Figure 6.5. Petu' 227's worst embroidery, done in 1992. Petu' is the daughter of Maruch 24. Nabenchauk, 1993. Photograph by Patricia Greenfield.

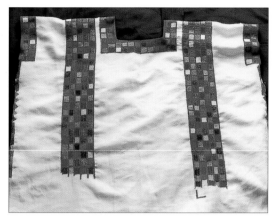

Figure 6.6. One of Maruch 24's two best embroideries. She made it to wear at the August 1993 fiesta in Nabenchauk. Photograph by Patricia Greenfield.

Figure 6.7. Petu' 227's best weaving, made for the August 1993 fiesta. Photograph by Patricia Greenfield.

pattern and colors, they had woven quite different items. Petu' had made a servilleta, whereas Loxa had made a bag (see fig. 5.19).

Over the next two years, Petu', in particular, seemed to interact with her mother's model. Petu' made two blouses. One, which she identified as her worst embroidery (fig. 6.5), was made before her mother made a similar blouse (fig. 6.6). It is therefore possible that Maruch looked at her daughter's blouse and copied it with greater technical skill. It is also possible that she helped Petu' make her blouse. For the August 1993 fiesta, Petu' wove a blouse (fig. 6.7) on which the neckline and sleeve embroidery closely resembled that on her mother's blouse (see fig. 6.6). Perhaps the mixing and matching of separate elements bespoke socialization

Figure 6.8. Lupa Z'us (right) and her older sister Xunka' (left) wearing similar blouses. Nabenchauk, 1993. Photograph by Patricia Greenfield.

Figure 6.9. Detail of Lupa's blouse with the paper pattern that inspired it. Nabenchauk, 1993. Photograph by Patricia Greenfield.

creativity to an implicit model of family creativity.

Another example of copying occurred between Lupa Z'us and her older sister Xunka' (fig. 6.8). Lupa used a paper pattern to make her blouse (fig. 6.9). Again, she consciously transformed the pattern, telling me that she had made the concentric diamond shapes more numerous: "*Ihpas mas ep li*" (I made more numerous here). Her sister's version (see fig. 6.8, left) does not have concentric diamonds. Most likely, she subsequently looked at Lupa's blouse and transformed it into her own version.

In another instance, two cousins and one cousin's mother took part in a similar

by a mother whose elementary school education had inculcated in her a more analytical approach or a more Western idea of creativity.

A second point is that the notion of individual uniqueness is unimportant to Zinacantecs. In this family, as in others, there are instead family styles. Family members are content to copy each other's designs. They are proud to produce models for other family members, and other family members are happy to copy from them. Perhaps the historical shift has been from an implicit model of community

Figure 6.10. Blouse made by one cousin, Maruch 205, for the May 1993 fiesta. Photograph by Patricia Greenfield.

Figure 6.11. Cousin Loxa 2's version of the blouse shown in figure 6.10, made for the Guadalupe fiesta in December 1992. Photograph by Patricia Greenfield.

Figure 6.12. Version of the same blouse made by Loxa's mother, Paxku' 1, for the Guadalupe fiesta in December 1992. Photograph by Patricia Greenfield.

process. One cousin, Maruch 205, age seventeen, told me that she had neither used paper patterns nor looked at another textile for her design (fig. 6.10). She also distinguished her type of design from her mother's, saying that her mother pulled threads to make an embroidery grid for her geometric designs. When I interviewed the other cousin, Loxa 2, age sixteen, I found essentially the same blouse (fig. 6.11). Loxa told me she had used two paper patterns in designing it. When I mentioned that Maruch 205 had made the same blouse but said she had not used patterns, Loxa told me that her cousin had looked at her blouse. Indeed, Maruch had

had an opportunity to observe Loxa's blouse because Loxa had made hers for the Guadalupe fiesta in December 1992, whereas Maruch had made hers for the May 1993 fiesta. Interestingly, Loxa's mother made essentially the same blouse (fig. 6.12) for the December 1992 fiesta. Unlike her daughter, she had not looked at paper patterns; most likely, she used Loxa's blouse as a model.

Note that the mother's blouse is a bit simpler than those of her daughter and niece. Her vertical lines of embroidery each contain two columns of stars, whereas the young cousins each embroidered three columns of stars. This greater sim-

plicity is considered appropriate for an older woman. Note, too, that the neckline and armhole embroidery is different on each of the three blouses—the blouses are strongly similar but not identical. Again, a family style indicates that individuation is unimportant. The practice of copying designs from family members indicates that helping family members, or perhaps expressing a family identity, may be more important than unique, individual expression.

One important arena of collaboration in 1993 was the apprenticeship process. For example, an older sister, Petu' 201, about sixteen, drew a pattern on a blouse

Figure 6.13. Maruch 201's best embroidery follows a pattern drawn by her older sister on a blouse sewn by their mother. Maruch made the blouse for her younger sister, Lupa, and I bought it for twenty-five pesos. Maruch worked on the embroidery two or three hours a day, two days a week, for three weeks while she attended school. Nabenchauk, 1993. Photograph by Don Cole.

sewn by her mother. A younger sister, Maruch 201, about twelve, then embroidered the pattern (fig. 6.13). Some of the designs came from paper patterns, and others from another blouse belonging to Petu'. During her interview with me, Maruch 201 selected this blouse as her best one. Her choice is interesting because it shows that she felt no need to display "independent" work; collaborative work was just as highly valued. Significantly, the blouse was made for the youngest sister in the family, two-year-old Lupa, so the collaboration was not for self but for a family goal. This example shows how, by being given a small part of the total task, girls can begin to master elements of textile creation before they are ready to carry out the whole process of designing and creating a textile. They can also contribute something of value to their families before they are ready to complete an entire task independently.

Figure 6.14. Example of a cross-stitch pattern used for brocade weaving as well as for embroidery. Nabenchauk, 1991.

REPRESENTATIONAL TOOLS

Much of the recent efflorescence of elaborate woven and embroidered designs in Nabenchauk—that is, the efflorescence of creativity—relates to the use and invention of representational tools, or tools for creating designs. None of these, including paper and pencil, was present at the time of our earlier studies. Indeed, our own experiment in 1969 and 1970, reported in the last chapter, seemed to have introduced the external representation of woven patterns (by placing sticks in a frame) into the community. When we returned in 1991, external representation of woven and embroidered designs was rife.

First among the new representational tools is the printed pattern. Printed cross-stitch patterns are used for both embroidery (see fig. 6.2) and weaving (see fig. 3.6). When cross-stitch patterns are used for weaving, new complications arise.

Figure 6.15. A girl draws designs to use for embroidery as her sister looks on. Designs that have already been drawn and cut out lie on the ground beside them. Nabenchauk, 1991. © Lauren Greenfield/VII.

Because these patterns are presented in a grid of squares (fig. 6.14), it is necessary to develop some mathematical equivalence rules in order to translate them onto a loom made up of warp and weft threads. Girls with little or no schooling have done just this. Some, for example, use one warp thread to one square in one dimension and four weft threads to one square in the other dimension.

Thinking in grids involves representational conventions closely tied to school, so it is no wonder that mothers who have been to school are more apt to use such patterns. One girl, Petu' 201, who had completed elementary school but who preferred to weave rather than travel to Hteklum, the Zinacantec ceremonial center, for junior high school, said that weaving was worse in the old days because there was not yet "paper to look at" (that is, patterns to use).

Many other techniques are used for embroidery. For example, girls cut out designs (fig. 6.15) and trace them onto their clothing to embroider. They copy the internal lines of the design. They utilize the skills with pen and paper that they have learned and practiced in school (fig. 6.16). Indeed, one girl had her patterns written in a school notebook. Writing has come to be highly valued in the domain of embroidery. One mother told me that she selected a blouse as her worst embroidery because she had not drawn (literally, written) designs to embroider on it.

Other girls have invented tracing systems. For example, Paxku' Pavlu, age eleven in 1993, had developed a tracing system to utilize designs from one textile for embroidering others. She showed me designs she had traced from a poncho to use on blouses. She used wax paper for the tracing (fig. 6.17), then took a ballpoint pen and retraced the design hard enough on notebook paper to leave an impression. She then followed the impression with a pen . Paxku', who has never been to school, invented her tracing system herself (*yul ta hol,* "it arrived at my head").

Figure 6.16. The same girl shown drawing in figure 6.15 writes in her notebook at school. Nabenchauk, 1991. © Lauren Greenfield/VII.

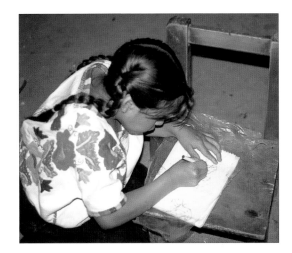

Figure 6.17. Paxku' Pavlu uses her tracing system. Nabenchauk, 1993. Photograph by Patricia Greenfield.

Figure 6.18. Loxa 227's tracing system, with its results on a servilleta, ready to embroider. Top: *a close-up of the design on the wax paper, with periodic holes along the design.* Bottom: *the design after it has been transferred in sets of three to make bouquets. Nabenchauk, 1993. Photograph by Patricia Greenfield.*

Similarly, Loxa 227, age twelve, had made a tracing system from wax paper. She drew designs directly onto the paper, then made tiny holes with a ballpoint pen to transfer the design. This was what she did to prepare a lavender servilleta for embroidery (fig. 6.18).

Another important design tool is a practice called *bozbil,* "pulling threads." In this technique, evenly spaced threads

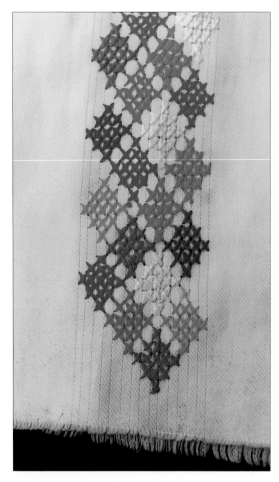

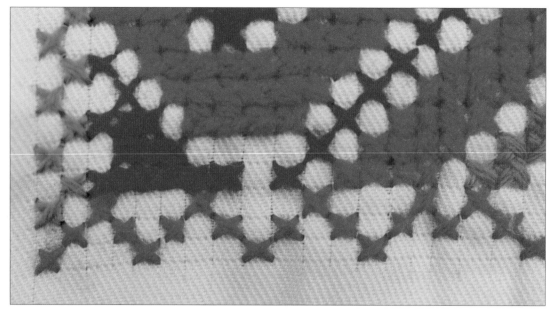

Figure 6.20. Pulled threads in two dimensions on a white background cloth form a grid that aids in the design process. This example is by Paxku' 136. The pulled threads form a grid that is analogous to the embroidery pattern shown in figure 6.14. Nabenchauk, 1993. Photograph by Patricia Greenfield.

Figure 6.19. Pulled threads in evenly spaced, parallel lines guide geometric embroidery. Detail from a blouse by Maruch 205. Nabenchauk, 1993. Photograph by Patricia Greenfield.

are pulled out in the design area to guide the embroidery of a geometric design (fig. 6.19). Some embroiderers also pull threads at right angles, in order to have something like a cross-stitch grid of pulled threads (fig. 6.20).

Still other representational tools have been spontaneously developed for color planning. One is the placing of small balls of colored thread in different areas of the design (fig. 6.21). A more sophisticated technique was developed by X 201, who had finished sixth grade; she sewed short pieces of colored thread into the various color areas (fig. 6.22). Indeed, colored pictures were common in school (fig. 6.23), and picture books were also to be found in X 201's home (fig. 6.24), a rather exceptional situation in Nabenchauk. Note that these indigenous representational tools have all been developed in the context of the ancient backstrap loom and traditional

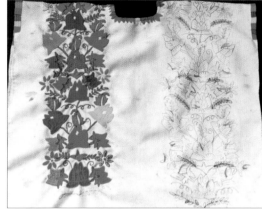

Figure 6.22. X 201's color planning system, in which she sewed bits of colored thread onto the design. Nabenchauk, 1993. Photograph by Patricia Greenfield.

Figure 6.21. Xunka 3's color planning system, involving balls of colored thread placed on parts of the design. Nabenchauk, 1991. Photograph by Patricia Greenfield.

clothing items. Yet the efflorescence of design could not have happened without them.

CONCLUSION

The creative process in textile design in Nabenchauk is both social and technological. Social apprenticeship within the community and social influence from without have helped forge the new designs. Although designs have become more individuated, the processes for creating them are highly social. The family processes identified in this chapter seem to indicate an intermediate step between community creativity and individual creativity. I call this step family creativity. Families try to distinguish themselves from other families, but individual family members do not try to distinguish themselves from other members of the nuclear or extended family.

The creative process in textile design makes use of new technologies such as paper patterns and combines them with old ones such as observing existing textiles. In the course of this creative process, Zinacantec girls and women integrate diverse sources into a single design that conforms to the norms for a particular piece of Zinacantec clothing.

In chapter 5, I documented changing skills in visual representation of textile patterns in Nabenchauk. Now we have seen that new skills in visual representation

Figure 6.23. Pictures in a classroom, Nabenchauk, 1991. © Lauren Greenfield/VII.

are also manifest in new techniques and tools for creating novel textile designs. Interestingly, many of the new technologies for design transfer have been developed by individuals. Technological development, like schooling and commerce, may be a force in moving the culture in a more individualistic direction. Because of technological innovation, the younger generation now teaches the older, undermining older people's traditional authority as experts while teaching them new skills.

Researchers in many fields observe and comment on culture change. What they infrequently note and rarely study are historical changes in processes of cognition and learning. These internal changes reflect and enable external changes in material culture, changes such as the development of novel and varied textile designs.

Figure 6.24. Three girls peruse an illustrated book at home. Nabenchauk, 1991. © Lauren Greenfield/VII.

Figure 7.0. © *Lauren Greenfield/VII.*

Cross-Cultural Perspectives

I wrote this book in Santa Fe, New Mexico. Living there taught me what I had suspected on purely theoretical grounds. Artists and artisans all over the world (and particularly in the world of indigenous peoples) are going through the same process of individuation, the same sort of movement from community expression to self-expression, and the same kinds of changes in what it means to create art and craft as are the Zinacantec Mayas in Chiapas, Mexico. As in the case of the Zinacantecs, we find a tight relationship between these shifts and increasing participation in a commercial economy.

During the nine months I spent in Santa Fe, I was able to see parallels in the paths taken by native arts in the United States and that taken by Zinacantec textiles in Chiapas. Because of the differences between the external structures of Mexico and the United States, Native Americans in the north have moved much farther in the direction of individuation and self-expression than have Zinacantecs. The basic processes and their direction, however, are the same; only the forces pushing these changes are stronger in the United States.

INCREASING INDIVIDUATION AND RATES OF CHANGE IN PUEBLO AND NAVAJO ARTS

In the late nineteenth century, the makers of pottery "gods" at Tesuque Pueblo, just north of Santa Fe, molded figures following a standard formula for each type of god—the god of hunger, the god of rain, and so forth. Showing some continuity with pre-Columbian figurine traditions, these clay images were sold wholesale by their makers as tourist souvenirs. Beginning in the 1920s, individual expression and variability became increasingly important in the representation of the rain god, the only such figure being produced by that time. Rain gods, which their makers began to sell retail, now included different shapes, painted motifs, and colors.[1] The history of rain gods seems to incorporate historical trends in Pueblo pottery more generally. Viewing the entire history of Pueblo pottery from 400 C.E., Richard Anderson of the Kansas City Art Institute notes that the pace of change has accelerated: "Pueblo pottery, after 1,500 years of evolutionary development, has gone through rapid and substantial changes in the twentieth century."[2]

The Pueblo sociologist Tessie Naranjo sees important links between commerce and individual expression. She writes that outside institutions such as the Santa Fe Indian Market

strongly emphasized individualism, or the focus on the self and one's own product—or pot. Communal or group production of pottery declined as Pueblo people, encouraged by outsiders, began to sign pots.

When an individual makes and claims pots, he precludes the interactive process of the old ways. Competition is a by-product of that individualization. Today competition is a strong element of Pueblo pottery. Non-Indian institutions clearly encouraged competition, telling Pueblo people to make better pots that could sell for more money....

Contrary to traditional Pueblo thought, competition is an exclusionary act that dilutes interaction and leads to the pursuit of perfection....

Individualism, competitiveness, and the pursuit of perfection set the stage for the economics of Pueblo pottery making. Economics takes Pueblo people solidly into the non-Indian world and further from that old world where clay is sacred, where Clay-Old-Lady is considered alive—where we flow with her and where we need to breathe as a partner with her.[3]

In her study of three age groups of potters in the pueblo of Santa Clara, Naranjo found evidence of social change in this direction over time. The youngest group (from twenty to thirty-nine years) "expressed the most European behaviors through pursuit of technical excellence, earlier self-identification as potter, engaging in the pottery-making process individually, and not fully understanding or applying Tewa cosmology in their pottery-making."[4] Zinacantecs are moving in the same direction, although no one yet signs her name to a piece of weaving.

Katsina dolls, a tradition of Hopis and some other Pueblo Indians, are supposed to be given to children by the *katsinas,* or spirit helpers. Therefore, katsina makers were traditionally not allowed to put their names on their dolls.[5] As one katsina carver put it, "the spirits don't need to know your name." But at the School of American Research in November 1999, a Hopi katsina carver who had entered the Santa Fe Indian Market for the first time the prior September told me, "I came to Santa Fe because I wanted to make my name. I wanted to get respect." He won first prize. Having a name and standing out are further steps along the path of individualism that Zinacantec weavers have yet to travel.

For Euro-Americans, part of the value of a work of art is to know it as the creation of an individual artist. Edgar Lee Hewett, founding director of the School of American Research and the Museum of New Mexico in the first decades of the twentieth century, not only introduced native artists in the Santa Fe area to easel painting but also encouraged individuality and personality and "taught" native artists to sign both their paintings and their pottery. He did this to make the work more salable. What Hewett probably did not realize was that in doing so, he was encouraging attitudes and practices that were diametrically opposed to the traditional native value system. That system valued fitting into the whole—both the natural whole and the social whole—rather than standing out as an individual. As one native artist put it, "European values center on the individual; native values center on the community."[6]

These are not either-or distinctions, however. Many people adapt by combining elements from both worlds. A potter at Acoma Pueblo socializes her children to make pottery by combining motivations from both value systems. She told me that she encourages her children to pot by emphasizing that they are part of the Bear Clan and that this is the significance of the bear symbol they put on their pots. This approach makes the whole family feel part of something larger. Theirs is a collectivistic motivation. Yet on the more individualistic and commercial side, her son was encouraged when someone bought a pot he made at the age of five. He received a letter from the purchaser telling him he would grow up to be a great potter.

Individuation has also entered the weavings that Pueblo Indians both make and wear. Pueblo belts, woven on the backstrap loom, used to be uniformly red and green. Indeed, they strongly resembled Zinacantec belts, for whatever historical reason. However, as I found out at the feast day of San Felipe Pueblo on May 1, 2000, these belts have now become highly individuated in color and design, and women look to coordinate belt and petticoat color and design. A concept of individuated beauty, different from the prior idea of a group "look," has emerged. As we have seen, this type of color coordination is a product of rapidly changing styles.

Looking like a member of a group contrasts with standing out from the group as an individual. Looking and behaving like a group member is closely related to the idea of individual anonymity. Indeed, people of the American Southwest used to create anonymously. Navajo weavers used to re-create culturally defined designs such as the so-called chief blanket. They did not sign their names to their work. In Chimayó, a Hispanic town north of Santa Fe, "it was not until recent years that the weaving establishments encouraged individual weavers to include their 'signatures' on their weavings."[7] Pueblo potters had

community designs and did not sign their pieces as recently as the 1960s.

COMPARING ZINACANTEC WEAVERS WITH NATIVE AMERICAN ARTISTS

Zinacantec weavers have not yet traveled this far on the road to individuation, self-expression, independence, and commercialization, although they started at the same point. They, too, are Native Americans with common artistic roots in the backstrap loom. Theirs, too, is a story of cultural transformation in the process of economic development.

Fundamental to human culture, to its preservation and transformation, are processes by which knowledge gets passed down or transformed from generation to generation. In November 1999, a potter at Zia Pueblo sadly told a group from the School of American Research that her daughters never wanted to watch her make pottery or showed any interest in participating. "You need to want to pot—it can't be forced," she explains. The daughters have made other choices: one is an optometrist, one a financial manager, and one a house cleaner.

Zinacantec girls, as if by a miracle of the common will, all still "want" to weave. They still watch other expert weavers in

their families and participate in step-by-step tasks that lead to weaving expertise. Why? "Because it is good," they tell us. As of yet, Zinacantecs have no concept of different or individual "goods." But they are moving inexorably along the road the Pueblos and Navajos have already traveled, together with many other peoples around the world, toward individuation, self-expression, and independence—toward creativity as North Americans or Europeans might define it. It was not always so. Until a few years ago, the Tzotzil term "different" (tos 'o), when applied to textiles (as to life in general), was a term of opprobrium. To be "different" was to be "bad."

The potter at Zia can work only on her local clay. She must now dig it alone, she says, because her young nephews and nieces, who might help her, spend the day in school and love TV. Education and electronic media are killing the way she learned to pot—by watching—and they are killing the motivation to pot. The virtual world of TV is driving out the native world of mother earth, where potting connects a person to the earth and is not merely an art or a craft. Even in Zinacantán, time spent watching television has increased exponentially since 1970, whereas time spent watching a mentor weave has declined.

But formal education is not just a negative force in relation to Pueblo pottery. Education is also creating a phoenix out of the old ways. Some potters at San Felipe and Santo Domingo Pueblos have studied art and art history. They research their roots. At San Felipe they are re-creating a pottery tradition using the local clay. At Santo Domingo they are using clay from the ancestral Anasazi site of Mesa Verde and even embedding ancestral Pueblo pottery shards into their own pots. At San Felipe, Daryl Candelaria makes pots out of "virtual" shards. He makes shard-shaped indentations in the clay and then fills in each "shard" with a design from a different pueblo and a different historical period. His is a postmodern example of creativity in which the creation comes from combining old images into new forms and in which there are multiple sources.

Zinacantecs are just beginning to follow this route. Their embroidered and woven textiles now incorporate multiple sources—printed patterns from Mexico City, other people's textiles, and their own imaginations. In former times only their own textiles and those of other community members would have been used to inspire their textile production. Influenced by

schooling and TV, they have entered the world of postmodern creativity.

For Daryl Candelaria and for Robert Tenorio of Santo Domingo Pueblo, the sources for learning to design pottery have expanded beyond their families to the Institute of American Indian Art and the School of American Research in Santa Fe. In contrast, Eusebia Shije of Zia, an older potter, learned by watching her mother. Such changes in the process of cultural learning support changes in the artistic products and make them possible.

For the Pueblo Indians, as for the Zinacantecs, changes in apprenticeship involve changes in relations between parents and children, between individual and community. Correlated with these transformations in both the Southwestern United States and Zinacantán is a movement from a definition of creativity on the level of community ("Our pottery is one way, theirs is another; our clothes are like this, theirs are like that") to a definition of creativity on the level of the family and ultimately on the level of the individual. At the limit, in recognizing "distinction" (individual distinctiveness), prizes and awards separate individuals from each other and from the community.

The driving force is economic development—the transition from subsistence to commerce, money, and markets. For katsina carvers (most of whom now want to be called artists), a "name" translates into market value, monetary gain. Zinacantec weavers have not traveled so far. Their acrylic textiles in fluorescent colors are not what the upscale market thinks indigenous crafts should be: pieces made with natural materials and natural dyes. Commerce, money, and formal education, however, have led to individuated design, market responsiveness, and more independent ways of learning the art and craft of textile production.

Like Pueblo potters and Navajo weavers, Zinacantec weavers are helping to re-create and transform Zinacantec culture. A guide in the Zinacantec museum in Zinacantán Center said to the anthropologist Jane Collier in 1997, "This is how we used to dress."[8] A separation between then and now, between self and tradition, between parent teacher and child learner has been born. New generations of weavers may eventually go to a museum to learn, instead of learning in the practice of everyday life.

Notes

PREFACE

1. Fadwa El Guindi, "From Pictorializing to Visual Anthropology," in *Handbook of Methods in Cultural Anthropology*, 459–511 (Walnut Creek, Calif.: Altamira Press, 1998).

2. Jon Wagner, "Constructing Credible Images: Documentary Studies, Social Research and Visual Studies," edited by Gregory Stanczak, special issue of *American Behavioral Scientist* (in press).

CHAPTER ONE: CHANGES IN THE FABRIC OF LIFE

1. *Gringos* are North Americans in Mexico; *gringa* is the feminine form.

2. Sometimes these "mistakes" were woven by children (Frank Cancian, personal communication, February 12, 2000). Leslie Haviland Devereaux (notes, December 15, 1993, 5) observed that good items were sometimes sold in times of crisis.

3. The apostrophe at the end of the name Xulumte' indicates a glottal stop in the pronunciation. Glottal stops also occur in Tzotzil after consonants such as *k'* or *t'*, where they make an explosive sound. The *x* denotes *sh*. I generally use orthography developed by Sna Jtz'ibajom (House of the Writer) for writing Tzotzil, an oral language until recently. However, I use *h* instead of *j* to make reading easier for English speakers. Sna Jtz'ibajom is a cooperative of Tzotzil speakers founded with the aid of Robert M. Laughlin, Smithsonian anthropologist and alumnus of the Harvard Chiapas project.

4. See Carla P. Childs and Patricia M. Greenfield, "Informal Modes of Learning and Teaching: The Case of Zinacanteco Weaving," in *Studies in Cross-Cultural Psychology*, vol. 2, edited by N. Warren, 269–316 (London: Academic Press, 1980).

5. Xunka is the Tzotzil version of Juana, her official Spanish name for civil and church purposes. All Tzotzil names are based on Spanish names.

6. Leslie K. M. Haviland, "The Social Relations of Work in a Peasant Community" (Ph.D. dissertation, Harvard University, 1978). Leslie Haviland subsequently changed her name to Devereaux. She made field notes for the present research under the name of Devereaux and is referred to in the text as Leslie Haviland Devereaux.

7. Evon Z. Vogt, *Zinacantán: A Maya Community in the Highlands of Chiapas* (Cambridge, Mass.: Harvard University Press, 1969).

8. *Ladino* is a term used in Chiapas to denote Mexicans who do not live in Indian communities. Ladinos can be of Indian heritage but have decided to leave their communities, their traditional dress, and their indigenous languages.

9. The Zinacantecs also had a long history of trade in specialized weavings, such as ritual garments and wedding costumes, both within their villages and with other Maya communities (Haviland Devereaux, notes, December 15, 1993, 4).

10. The notion of the debasement of crafts by the tourist market (Nash, introduction to *Crafts in the World Market: The Impact of Global Exchange on Middle American Artists,* edited by June Nash, 10 [Albany: State University of New York Press, 1993]) does not take into account production for the internal community, which may also become commercialized.

11. Zinacantec weavers also recognize that strangers "do not know careful, detailed weaving

from less careful, detailed weaving" (Haviland Devereaux, notes, September 11, 1991, 2).

12. Haviland Devereaux, personal communication, September 1, 1991.

13. Haviland, "Social Relations"; Haviland Devereaux, notes, December 15, 1993, 2, 3.

14. Haviland Devereaux, personal communication, September 1–2, 1991.

15. Leslie Haviland Devereaux remarked that young Zincantecs were "entering an image-ful and (dare I say it) post-modern world much more fully than they took up literacy and classic modernism" (notes, September 11, 1991, 4).

16. Haviland, "Social Relations," 37.

17. Haviland Devereaux, personal communication, September 2, 1991.

18. Between our first and second period of fieldwork, the civil war in Guatemala had created many Guatemalan Maya refugees in Chiapas. Most of them were living near Comitán, the Chiapanecan city nearest to the Guatemala border.

CHAPTER TWO: FOUNDATIONS OF CULTURAL CONTINUITY

1. Marta Turok, "Le Geste des Tisserandes: Transmission et Renouvellement," in *Textiles Mayas: La Trame d'un Peuple,* edited by Danielle Dupiech-Cavaleri, 34–49 (Paris: Editions Unesco, 1999); Frank Cancian, *The Decline of Community in Zinacantán: Economy, Public Life, and Social Stratification, 1960–1987* (Stanford, Calif.: Stanford University Press, 1992); Walter F. Morris, Living Maya (New York: Harry N. Abrams, 1987); Evon Z. Vogt, *Zinacantán: A Maya Community in the Highlands of Chiapas* (Cambridge, Mass.: Harvard University Press, 1969).

2. Newborn and weaving tools: Mary Anschuetz, "To Be Born in Zinacantán" (manuscript on file, Harvard Chiapas Project, Department of Anthropology, Harvard University, 1966). Stacy Schaefer, in her beautiful study of Huichol weavers, *To Think with a Good Heart: Wixarika Women, Weavers, and Shamans* (Salt Lake City: University of Utah Press, 2002), also saw weaving as an agent of enculturation and the core definition of Huichol womanhood. White Flower: Turok, "Le Geste des Tisserandes," 34–49; 1540 description: Fray Toríbio de Motolonía, "Indians of New Spain," translated and edited by E. A. Foster, The Cortes Society, (Berkeley, Calif.: Bancroft Library, 1950).

3. T. Berry Brazelton, John S. Robey, and George Collier, "Infant Development in the Zinacanteco Indians of Southern Mexico," *Pediatrics* 44 (1969): 274–283.

4. This section on the body is based on Ashley E. Maynard, Patricia M. Greenfield, and Carla P. Childs, "Culture, History, Biology, and Body: Native and Non-native Acquisition of Technological Skill," *Ethos* 27 (1999): 379–402.

5. Patricia M. Greenfield, T. Berry Brazelton, and Carla P. Childs, "From Birth to Maturity in Zinacantan: Ontogenesis in Cultural Context," in *Ethnographic Encounters in Southern Mesoamerica: Essays in Honor of Evon Zartman Vogt, Jr.,* edited by V. R. Bricker and G. H. Gossen, 135-159. (Albany: Institute for Meso-American Studies, State University of New York at Albany, 1989); Patricia M. Greenfield and Carla P. Childs, "Developmental Continuity in Biocultural Context," in *Context and Development,* edited by R. Cohen and A. W. Siegel, pp. 135–159. (Hillsdale, N.J.: Erlbaum, 1991).

6. Brazelton, Robey, and Collier, "Infant Development"; Patricia M. Greenfield, "Studies of

Mother-Infant Interaction: Towards a Structural-Functional Approach," *Human Development* 15 (1972): 131–138. These body movement characteristics are even visible in the signing of deaf Mayas who develop their own simple sign language, as well as in standard Maya sign language. According to research by Eve Danziger ("The Communicative Creation of Language: A Mayan Case Study," paper presented at the annual meeting of the American Anthropological Association, 1996), they use a small signing space for their arms, which would keep their arms close to their bodies. "Local biology": Arthur Kleinman, "General Discussion," conducted at the colloquium "Culture and the Uses of the Body," Saint-Germain-en-Laye, France, March 1996.

7. Walter Morris, Jr., (personal communication, September 27, 1997) pointed out this parallel between body position in placing a tortilla on the grill and lifting up the heddle.

8. Maintaining the capacity to kneel: Theya Molleson, "The Physical Anthropology of Role Specialization from Neolithic Times," paper presented at the colloquium "Culture and the Uses of the Body," St. Germain-en-Laye, France, March 1996. Squatting as a developmental stage: Blandine Bril, "Learning Cultural Motor Skills," paper presented at the colloquium "Culture and the Uses of the Body," Saint-Germain-en-Laye, France, March 1996.

9. Ashley E. Maynard, "An Ethnomodel of Teaching and Learning: Apprenticeship in Zinacantecan Maya Women's Tasks," 22 (M.A. thesis, University of California, Los Angeles, 1996); Nancy Modiano, *Indian Education in the Chiapas Highlands* (New York: Holt, Rinehart and Winston, 1973).

10. Childs and Greenfield, "Informal Modes." Vera John-Steiner, in *Notebooks of the Mind: Explorations of Thinking*, 14–15 (New York: Oxford University Press, 1997), associates heavy reliance on observation in apprenticeship with nonindustrial societies where adults include children in most of their activities. This relationship holds true in Kpelleland, Liberia (David F. Lancy, *Playing on the Mother-Ground: Cultural Routines for Children's Learning* [New York: Guilford Press, 1996]). Mariëtte de Haan provides an example of an indigenous Mazahua mother in Mexico who conceptualizes her son's apprenticeship of a technical task as based on observation and imitation of her model ("Instruction and Cultural Meaning: A Study of Teaching Practices of a Native American Group, the Mazahuas," paper presented at the Second Socio-Cultural Conference, Geneva, September 1996).

11. Patricia M. Greenfield and Jean Lave, "Cognitive Aspects of Informal Education," in *Cultural Perspectives on Child Development*, edited by D. Wagner and H. Stevenson, 181–207 (San Francisco: Freeman, 1982).

12. Marta Turok, "Handicrafts: A Case Study of Weaving in the Highlands," 1–2 (manuscript on file, Harvard Chiapas Project, Department of Anthropology, Harvard University, 1972).

13. Francesca Cancian, "Family Interaction in Zinacantán" (Ph.D. dissertation, Harvard University, 1963).

14. For our 1993 interviews, we went back to the same sample of girls we had videotaped learning to weave, mostly in 1991. Twenty-nine mothers and fifty-four girls in our sample of weaving learners answered this question about play weaving. There were a lot more girls than mothers because many mothers had more than one daughter, and some mothers were unavailable. Fifty-four girls and thirty-two mothers answered a similar question about play embroidery (discussed two paragraphs later).

15. Ashley E. Maynard, "Cultural Teaching" (Ph.D. dissertation, University of California, Los Angeles, 1999). Parts of this dissertation have been published in Maynard's "Cultural Teaching: The Development of Teaching Skills in Maya Sibling Interactions," *Child Development* 73 (2002): 969–982.

16. This minimum age for play weaving agrees with that observed by Walter Morris, who studied a number of Maya communities in highland Chiapas (Morris, Living Maya, 67). The late Nancy Modiano (*Indian Education*) also observed play weaving in highland Chiapas. Whereas Morris saw the mothers as giving carved weaving sticks to the young girls to play with, Modiano noted that girls constructed their own looms out of sticks. Undoubtedly, both were true in different cases. Marie-Noëlle Chamoux posits that a play stage before active apprenticeship, sometimes including toy tools, is typical of Indian groups in Mexico and Guatemala ("Apprendre Autrement," in *Demain L'Artrisanat?. Cahiers de L'Institut Universitaire d'Etudes du Développement* [Paris: Presses Universitaires de France, 1986]).

17. For research subjects, as opposed to people with whom I had a collaborative relationship, I retain both identity and anonymity by using unique family numbers here and elsewhere. For those who were proud of our collaboration and wanted to be identified, I use first and last, or fathers', names. Family numbers under 200 indicate nuclear families that existed in 1969 and 1970; family numbers over 200 are nuclear families that had come into existence by 1991. In a few cases, parents who already had children in our studies by 1970 also had children young enough to be in our 1991 cohort; in these cases, they retained their family numbers under 200. When surnames are given, I use Tzotzil where possible. When the only surname is Spanish, I use the Spanish spelling. For first names, I use either the Tzotzil or the Spanish version according to the way community members address a person.

18. Lynn Fairbanks, "Behavioral Development of Nonhuman Primates and the Evolution of Human Behavioral Ontogeny," in *Biology, Brain, and Behavior: The Evolution of Human Development*, edited by Sue Parker, Jonas Langer, and Michael Mackinney (Santa Fe, N.M.: SAR Press, 2000).

19. Ashley E. Maynard, "An Ethnomodel of Teaching and Learning," 31, 32.

20. Ashley E. Maynard and Patricia M. Greenfield, "Implicit Cognitive Development in Cultural Tools and Children," *Cognitive Development* 18 (2003): 489-510.

21. Marida H. Blanco and Nancy J. Chodorow, "Children's Work and Obedience in Zinacantán" (manuscript on file, Harvard Chiapas Project, Department of Anthropology, Harvard University, 1972).

22. Based on his study of a number of Maya communities in Chiapas, Morris (*Living Maya, 67*) asserted that "no child is expected to produce a usable piece of cloth until she is seven, when a mother will begin to correct and criticize her daughter's work." According to McVey-Dow's 1984–85 field observations ("Indian Women and Textile Production," 92 [Ph.D. dissertation,

Department of Geography, University of Colorado, Boulder]), the neighboring Chamulas, who weave entirely in wool, which may be more difficult, start girls weaving at about age eleven. The developmental notion that a child must be ready before adults assign him or her tasks is also important in Maya Guatemala (James Loucky, "Children's Work and Family Survival in Highland Guatemala" [Ph.D. dissertation, University of California, Los Angeles, 1988]) and in other subsistence communities, for example, among the Kpelle of Liberia (David F. Lancy, *Playing on the Mother-Ground*).

23. Isabel Zambrano and Patricia Greenfield, "Ethnoepistemologies at Home and at School," in *Culture and Competence*, edited by Robert J. Sternberg and Elena Grigorenko (Washington, D.C.: American Psychological Association, 1999a); Isabel Zambrano, "From *Na'* to Know: Power, Epistemology, and the Everyday Forms of State Formation in Mitontik, Chiapas" (Ph.D. dissertation, Harvard University, 1999b).

24. Robert M. Laughlin, *The Great Tzotzil Dictionary of San Lorenzo Zinacantán*, Smithsonian Contributions to Anthropology, no. 19 (Washington, D.C.: Smithsonian Institution Press, 1975).

25. Childs and Greenfield, "Informal Modes."

26. Interrater reliability was also established with additional coders. Interrater reliability relates to the agreement in applying different coding categories that can be reached when two people independently code the same data, here, the same video records. It is considered a measure of adequacy of the operational definition of variables. If agreement is high enough, it means that results do not depend on one single person but, given the same data, could be replicated by other researchers.

Interrater reliability was excellent; reliability statistics are presented in Greenfield, Maynard, and Childs, "Historical Change, Cultural Learning and Cognitive Representation in Zinacantec Maya Children."

27. This section is taken from Maynard, Greenfield, and Childs, "Culture, History, Biology, and Body."

28. See Fairbanks, "Behavioral Development," 131–158; Patricia M. Greenfield, "Culture and Universals: Integrating Social and Cognitive Development," in *Culture, Thought, and Development*, edited by Larry P. Nucci, Geoffrey B. Saxe, and Elliot Turiel, 231-277 (Mahwah, N.J.: Lawrence Erlbaum Associates, 2000).

29. This section is drawn from Childs and Greenfield, "Informal Modes."

30. Manning Nash, in *Machine Age Maya: The Industrialization of a Guatemalan Community* (Chicago: University of Chicago Press, 1967; originally published 1958, Free Press), also noted the importance of observational learning for Maya adults learning to weave in Guatemala; James Loucky ("Children's Work and Family Survival in Highland Guatemala") makes the same point with respect to Maya children in Guatemala. Based on experience in nonindustrial societies, Alan Page Fiske has also made a general case for the importance of observational learning in cultural learning ("Learning a Culture the Way Informants Do: Observing, Imitating, and Participating," paper presented at National Institutes for Mental Health workshop, Washington, D.C., 1995). David F. Lancy's ethnography of childhood in Kpelleland, Liberia, notes the importance of adult models to observe, specifically in learning how to weave (*Playing on the Mother-Ground*).

31. David Wood, Jerome S. Bruner, and Gail Ross, "The Role of Tutoring in Problem Solving," *Journal of Child Psychology and Psychiatry* 17 (1976): 89–100.

32. Childs and Greenfield, "Informal Modes." Scaffolding also fits the observations of Esther Goody on learning to weave among the Daboya in West Africa ("Daboya Weavers: Relations of Production, Dependence and Reciprocity," in *From Craft to Industry: The Ethnography of Proto-Industrial Cloth Production* [New York: Cambridge University Press, 1982] 50–84).

33. Alan Page Fiske ("Learning a Culture") posits the nonverbal nature of cultural learning. In contrast, Chamoux ("Apprendre Autrement") emphasizes the absence of one particular type of teaching verbalization, the explanation, in indigenous weaving apprenticeship in Mexico and Guatemala.

Although we did not find verbal explanations totally nonexistent, they were indeed rare. In the past, anthropologists may have overgeneralized from the lack of verbal explanation to the lack of all kinds of verbalization. By making the distinction between various types of verbalization, we have shown how important verbal instruction is to Zinacantec weaving apprenticeship. Even more important, anthropologists have not generally recognized the integration of verbal and nonverbal means of communication in cultural learning in nonindustrial societies. See Childs & Greenfield (1980) for a discussion of the importance of such integration in Zinacantec weaving apprenticeship.

34. The relative absence of verbal explanation is similar to the findings of Chamoux ("Apprendre Autrement") for indigenous weaving apprenticeship elsewhere in Mexico and in Maya Guatemala.

35. The analysis of modes of communication in weaving apprenticeship in 1970 comes from Childs and Greenfield, "Informal Modes." Silvia Scribner and Michael Cole, in *The Psychology of Literacy* (Cambridge, Mass.: Harvard University Press, 1981), note the crucial role of school-based learning in developing the habit of verbal explanation.

36. Maynard, "An Ethnomodel."

37. Maynard, "An Ethnomodel," 22.

38. Maynard, "An Ethnomodel"; "Cultural Teaching" (Ph.D. dissertation); "Cultural Teaching: The Development."

39. Greenfield and Lave, "Cognitive Aspects"; Jean Lave and E. Wenger, *Situated Learning: Legitimate Peripheral Participation* (Cambridge: Cambridge University Press, 1991); Anderson, *Art in Primitive Societies* (Englewood Cliffs, N.J.: Prentice-Hall, 1979). This section is based on "Learning to Weave in Zinacantán: A Two-Decade Study of Historical Change in Informal Education," by Patricia M. Greenfield and Carla P. Childs, paper presented at the annual meeting of the American Anthropological Association, November 1996, San Francisco.

40. Maynard, "An Ethnomodel." James Loucky identified the same model of teaching and learning in Maya Guatemala in his 1988 dissertation research ("Children's Work and Family Survival in Highland Guatemala"); thus, the indication is that the model is Maya, not merely Zinacantec.

41. Zambrano, "From *Na'* to Know."

42. Patricia M. Greenfield, "A Theory of the Teacher in the Learning Activities of Everyday Life," in *Everyday Cognition,* edited by Barbara Rogoff and Jean Lave, 117–138 (Cambridge, Mass.: Harvard University Press, 1984); Barbara

Rogoff, *Apprenticeship in Thinking* (Cambridge: Cambridge University Press, 1990); Childs and Greenfield, "Informal Modes."

43. Modiano, *Indian Education,* 118.

44. Modiano, *Indian Education,* 118; Elias Pérez Pérez, "Los Maestros Bilingües Frente a un Conflicto Cultural: Críticas y Reflexiones," paper presented at the Regional Congress of Psychology for Professionals in the Americas, Mexico City, 1997b; Elias Pérez Pérez, discussion conducted at the Regional Congress of Psychology for Professionals in the Americas, Mexico City, 1997a.

CHAPTER THREE: APPRENTICESHIP TRANSFORMED

1. This chapter draws on material from the following sources: Patricia M. Greenfield, T. Berry Brazelton, and Carla P. Childs, "From Birth to Maturity in Zinacantan: Ontogenesis in Cultural Context," in *Ethnographic Encounters in Southern Mesoamerica: Essays in Honor of Evon Zartman Vogt, Jr.,* edited by V. R. Bricker and G. H. Gossen, 177–216 (Albany: Institute for Meso-American Studies, State University of New York at Albany, 1989); Patricia M. Greenfield and Carla P. Childs, "Developmental Continuity in Biocultural Context," in *Context and Development,* edited by Robert Cohen and Alexander W. Siegel, 135–159 (Hillsdale, N.J.: Erlbaum, 1991); Patricia M. Greenfield and Jean Lave, "Cognitive Aspects of Informal Education," in *Cultural Perspectives on Child Development,* edited by D. Wagner and H. Stevenson, 181–207 (San Francisco: Freeman, 1982); Patricia M. Greenfield, Ashley E. Maynard, and Carla P. Childs, "History, Culture, Learning, and Development," *Cross-Cultural Research* 34

(2000): 351–374; Patricia M. Greenfield, Ashley E. Maynard, and Carla P. Childs, "Historical Change, Cultural Learning, and Cognitive Representation in Zinacantec Maya Children," *Cognitive Development* 18 (2003):455–487; Patricia M. Greenfield, "Culture and Universals: Integrating Social and Cognitive Development," in *Culture, Thought, and Development,* edited by L. P. Nucci, G. B. Saxe, and E. Turiel, 231–277 (Mahwah, N.J.: Lawrence Erlbaum Associates, 2000).

2. Evon Z. Vogt, *Zinacantán: A Maya Community in the Highlands of Chiapas* (Cambridge, Mass.: Harvard University Press, 1969).

3. Leslie K. M. Haviland, "The Social Relations of Work in a Peasant Community," 191 (Ph.D. dissertation, Harvard University, 1978).

4. Vogt, *Zinacantán.* In "Children's Work and Family Survival in Highland Guatemala" (Ph.D. dissertation, University of California, Los Angeles, 1988), James Loucky notes that respect, especially deference to elders, is key to a child's conceptualization of family relations in two Tzutujil Maya communities in Guatemala. Such an orientation goes beyond the Maya world to other subsistence communities, for example, David F. Lancy's study of development and socialization among the Kpelle of Liberia (*Playing on the Mother-Ground: Cultural Routines for Children's Development* [New York: The Guilford Press, 1996]).

5. Vera John-Steiner emphasizes intergenerational relations as a characteristic of the apprenticeship process; see *Notebooks of the Mind: Explorations of Thinking,* (New York: Oxford University Press, 1997): 51.

6. This pattern of socialization, in which the mother supervises an intermediary (in function,

age, and status) who has responsibility to more directly care for, socialize, or teach a still younger sibling, is similar to that described by Elinor Ochs for western Samoa, by Patricia Zukow-Goldring for central Mexico, and by Beatrice Whiting and Carolyn Edwards for still other cultures. See Elinor Ochs, *Culture and Language Development: Language Acquisition and Language Socialization in a Samoan Village* (Cambridge: Cambridge University Press, 1988); Patricia Zukow-Goldring, "Siblings as Effective Socializing Agents: Evidence from Central Mexico," in *Sibling Interaction across Cultures,* edited by P. G. Zukow, 79–105 (New York: Springer-Verlag, 1989); and Beatrice Blyth Whiting and Carolyn Pope Edwards, *Children of Different Worlds: The Formation of Social Behavior* (Cambridge, Mass.: Harvard University Press, 1988).

7. Marida H. Blanco and Nancy J. Chodorow, "Children's Work and Obedience in Zinacantán" (manuscript on file, Harvard Chiapas Project, Department of Anthropology, Harvard University, 1972). James Loucky made the same observation in two Tzutujil Maya communities in Guatemala, while Suzanne Gaskins drew the same conclusion in a Maya community in Yucatán. This basic ethnotheory of development therefore appears to be PanMaya, instead of Zinacantec. (See Loucky's "Children's Work and Family Survival"; see also Gaskins's "Children's Daily Lives in a Mayan Village: A Case Study of Culturally Constructed Roles and Activities," in *Children's Engagement in the World: Sociocultural Perspectives,* edited by A. Göncü, 25–64 (New York: Cambridge University Press, 1999), and "Historical Change and Developmental Change," *Mind, Culture, and Activity* 6 [1999b]: 109–112). Two major studies

of maternal teaching in a Maya community, these in Guatemala, were carried out by Barbara Rogoff and colleagues; see Barbara Rogoff, J. J. Mistry, A. Göncü, and C. Mosier, "Guided Participation in Cultural Activities by Toddlers and Caregivers," *Monographs of the Society for Research in Child Development,* vol. 7, series no. 236, 58 (1993), and Pablo Chavajay and Barbara Rogoff, "Schooling and Traditional Collaborative Social Organization of Problem Solving by Mayan Mothers and Children," *Developmental Psychology* 38 (2002): 55–66.

8. Pre-Columbian history of commerce: Haviland, "Social Relations"; Robert Wasserstrom, *Class and Society in Central Chiapas* (Berkeley: University of California Press, 1983). Recent history of commerce: Frank Cancian, The *Decline of Community in Zinacantán: Economy, Public Life, and Social Stratification, 1960–1987* (Stanford, Calif.: Stanford University Press, 1992); Benjamin N. Colby, "Social Relations and Directed Culture Change among the Zinacantán," *Practical Anthropology* (November–December, 1960): 241–250.

9. Haviland, "Social Relations," 206. Frank Cancian (personal communication, June 2003) remembers being told that the bad Zinacantec clothing for sale in San Cristóbal was woven by girls who were in the process of learning to weave.

10. In Tzotzil, this type of buying and selling has a distinct term, *chonalah.* It is different from simply selling something that one has produced oneself *(chon).* (There is a syntactic, as well as a pragmatic difference, in that chonolah is intransitive, whereas chon is transitive.)

11. G. A. Collier, "Seeking Food and Seeking Money: Changing Productive Relations in a

Highland Mexican Community," *Discussion Paper* 11 (Geneva, Switzerland: United Nations Research Institute for Social Development, 1990).

12. Increasing importance of money: Devereaux, notes, December 15, 1993, 4. Decline of cargo system: Cancian, *Decline of Community.*

13. Jane Collier, paper presented at UCLA Sloan Center Workshop on Kinship and Family, January 31, 2003.

14. Another inspiration for my hypothesis was James and Maria Loucky's observations on Maya weaving apprenticeship in a Guatemalan community where pattern innovation was valued. There, after a period when miniature looms were set up for girls and they were given leftover scraps of grass to weave, girls were left alone to learn "real" weaving.

15. Initials are being used here instead of first names to provide additional anonymity, in accord with the request of the participants.

16. George Simmel, *The Philosophy of Money,* translated by T. Bottomore and D. Frisby (New York: Routledge, 1990).

17. For the increase in independent weaving, we used a repeated-measures analysis of variance, with historical period as the independent variable. The dependent variables (considered as two temporally distinct or repeated measures of independence for each learner) were the amount of time the learner worked independently while attaching the end-stick and the amount of time the learner worked independently while putting in the first weft thread. The results were statistically adjusted for weaving experience, which served as a covariate. $F = 4.22$, $p = .045$, $n = 60$. Weaving experience exerted a significant effect on independence: $F = 36.63$, $p < .001$ The sample was reduced

from seventy-two to sixty for this analysis because we did not observe twelve weaving learners winding the end-stick.

18. For the decrease in observation, we again used a repeated-measures analysis of variance, with historical period as the independent variable. The dependent variables were the amount of time the learner observed a model while attaching the end-stick and while putting in the first weft thread. The results were statistically adjusted for weaving experience, which served as a covariate. F = 10.91, p = .002, n = 60 (see explanation of sample size in the preceding note). Weaving experience was negatively related to the proportion of time spent observing, as we expected (F = 14.34, p < .001). The role of observation has been highlighted by A. P. Fiske, "Learning a Culture the Way Informants Do: Observing, Imitating, and Participating" (paper presented at the National Institutes for Mental Health Workshop, Washington, D.C., 1955); John-Steiner, *Notebooks of the Mind,* 13; and R. L. Anderson, *Art in Primitive Societies* (Englewood Cliffs, N.J.: Prentice-Hall, 1979).

19. Devereaux, notes, September 11, 1991.

20. E. Pérez Pérez, "Los Maestros Bilingüe Frente a un Conflicto Cultural: Críticas y Reflexiones" (paper presented at the Regional Congress of Psychology for Professionals in the Americas, "Interfacing the Science and Practice of Psychology" Mexico City, 1997b); Catherine Raeff, Patricia Greenfield, and Blanca Quiroz, "Conceptualizing Interpersonal Relationships in the Cultural Contexts of Individualism and Collectivism," in *Variability in the Social Construction of the Child: New Directions in Child Development,* edited by Sara Harkness, Catherine Raeff, and Charles R. Super, 59–74 (San Francisco: Jossey-Bass, 2000);

Patricia M. Greenfield, Blanca Quiroz, and Catherine Raeff, "Cross-Cultural Conflict and Harmony in the Social Construction of the Child," in *Social Construction of the Child,* edited by Harkness, Raeff, and Super, 93–108 (San Francisco: Jossey-Bass, 2000).

21. Paired t-test, n = 36 mother-daughter pairs, t = 2.65, p = .006, one-tailed.

22. Colby, "Social Relations."

23. Generational status of the learner's oldest teacher or helper was coded into one of three categories: older generation, teenager, and younger child. Cases with no helper were eliminated from the analysis, yielding a sample size of sixty. A two-sample t-test showed that inexperienced learners in the later historical period more frequently lacked a teacher of the older generation (t, adjusted for unequal variances, = 2.21, p = .039, two-tailed test).

24. A t-test for paired mother-daughter samples showed this shift to be statistically significant (n = 38 mother-daughter pairs, t = -2.27, p = .015, one-tailed test). Although each pair was a unique combination of mother and daughter, some mothers had more than one daughter in the sample.

25. Haviland Devereaux, notes, September 11, 1991.

26. Haviland Devereaux, notes, September 3, September 11, 1991.

27. Greenfield, Maynard, and Childs, "History, Culture, Learning, and Development"; Greenfield, Maynard, and Childs, "Historical Change."

28. Haviland, "Social Relations," 222. Haviland also points out that prices were low and that they bore no relationship to the amount of time a piece took to weave. Usually, a woman wove for her immediate family as subsistence labor. Occasionally, she wove for money in order to

maintain distance between herself and a man—for example, a sister's husband. Otherwise, weaving for a man would be considered a suggestive activity.

29. Christine Eber and Brenda Rosenbaum noted the systematically later marriage ages in highland Chiapas; see their "That We May Serve Beneath Your Hands and Feet: Women Weavers in Highland Chiapas, Mexico," in *Crafts in the World Market: The Impact of Global Exchange on Middle-American Artisans,* edited by June Nash, 165 (Albany: State University of New York Press, 1993). Leslie Haviland Devereaux made me aware of the impact of the development of indigenous transportation (with familiar, Tzotzil-speaking drivers) on women's independence (Devereaux, notes, December 15, 1993).

30. In her introduction to *Crafts in the World Market,* 1–22, June Nash notes that crafts have been a means for the economic independence of Maya women in Chiapas. In "Crafting Selves: The Lives of Two Mayan Women" (*Annals of Tourism Research* 24 [1995]: 314–327), Cynthia Cone provides two case studies in which commerce and professionalism in traditional crafts led Maya women to economic independence and varying degrees of isolation from their own communities. Diane Rus has carried out extensive studies of Chamula women and their engagement in crafts, emphasizing the difficulty of earning a living from craft sales to tourists; see her "La Crisis Ecónomica y la Mujer Indígena: El Caso de Chamula, Chiapas" (San Cristóbal de las Casas: Instituto de Asesoría Antropológica para la Región Maya, A.C., 1990). According to Jane Collier, in a talk she prepared for presentation at the UCLA Sloan Center Workshop on Kinship and Family, January 31, 2003, the dynamic of men investing in their own

commercial enterprises and feeling less obligation to support their families is part and parcel of the new economic environment in Zinacantán.

31. Walter F. Morris, Jr., *Handmade Money,* 35 (Washinton, D.C.: Organization of American States, 1996). The translation of Sna Jolobil is based on Laughlin, *The Great Tzotzil Dictionary.* Christine Eber and Brenda Rosenbaum provide an overview of weaving cooperatives in highland Chiapas that focuses on their political and marital effects; see their "That We May Serve." An interesting contrasting case of the commercialization of handweaving is presented by Esther Goody in *From Craft to Industry: The Ethnography of Proto-Industrial Cloth Production,* 50–84 (New York: Cambridge University Press, 1982).

32. Tsuh-Yin Chen, "Informal Education in San Pedro Chenalho: A Comparative Study of Weaving between Families Belonging to and Families Not Belonging to Weaving Cooperatives," 6 (M.A. thesis, Department of Psychology, University of California at Los Angeles, 1991).

33. Chen, "Informal Education." Diane Rus studied Chamula women who left their community, next to Zinacantán, to sell crafts in San Cristóbal. She noted that this process reduced mothers' opportunities to transmit Chamula culture, because children spent so much time with their mothers outside the natal community. See Rus, "La Crisis Ecónomica."

34. Jane Collier, personal communication, July 27, 1997.

35. Isabel Zambrano, "From *Na'* to Know: Power, Epistemology, and the Everyday Forms of State Formation in Mitontik, Chiapas" (Ph.D. dissertation, Harvard University, 1999b); Chen, "Informal Education."

36. Chen, "Informal Education," 10.

37. Isabel Zambrano ("From *Na'* to Know") develops the idea of school creating a second authority system.

38. Haviland, "Social Relations."

39. The figure of 1 percent nonweavers for Nabenchauk is derived from 3 weavers out of 225 households. Therefore, the actual percentage of nonweaving females is probably less, because some households undoubtedly contained more than one adult woman, which would increase the denominator of the nonweaving rate. The nonweaving rate in Apas could have been less than 2 percent because Collier was measuring current weaving, and Haviland ("Social Relations," 213) notes that virtually all women drop out of weaving for years at a time.

40. John Haviland (personal communication, September 19, 1997) has pointed out that in the lower Zinacantec hamlets with inadequate water, weaving is relatively simple and rarer. (Residents of Nabanchauk and other hamlets sell old weavings to people there.) Therefore, weaving is not universal in Zinacantán as a whole.

41. Pérez Pérez, "Maestros bilingües."

CHAPTER FOUR: THE TEXTILES

1. Irmgard Weitlaner Johnson, "Chiptic Cave Textiles from Chiapas," *Journal de la Societé des Américanistes* 43 (1954): 137–147.

2. Marguerite Porter Davison, *A Handweaver's Pattern Book for Four Harness Loom* (Swarthmore, Pa.: Author, 1944); Chloë Sayer, *Arts and Crafts of Mexico,* 27 (San Francisco: Chronicle Books, 1990).

3. A figure from Jaina, Campeche, on the

Yucatán peninsula clearly shows these same two articles of clothing in a pottery figurine from the same general period (Sayer, *Arts and Crafts of Mexico,* 18).

4. All purported connections between ancient and current clothing designs have been corroborated by current weavers in Nabenchauk. Any connections that could not be seen by current informants were not considered to be reliable/valid and are not presented in this work.

5. Quote from Walter F. Morris, *A Millennium of Weaving in Chiapas,* 22 (San Cristóbal de las Casas: Sna Jolobil, 1984). Aztec huipil from B. de Sahagun, *Florentine Codex, Book 10: The People,* Monographs of the School of American Research and the Museum of New Mexico, translated by Charles E. Dibble and Arthur J. O. Anderson, Figure 139 (Santa Fe, N.M.: School of American Research Press and the University of Utah, 1961).

6. E. Z. Vogt, *Zinacantán: A Maya Community in the Highlands of Chiapas* (Cambridge, Mass.: Harvard University Press, 1969); Gene S. Stuart and George S. Stuart, *Lost Kingdoms of the Maya* (Washington, D.C.: National Geographic Society, 1993).

7. Donald Cordry and Dorothy Cordry, *Mexican Indian Costumes,* 9 (Austin: University of Texas Press, 1968). This notion is bolstered by evidence that land reform in the twentieth century "let rank-and-file Zinacantecos embrace prestigious practices of their elites and generalize them as Zinacanteco custom. Property-owning elites once had reserved stately marriage feasts, church weddings, grace-imparting service to Our Lord, and colloquy with ancestor and earth spirits for themselves, using these to justify their superiority over rank and file compatriots. But the reform raised

former poor, debt-indentured Zinacanteco workers to the status of property-owners who farmed milpa [corn fields]. Zinacanteco rank and file then adopted lengthy courtships and bridewealth and began to compete for the right to take costly cargos [offices in the religious hierarchy]." (George Collier, "Zinacantecos at Home in the World," unpublished manuscript, no date, 12; in Spanish "Los Zinacantecos en su mundo contemporáneo," in *Antropología Mesoamericana: Homenaje a Alfonso Villa Rojas,* edited by M. Esponda, S. Pincemin, and M. Rosas, 189-215 (Tuxtla Gutierrez, Mexico: Instituto Chiapaneco de Cultura, 1992).

8. Stuart and Stuart, *Lost Kingdoms,* 192, 198, 199 (Washington, D.C.: National Geographic Society, 1993).

9. R. M. Laughlin and C. Karasik, *The People of the Bat: Mayan Tales and Dreams from Zinacantán,* 1–2 (Washington, D.C.: Smithsonian Institution Press, 1988).

10. L. K. M. Haviland, "The Social Relations of Work in a Peasant Community," 25–26 (Ph.D. dissertation, Harvard University, Cambridge, Mass., 1978).

11. Haviland, "Social Relations," 37.

12. Marta Turok, "Le Geste des Tisserandes: Transmission et Renouvellement," in *Textiles Mayas: La Trame d'un Peuple,* edited by D. Dupiech-Cavaleri (Paris: Editions Unesco, 1999).

13. Barbara Tedlock and Dennis Tedlock, "Text and Textile: Language and Technology in the Arts of the Quiché Maya," *Journal of Anthropological Research* 41 (1985): 121–146.

14. R. Wasserstrom, *Class and Society in Central Chiapas* (Berkeley: University of California Press, 1983).

15. Wasserstrom, Class and Society; Frank

Cancian, *The Decline of Community in Zinacantan: Economy, Public Life, and Social Stratification, 1960–1987,* 17 (Stanford, Calif.: Stanford University Press, 1992).

16. Cordry and Cordry, *Mexican Indian Costumes.*

17. Although they look alike, the narrow woven edges of the poncho (or shawl) and the thin line of brocade are technically very different. The edges are a striped pattern created in winding the warp. Brocading, in contrast, is a technique that utilizes supplementary wefts and has the potential for highly complex designs. However, the earlier bottom borders in figures 4.9 and 4.11 are not brocade; they do not involve a supplementary weft technique and are simple weft stripes.

18. Leslie Haviland Devereaux, notes, September 11, 1991. In *Art in Primitive Societies,* Richard L. Anderson raises the possibility that innovation in art is universal, but the degree or emphasis on innovation varies from culture to culture (Englewood Cliffs, N.J.: Prentice-Hall, 1979); Haviland, "Social Relations."

19. Evon Z. Vogt, "The Harvard Chiapas Project: 1957–1975," in *Long-Term Field Research in Social Anthropology,* edited by George M. Foster, Thayer Scudder, Elizabeth Colson, and Robert V. Kemper, 279–301 (New York: Academic Press, 1979).

20. Maya cutting: Patricia Altman and Caroline D. West, *Threads of Identity* (Los Angeles: Fowler Museum of Cultural History, 1992). Exceptions: Leslie Devereaux (e-mail, July, 2003). For discussion of the complex history of cutting blouse neckholes, see caption to figure 4.37.

21. Anderson, in *Art in Primitive Societies,* cites evidence for implicit rules concerning Pueblo pottery design from the ethnography of Ruth Bunzel,

first published in 1929. Anderson also considers the generative approach to "primitive" art. He discusses its origins in the linguistics of Chomsky and the anthropological structuralism of Claude Lévi-Strauss, as well as its application to Nuba body decoration by James Faris. Perhaps the breakdown of rules over time, described in this chapter, is also analogous to the ways languages change over time.

22. In both Chiapas and Guatemala, particular woven articles of clothing identify the wearer as coming from a particular Maya community (Altman and West, *Threads of Identity;* M. de Orellana, "A Weft of Voices: The Weaver at Her Loom," in *Artes de Mexico,* translated by C. Castelli, No. 19 (1993): 88–93; Margot Blum Schevill, *Maya Textiles of Guatemala* [Austin: University of Texas Press, 1992]). At the same time, Schevill also notes longstanding interethnic commerce in handwoven clothing between Maya communities in Guatemala. Anderson *(Art in Primitive Societies)* notes that although we think of art as innovative, art in slowly changing societies may function instead to support cultural homeostasis.

23. On July 20, 2003, Ashley Maynard sent me an electronic message reporting that some girls in Nabenchauk were making green skirts to wear to the next fiesta. From 1969 to 1991, the Zinacantec skirt had changed not at all; it was still an indigo blue tube. By 2000 dark embroidery had begun to be added, but the Zinacantec skirt was still indigo blue or black, as was the case throughout Maya communities in Chiapas. Although they were dark green, these skirts were a somewhat radical departure, another sign of accelerating change led by the younger generation. Ashley reported: "The younger girls and women like the green skirts, but

the older women are not so sure about it."

24. Aztec influence: Morris, *Millennium of Weaving;* Margarita de Orellana, "A Weft of Voices," *Artes de Mexico,* 89.

25. Sylvanus Griswold Morley, *The Ancient Maya,* 405 (Stanford, Calif.: Stanford University Press, 1946).

26. Devereaux, notes, December 15, 1993, 7.

27. Collier, "Zincantecs at Home," unpublished paper.

28. Robert M. Laughlin, *The Great Tzotzil Dictionary of San Lorenzo Zinacantán,* in Smithsonian Contributions to Anthropology, no. 19. (Washington, D.C.: Smithsonian Institution Press, 1975).

29. The stripes of the red-and-white shawl or baby carrier are wound into the warp, making this shawl more difficult to weave than the basket weave shawl.

30. Devereaux, notes, December 15, 1993, 7.

31. Devereaux, notes, December 15, 1993, 7; Haviland, "Social Relations," 219. Allen W. Johnson and Timothy Earle, in *The Evolution of Human Societies: From Foraging Group to Agrarian State* (Stanford, Calif.: Stanford University Press, 1987), hypothesize that population growth is the primary motor for economic and cultural evolution. Clearly, in the Zinacantec case, it was at very least a correlate.

32. The notion of the reemergence of ancient designs in highland Maya textiles comes from William F. Morris, Jr., *Living Maya* (New York: Harry N. Abrams, 1987).

33. Vogt, *Zinacantán.*

34. Vogt, *Zinacantán.* The ancient migration from mountains to lowlands stimulated pyramids as substitutes for mountains. Mountains and caves

as transitions between the physical world and the spirit world were a Mesoamerican concept, already ancient when Maya culture developed. "Some symbols on temples and pyramids proclaim them manmade mountains and centers of power"(Stuart and Stuart, *Lost Kingdoms,* 48). This equation of mountains and pyramids is alive today. The Chamulas, a neighboring Tzotzil-speaking group with close connections to Zinacantán, "for instance, are now building pyramids. They did not go to the ruins and decide to copy them; they simply arrived at a moment when they have enough people and money to create monumental architecture once again. Since these structures are being built to honor their ancestors and community, just as the earlier pyramids were, it is not surprising that they are similar in form as well as meaning. The Chamulas are now making the pyramids by terraforming the three sacred mountains, all called Calvario, around Chamula center. Each of these mountains has on its top a cross shrine to the Ancestors of the three districts of Chamula. Platforms have been built on the summit around the shrine, and wide sets of stairs rise from the base of the hills, giving the appearance of pyramids with crosses on top" (Morris, *Living Maya,* 212–213).

35. Walter F. Morris, Jr., *Luchetik: El Lenguage Textil de los Altos de Chiapas (The Woven Word from Highland Chiapas),* 31 (San Cristóbal de Las Casas, Chiapas, Mexico, n.d.).

36. Jane Collier, personal communication, July 26, 1997.

37. Devereaux, notes, December 15, 1993, 8.

38. Leslie Haviland Devereaux found that older people preferred the old styles (notes, September 1, 1991). This may be because she had some older informants than I had in my sample of girls and

their mothers. It might also be because her informants have stronger agrarian connections and are part of a more conservative element in the village.

39. Haviland, "Social Relations," 206, 207.

40. The first two sentences of this paragraph are based on ideas from Pierce Butler, personal communication, no date. The relationships between Zinacantecs and other Maya communities in Chiapas tend to be few and specific. For example, Zinacantecs have traditionally bought pox (a liquor used for ceremonies) and ceremonial leather sandals from their neighbors in Chamula. They also hire Chamulas to work in their fields. Apart from the Guatemalan blouses that appeared for a few years in Nabenchauk, I have not observed any other relationship between Guatemalans and Zinacantecs.

41. The Zapatista uprising began January 1, 1994. When Zapatistas helped expelled members of Nabenchauk return to their village, the Zapatistas had the direct political effect of turning those members of the community away from the ruling PRI (who had refused to help them fight their expulsion) to membership in the PRD, the Zapatistas' allied political party. The Zapatista uprising also seemed to have an indirect liberating effect, resulting in increased communal entrepreneurship. For example, in 1997 eight men in Nabenchauk bought one car each and formed a taxi cooperative. Before the Zapatista uprising, taxis, like many other forms of commerce, had been the prerogative of non-Indian Mexicans, called Ladinos.

42. June Nash, introduction to *Crafts in the World Market: The Impact of Global Exchange on Middle American Artists* (Albany: State University of New York Press, 1993).

43. Vicki McVey-Dow, "Indian Women and Textile Production: Adaptation to a New Environment in Chiapas, Mexico" (Ph.D. dissertation, Department of Geography, University of Colorado, 1986); Diane Rus, "La Crisis Ecónomica y la Mujer Indígena: El Caso de Chamula, Chiapas" (Instituto de Asesoría Antropológica para la Región Maya, A.C., San Cristóbal de las Casas, Chiapas, Mexico, 1990).

44. Barbara de Arathoon, "A Wave of Change in Backstrap Weaving," in *Friends of the Ixchel Museum* 12, no. 1 (2001): 1–2; Altman and West, *Threads of Identity*, preface.

CHAPTER FIVE :
INSIDE THE MIND

1. In Tzotzil, *(Ta 'ora) Ha chak'el li pok' mochebal li'e. Chak'el k'u x 'elan. Ha' ko'ol schi'uk li'e cha laz li te'etike.* (Until recently, Tzotzil speakers did not write their own language. Now that they have begun to do so, I have tried to stay with the transcription system used by Sna Jtz'ibajom, House of the Writer. However, I have made one departure in deference to English readers. Whereas Sna Jtz'ibajom publications use *j* where we would use *h* in English, I have used *h*.) Before these instructions, there was a warm-up item in which the participants practiced filling the frame with sticks placed in the proper orientation.

2. Jerome S. Bruner, Jacqueline Goodnow, and Georget Austin, *A Study of Thinking* (New York: Science Editions, Wiley, 1956).

3. Eleanor J. Gibson, "An Ecological Psychologist's Prolegomena for Perceptual Development: A Functional Approach," in *Evolving Explanations of Development: Ecological*

Approaches to Organism-Environment Systems, edited by Patricia Zukow-Goldring, 23–45 (Washington, D.C.: American Psychological Association, 1997). Patricia Goldring-Zukow, "A Social Ecological Realist Approach to the Emergence of the Lexicon: Educating Attention to Amodal Invariants in Gesture and Speech," in *Evolving Explanations of Development: Ecological Approaches to Organism-Environment Systems*, edited by Patricia Zukow-Goldring, 199–250 (Washington, D.C.: American Psychological Association, 1997).

4. Some basic works in cultural and cross-cultural psychology include the following: James W. Stigler, Richard A. Shweder, and Gilbert Herdt, *Cultural Psychology: Essays in Comparative Human Development* (New York: Cambridge University Press, 1990); Michael Cole, *Cultural Psychology: A Once and Future Discipline* (Cambridge, Mass.: Harvard University Press, 1996); and John W. Berry, Ype H. Poortinga, Janak Pandey, Pierre R. Dasen, T. S. Saraswathi, Marshall H. Segall, and Cigdem Kagitcibasi, eds., *Handbook of Cross-Cultural Psychology*, 3 vols. (Boston: Allyn and Bacon, 1997).

The classic work on culture and perception is *Influence of Culture on Visual Perception* by Marshall H. Segall, Donald T. Campbell, and J. M. Herskovitz (Indianapolis: Bobbs-Merrill, 1966). An even earlier antecedent was the notion that psychological needs stemming from the conditions of everyday life could influence perception (Jerome S. Bruner, "Value and Need as Organizing Factors in Perception," *Journal of Abnormal and Social Psychology* 42 (1947): 33–44.

The pioneering book on the cultural study of everyday cognition is *Everyday Cognition: Its*

Development in Social Context, edited by Barbara Rogoff and Jean Lave (Cambridge, Mass.: Harvard University Press, 1984). Our study was inspired by Douglas Price-Williams, W. Gordon, and M. Ramirez, "Manipulation and Conservation: A Study of Children from Pottery-Making Families in Mexico," *Memorias del XI Congreso Interamericano de Psyicologia* (1967), pp. 106–126.

Other studies of the cognitive implications of weaving include: Barbara Rogoff and Mary Gauvain, "The Cognitive Consequences of Specific Experiences: Weaving vs. Schooling among the Navaho," *Journal of Cross-Cultural Psychology* 15 (1984): 453–475; Geoffrey B. Saxe and Maryl Gearhart, "The Development of Topological Concepts in Unschooled Straw Weavers," *British Journal of Developmental Psychology* 8 (1990): 251–258.

5. With paper and pencil, we recorded each stick placement. We followed a similar recording procedure for all the participants and all the parts of the experiment. Much of the material in this chapter, including more detailed description of the procedures and materials, can be found in Patricia M. Greenfield and Carla P. Childs, "Weaving, Color Terms, and Pattern Representation: Cultural Influences and Cognitive Development among the Zinacantecos of Southern Mexico," *International Journal of Psychology* 11: 23–48, and in Patricia M. Greenfield, Ashley E. Maynard, and Carla P. Childs, "Historical Change, Cultural Learning, and Cognitive Representation in Zinacantec Maya Children," in *Cognitive Development,* 18 (2003): 455–489.

6. Right before the experimenter presented the novel patterns, she presented a couple of pattern continuation items that were culturally familiar.

The first pattern was a simple red-and-white alternation of the narrow sticks; the second also used narrow sticks and had a repeating unit of three narrow reds and one narrow white. Data from these two items were not used in any analyses in this chapter.

7. *(Ta'ora) Tahlaz li te'etik li vo'one. 'A li vo'ote chak'el k'u x 'elan tahlaz. Ha' chalaz li te'etik ko'ol schi'uk li'e or Ha' ko'ol schi'uk li'e chalaz. Ha chanohes yech chak li'e* ("The same as this you stack. You fill in that way like here.")

8. Unlike the other pattern continuations, we did not ask the participants to do it the same as our model. Instead, we said, "Now I start myself. As for you, you look at what the start is like" (or "how I start it"). "You finish what I have started." In Tzotzil, it was *Ta 'ora tahtam li vo'one. A li vo'ote chak'el k'u x 'elan stamel* [or *k'u x 'elan tahtam*]. *Ha' chalehes li k'usi htamoh.*

9. *Schi'uk li te'etik li'e, ha chalaz k'u x 'elan chak'an li vo'ote. 'Akbo lek lek sba. Ha' li mas lek lek sba xava'i, ha yech chalaz.*

10. Narrow was 1/4 inch, medium was 1 1/4 inch, and wide was 2 1/4 inch. The sticks fit into a frame with inside dimensions of 9 by 16 inches. In all, there were sixty white sticks, sixty red sticks, thirty light pink, thirty orange, sixteen olive green, sixteen yellow, three black, and three sky blue sticks. Other details of the full procedure are to be found in Greenfield and Childs, "Weaving, Color Terms, and Pattern Representation."

11. J. B. Carroll, ed., *Language, Thought, and Reality: Selected Writings of Benjamin Lee Whorf* (Cambridge, Mass.: MIT Press, 1956).

12. There was, however, an interesting study in which IQ tests were repeated ten years apart in the same community. The large rise in scores was attributed to important social change that had occurred in the preceding decades (L. R. Wheeler, "A Trans-Decade Comparison of the IQs of Tennessee Mountain Children," in *Cross-Cultural Studies of Behavior,* edited by I. Al-Issa and W. Dennis, 120–133 [New York: Holt, Rinehart & Winston, 1970]). Most recently, Daley and colleagues repeated cognitive tests years apart in Kenya (Tamara C. Daley, Shannon E. Whaley, Marian D. Sigman, Michael P. Espinosa, and Charlotte Neumann, "IQ on the Rise: The Flynn Effect in Rural Kenyan Children," *Psychological Science* 14 (2003): 215–219). However, unlike our study, these investigations did not repeat the tests on descendants of the same families originally tested.

13. Childs and Greenfield, "Informal Modes of Learning and Teaching: The Case of Zinacanteco Weaving," in *Studies in Cross-Cultural Psychology,* vol. 2, edited by N. Warren, 269–316 (London: Academic Press, 1980). A. E. Maynard, "Cultural Teaching" (Ph.D. dissertation, University of California, Los Angeles, 1999).

14. For the last 1991 participants, after Carla had left the field, I interacted with the participants.

15. Among participants in 1969 and 1970, all of the analytic representations of the shawl were detailed; in 1991 eight abstract analytic representations of the shawl appeared in the total sample: six abstract analytic representations of the old shawl and two abstract analytic representations of the new shawl.

There was also a highly significant association between formal schooling and the use of an abstract instead of a detailed (that is, thread-by-thread) analytic strategy to represent the old pok

mochebal (N = 39, df = 1, chi-square = 4.56, $p < .02$, one-tailed).

16. Greenfield, Maynard, and Childs, "Historical Change."

17. Mean, first historical period: 2.19, out of five patterns correctly completed. Mean, second historical period: 2.65, out of five patterns correctly completed. The effect of historical period on skill with novel patterns was statistically significant with age controlled (Greenfield, Maynard, and Childs, "Historical Change").

18. Statistical results concerning historical period and gender are in Greenfield, Maynard, and Childs, "Historical Change."

19. Controlling for age, we found a significant correlation between learner independence in weaving apprenticeship and correct completions of the five culturally novel patterns (Greenfield, Maynard, and Childs, "Historical Change").

20. The concept of going beyond the information given is from Bruner, Goodnow, and Austin, "A Study of Thinking."

21. A chi-square test showed this historical change to be statistically significant (chi-square = 10.54; N = 37, df = 2, $p = .0025$, one-tailed) (Greenfield, Maynard, and Childs, "Historical Change"). We counted as a strategy, the use of one of the three strategies—repetition, mirror image, and growing (or progression)—with up to three errors.

22. Controlling for age and commercial involvement, schooling was significantly correlated with the use of the progression strategy (with no errors) on the "growing pattern" (N = 173, r = .46, $p < .0005$, one-tailed). Conversely, controlling for age and schooling, commercial involvement was

correlated with the use of the progression strategy, but at a lower level of significance (N = 173, r = .15, *p* < .03, one-tailed).

Showing the importance of formal education, a U.S. college sample, tested after the 1969 Chiapas field season, uniformly used the progression strategy.

23. A breakdown of recognizable patterns goes as follows: Like ours and like a woven pattern, N = 23; like ours only, N = 0; like a woven pattern only, N = 50; original (like neither ours nor a woven pattern), N = 39.

24. Greenfield and Childs, "Weaving, Color Terms, and Pattern Representation."

25. Eleanor Rosch, "Natural Categories," *Cognitive Psychology* 7 (1973): 573–605.

26. Brent Berlin and Paul Kay, *Basic Color Terms: Their Universality and Evolution* (Berkeley: University of California Press, 1969).

27. Our longitudinal evidence for Berlin and Kaye's theory of the evolution of color terms among the Zinacantecs was foreshadowed by Sara Harkness's observations at a single point in time of Spanish borrowing in Mam, another Maya language (Sara Harkness, "Universal Aspects of Learning Color Codes," *Ethos* 1 [1973]: 175–200). Mam, like Tzotzil, had five basic color terms: black, white, red, green, and yellow. In Santiago Chimaltenango, Guatemala, Harkness found selective borrowing of Spanish color words in the order predicted by Berlin and Kay's evolutionary theory: Blue (azul or celeste), the sixth term in their evolutionary sequence, predominated in seven- and eight-year-olds' color naming, and blue and brown (brown being the following term in Berlin and Kay's evolutionary sequence) predominated in the color naming of adults. The difference between

children and adults also suggests that developmental ordering follows the ordering of cultural evolution.

28. In 1969 and 1970 eighty-nine participants were tested on the full array of color terms; in 1991 the number was 113.

CHAPTER SIX:
THE CREATIVE PROCESS

1. Howard Gardner, *Art, Mind, and Brain: A Cognitive Approach to Creativity*, 35 (New York: Basic Books, 1982).

2. For Western definitions of creativity, for example, see Mihaly Csikszentmihaly, *Creativity: Flow and the Psychology of Discovery and Invention* (New York: HarperCollins, 1996); Arthur J. Cropley, "Definitions of Creativity," in *Encyclopedia of Creativity*, vol. 1, edited by Mark A. Runco and Steven R. Pritzker, 511–524 (San Diego: Academic Press, 1999); Vera John-Steiner, *Notebooks of the Mind: Explorations of Thinking*, 206 (New York: Oxford University Press, 1997); Karen O'Quin and Susan P. Besemer, "Creative Products," in *Encyclopedia of Creativity*, vol. 1, edited by Mark A. Runco and Steven R. Pritzker, 413–422 (San Diego: Academic Press, 1999). This Western definition of creativity leads to corresponding personality traits, such as independence and nonconformity, that are characteristic of creative individuals (Vera John-Steiner, *Notebooks of the Mind*, 219).

3. Gardner, *Art, Mind, and Brain*.

4. Fifty-six out of fifty-eight learners, plus thirty of their mothers.

5. Lawrence Hirschfeld, in "Cuna Aesthetics: A

Quantitative Analysis," *Ethnology* 16: 147–166, takes a similar approach to *cuna molas* (reverse appliqué blouses). He finds agreement between the criteria identified by the technique of eliciting best molas and criteria identified by rating a series of molas.

6. Vera John-Steiner has a recent book (*Creative Collaboration* [Oxford: Oxford University Press, 2000]) in which she explores the concept of collaborative creativity in Western science and art. Here, as well as in her earlier book, *Notebooks of the Mind*, she points out that creative collaboration has not been heretofore recognized because of the Western bias toward individual creativity.

7. William F. Hanks, "Text and Textuality," in *Annual Review of Anthropology*, vol. 18, edited by B. J. Siegel, A. R. Beals, and S. A. Tyler, 95–127 (Palo Alto: Annual Reviews, Inc., 1989).

8. B. Tedlock and D. Tedlock, "Text and Textile: Language and Technology in the Arts of the Quiché Maya," *Journal of Anthropological Research* 41:121–146.

9. This use of multiple motifs or "texts," even from multiple media, is the postmodern process of "intertextuality" (Tedlock and Tedlock, "Text and Textile"; Hanks, "Text and Textuality"). The use of the rules and individual creativity to combine the texts creates a quality that in literary analysis is called "textuality" (Hanks, "Text and Textile").

10. Tedlock and Tedlock ("Text and Textile") speak of the iconic, indexical, and symbolic aspects of textiles as texts. This terminology analyzes the semantics of textiles as text, if you will. Translating this blouse into the terms of Tedlock and Tedlock, they would perhaps see its flowers as icons or images, the blouse itself as indexical of woman-

hood, and its overall style and construction as a conventional symbol of Zinacantán. However, Tedlock and Tedlock also analyze the "grammar" of Quiché Maya designs, particularly the belt. Although the grammar is different from Zinacantec textile grammar, like the Zinacantec conventions, Quiché conventions include a primary distinction between stripes (woven) and figures (brocaded with supplementary wefts).

11. Tedlock and Tedlock, "Text and Textile."

12. Tedlock and Tedlock, "Text and Textile," 142.

13. Yet Tedlock and Tedlock ("Text and Textile") tell us that the ancient Maya saw an identification between images in books and in woven cloth.

14. Patricia Greenfield and Ashley Maynard, "Women, Girls, Apprenticeship, and Schooling: A Longitudinal Study of Historical Change among the Zinacantecan Maya," paper presented to the American Anthropological Association, November, 1997, Washington, D.C. A chi-square test showed that mothers were more likely to use paper patterns in their embroidery if they had been to school, N = 39, chi-square = 16.632, df = 1, $p < .001$, two-tailed; mothers were also more likely to use

paper patterns in their weaving if they had been to school, N = 40, chi-square = 5.714, df = 1, $p < .02$, two-tailed. Mothers were more likely to use paper patterns in their embroidery if they had a TV in the house, N = 38, chi-square = 7.370, df = 1, $p < .01$. Mothers were also more likely to use paper patterns in their weaving if they had a TV in the house, N = 39, chi-square = 8.598, df = 1, $p < .01$.

15. F. Medardo Tapia Uribe, Robert A. LeVine, and Sarah E. Levine, "Maternal Behavior in a Mexican Community: The Changing Environments of Children," in *Cross-Cultural Roots of Minority Child Development,* edited by Patricia M. Greenfield and Rodney R. Cocking, 41–54 (Hillsdale, N.J.: Erlbaum, 1994).

CODA: CROSS-CULTURAL PERSPECTIVES

1. Duane Anderson, lecture presented at the School of American Research, Santa Fe, New Mexico, February 23, 2000; Duane Anderson, *When Rain Gods Reigned: From Curios to Art at Tesuque Pueblo* (Santa Fe: Museum of New Mexico Press, 2002).

2. Richard L. Anderson, *Art in Primitive Societies* (Englewood Cliffs, N.J.: Prentice-Hall, 1979).

3. Tessie Naranjo, "Pueblo Pottery Remains Down to Earth: Old Beliefs Wrestle with New Influences," Pasa 2000, in the *Santa Fe New Mexican,* 1 January 2000, pp. 8–9.

4. Tessie Naranjo, "Social Change and Pottery-Making at Santa Clara Pueblo" (Ph.D. dissertation, University of New Mexico, 1992).

5. Barton Wright, colloquium on the Katsina Convocation, School of American Research, Santa Fe, New Mexico, November 1999.

6. Quoted in Katherine Chase, "The Deep Remembering: Native American Painting in the Southwest" (School of American Research Membership Lecture, Santa Fe, New Mexico, February 17, 2000).

7. "Weaving the Threads: The Weaving Community and Traditions of Chimayó," (Chimayó History Museum, Chimayó, New Mexico, July 17–November 30, 1999).

8. Jane Collier, personal communication, San Cristóbal de las Casas, July 1997.

References

Altman, P. and C. D. West
1992   *Threads of Identity*. Los Angeles: Fowler Museum of Cultural History.

Anderson, D.
2002   *When Rain Gods Reigned: From Curios to Art at Tesuque Pueblo*. Santa Fe: Museum of New Mexico Press.

Anderson, R. L.
1979   *Art in Primitive Societies*. Englewood Cliffs, N.J.: Prentice-Hall.

Anschuetz, M.
1966   To Be Born in Zinacantán. Manuscript on file, Harvard Chiapas Project, Department of Anthropology, Harvard University, Cambridge, Mass.

Berlin, B. and P. Kay
1969   *Basic Color Terms: Their Universality and Evolution*. Berkeley: University of California Press.

Berry, J. W., Y. H. Poortinga, J. Pandey, P. R. Dasen, T. S. Saraswathi, M. H. Segall and C. Kagitcibasi, eds.
1997   *Handbook of Cross-Cultural Psychology*. 3 vols. Boston: Allyn and Bacon.

Blanco, M. H. and N. J. Chodorow
1972   Children's Work and Obedience in Zinacantán. Manuscript on file Harvard Chiapas Project, Department of Anthropology, Harvard University, Cambridge Mass.

Brazelton, T. B., J. S. Robey and G. Collier
1969   Infant Development in the Zinacanteco Indians of Southern Mexico. *Pediatrics* 44:274–283.

Bril, B.
1996   Learning Cultural Motor Skills. Paper presented eat the March colloquium "Culture and the Uses of the Body," Saint-Germain-en-Laye, France.

Bruner, J. S.
1947   Value and Need as Organizing Factors in Perception. *Journal of Abnormal and Social Psychology* 42:33–44.

Bruner, J. S., J. Goodnow and G. Austin
1956   *A Study of Thinking*. New York: Science Editions, Wiley.

Cancian, Francesca
1963   Family Interaction in the Zinacantán. Ph.D. diss., Harvard University, Cambridge, Mass.

Cancian, Frank
1974   *Another Place: Photographs of a Maya Community*. San Francisco: Scrimshaw Press.

1992   *The Decline of Community in Zinacantán: Economy, Public Life, and Social Stratification, 1960–1987*. Stanford, Calif.: Stanford University Press.

Carroll, J. B., ed.
1956   *Language, Thought, and Reality: Selected Writings of Benjamin Lee Whorf*. Cambridge, Mass.: MIT Press.

Chamoux, M.
1986   Apprendre Autrement. In *Demain L'Artisanat?. Cahiers de L'Institut Universitaire d'Etudes du Développement*, pp. 211–335. Paris: Presses Universitaires de France.

Chase, K.
2000   The Deep Remembering: Native American Painting in the Southwest. School of American Research Membershipo Lecture, February 17, Santa Fe, N.M.

Chavajay, P., and B. Rogoff
2002   Schooling and Traditional Collaborative Social Organization of Problem Solving by Mayan Mothers and Children. *Developmental Psychology* 38:55–66.

Chen, T.
1991   Informal Education in San Pedro Chenalho: A Comparative Study of Weaving between Families Belonging to and Families Not Belonging to Weaving Cooperatives. M.A. thesis, Department of Psychology, University of California, Los Angeles.

Childs, C. P., and P. M. Greenfield
1980   Informal Modes of Learning and Teaching: The Case of Zinacanteco Weaving. In *Studies in Cross-Cultural Psychology,* vol. 2, edited by N. Warren, pp. 269–316. London: Academic Press.

Chimayó History Museum
1999   "Weaving the Threads: The Weaving Community and Traditions of Chimayó," Chimayó History Museum, Chimayó, New Mexico, July 17–November 30.

Colby, B. N.
1960   Social Relations and Directed Culture Change among the Zinacantán. *Practical Anthropology* (November-December):241–250.

Cole, M.
1996   *Cultural Psychology: A Once and Future Discipline.* Cambridge, Mass.: Harvard University Press.

Collier, G. A.
1990   Seeking Food and Seeking Money: Changing Productive Relations in a Highland Mexican Community. Discussion Paper 11. United Nations Research Institute for Social Development.
n.d.   Zincantecs at Home in the World, unpublished manuscript. Published in Spanish as Los Zinacantecos en su mundo contemporáneo. *Antropología Mesoamericana: Homenaje a Alfonso Villa Rojas,* edited by M. Esponda, S. Pincemin, and M. Rosas, pp. 189-215. Tuxtla Gutierrez: Instituto Chiapaneco de Cultura, 1992.

Collier, J. F.
2003   Talk prepared by Jane F. Collier for presentation at UCLA Sloan Center Workshop on Kinship and Family, January 31, 2003.

Cone, C.
1995   Crafting Selves: The Lives of Two Mayan Women. *Annals of Tourism Research* 24:314–327.

Cordry, D., and D. Cordry
1968   *Mexican Indian Costumes.* Austin: University of Texas Press.

Cropley, A. J.
1999   Definitions of Creativity. In *Encyclopedia of Creativity,* vol. 1, edited by M. A. Runco and S. R. Pritzker, pp. 511–524. San Diego: Academic Press.

Csikszentmihaly, M.
        Creativity: Flow and the Psychology of Discovery and Invention. New York: HarperCollins.

Daley, T. C., S. E. Whaley, M. D. Sigman, M. P. Espinosa, and C. Neumann
2003   "IQ on the Rise: The Flynn Effect in Rural Kenyan Children," *Psychological Science* 14: 215-219.

Danziger, E.
1996   The Communicative Creation of Language: A Mayan Case Study. Paper presented at the annual meeting of the American Anthropological Association, San Francisco.

Davison, M. P.
1944   *A Handweaver's Pattern Book for Four Harness Looms.* Swarthmore, Pa.: Published by the author.

de Arathoon, B.
2001   A Wave of Change in Backstrap Weaving. *Friends of the Ixchel Museum* 12, no. 1: 1–2.

de Haan, M.
1996   Instruction and Cultural Meaning: A Study of Teaching Practices of a Native American Group, the Mazahuas. Paper presented at the Second Socio-Cultural Conference, Geneva.

de Motolonía, T.
1950   *Indians of New Spain.* Translated and edited by E. A. Foster, The Cortes Society. Berkeley, Calif.: Bancroft Library.

de Orellana, M.
1993   A Weft of Voices: The Weaver at Her Loom, translated by C. Castelli. *Artes de Mexico,* No. 19:88–93.

de Sahagun, B.

1961   *Florentine Codex: General History of the Things of New Spain.* Book 10, *The People*, in Monographs of the School of American Research and the Museum of New Mexico, translated by C. E. Dibble and A. J. O. Anderson. Santa Fe, N.M.: SAR Press and the University of Utah Press.

Devereaux, L. Haviland

1991   Unpublished field notes.

1993   Unpublished field notes.

Dibble, C. E., and A. J. O. Anderson, trans.

1961   *Florentine Codex.* Book 10, *The People*, in Monographs of the School of American Research and the Museum of New Mexico. Santa Fe, N.M.: SAR Press and the University of Utah Press.

Eber, C., and B. Rosenbaum

1993   That We May Serve Beneath Your Hands and Feet: Women Weavers in Highland Chiapas, Mexico. In *Crafts in the World Market: The Impact of Global Exchange on Middle-American Artisans*, edited by J. Nash, pp. 127–153. Albany: State University of New York Press.

El Guindi, F.

1998   From Pictorializing to Visual Anthropology. In *Handbook of Methods in Cultural Anthropology*, pp. 459–511. Walnut Creek, Calif.: Altamira Press.

Fairbanks, L. A.

2000   Behavioral Development of Nonhuman Primates and the Evolution of Human Behavioral Ontogeny. In *Biology, Brain, and Behavior: The Evolution of Human Development*, edited by S. Parker, J. Langer, and M. McKinney, pp. 131–158. Santa Fe, N.M.: SAR Press.

Fiske, A. P.

1995   Learning a Culture the Way Informants Do: Observing, Imitating, and Participating. Paper presented at the National Institutes for Mental Health Workshop, Washington, D.C.

Foster, G. M., T. Scudder, E. Colson, and R. V. Kemper

1982   *Long-Term Field Research in Social Anthropology.* New York: Academic Press.

Gardner, H.

1982   *Art, Mind, and Brain: A Cognitive Approach to Creativity.* New York: Basic Books.

Gaskins, S.

1999   Children's Daily Lives in a Mayan Village: A Case Study of Culturally Constructed Roles and Activities. In *Children's Engagement in the World: Sociocultural Perspectives*, edited by A. Göncü, pp. 25–64. New York: Cambridge University Press.

Gibson, E. J.

1997   An Ecological Psychologist's Prolegomena for Perceptual Development: A Functional Approach. In *Evolving Explanations of Development: Ecological Approaches to Organism-Environment Systems*, edited by Patricia Zukow-Goldring, pp. 23–45. Washington, D.C.: American Psychological Association.

Goody, E.

1982   Daboya Weavers: Relations of Production, Dependence and Reciprocity. In *From Craft to Industry: The Ethnography of Proto-Industrial Cloth Production*, edited by E. Goody, pp. 50–84. New York: Cambridge University Press.

Greenfield, P. M.

1972   Studies of Mother-Infant Interaction: Towards a Structural-Functional Approach. *Human Development* 15: 131–138.

1984   A Theory of the Teacher in the Learning Activities of Everyday Life. In *Everyday Cognition*, edited by B. Rogoff and J. Lave, pp. 117–138. Cambridge, Mass.: Harvard University Press.

1999   Historical Change and Cognitive Change: A Two-Decade Follow-Up Study in Zinacantan, A Maya Community in Chiapas, Mexico. *Mind, Culture, and Activity,* 6: 92–108.

2000   Culture and Universals: Integrating Social and Cognitive Development. In *Culture, Thought, and Development*, edited by L. P. Nucci, G. B. Saxe, and E. Turiel, pp. 231–277. Mahwah, N.J.: Lawrence Erlbaum Associates.

Greenfield, P. M., T. B. Brazelton, and C. P. Childs

1989   From Birth to Maturity in Zinacantán: Ontogenesis in Cultural Context. In *Ethnographic Encounters in Southern Mesoamerica: Essays in Honor of Evon Zartman Vogt, Jr.*, edited by V. R. Bricker and G. H. Gossen, pp. 177–216. Albany: Institute for Meso-American Studies, State University of New York at Albany.

Greenfield, P. M., and C. P. Childs

1977   Weaving, Color Terms, and Pattern Representation: Cultural Influences and Cognitive Development among the Zinacantecos of Southern Mexico. *International Journal of Psychology* 11:23–48.

1991   Developmental Continuity in Biocultural Context. In *Context and Development*, edited by R. Cohen and A. W. Siegel, pp. 135–159. Hillsdale, N.J.: Erlbaum.

1996   Learning to Weave in Zinacantán: A Two-Decade Study of Historical Change in Informal Education. Paper presented at the annual meeting of the American Anthropological Association, November, San Francisco.

Greenfield, P. M., and J. Lave

1982   Cognitive Aspects of Informal Education. In *Cultural Perspectives on Child Development*, edited by D. Wagner and H. Stevenson, pp. 181–207. San Francisco: Freeman.

Greenfield, P. M., and A. E. Maynard

1997   Women, Girls, Apprenticeship, and Schooling: A Longitudinal Study of Historical Change among the Zinacantecan Maya. Paper presented at the annual meeting of the American Anthropological Association, November, Washington, D.C.

2000   Cultural Apprenticeship and Cultural Change: Tool Learning and Imitation in Chimpanzees and Humans. In *Biology, Brains, and Behavior*, edited by S. Taylor Parker, J. Langer, and M. L. McKinney, pp. 237–277. Santa Fe, N.M.: SAR Press.

Greenfield, P. M., A. E. Maynard, and C. P. Childs

2000   History, Culture, Learning, and Development. *Cross-Cultural Research* 34:351–374.

2003   Historical Change, Cultural Learning, and Cognitive Representation in Zinacantec Maya Children. In *Cognitive Development* 18: 455–487.

Greenfield, P. M., B. Quiroz, and C. Raeff

2000   Cross-Cultural Conflict and Harmony in the Social Construction of the Child. In *The Social Construction of the Child, New Directions in Child Development*, edited by S. Harkness, C. Raeff, and C. R. Super, pp. 93–108. San Francisco: Jossey-Bass.

Hanks, W. F.

1989   Text and Textuality. In *Annual Review of Anthropology*, vol. 18, edited by B. J. Siegel, A. R. Beals, and S. A. Tyler, pp. 95–127. Palo Alto, Calif.: Annual Reviews, Inc.

Harkness, S.

1973   Universal Aspects of Learning Color Codes: A Study in Two Cultures. *Ethos* 1:175–200.

Haviland, L. K. M.

1978   The Social Relations of Work in a Peasant Community. Ph.D. diss., Harvard University, Cambridge, Mass.

Hirschfeld, L. A.

1977   Cuna Aesthetics: A Quantitative Analysis. *Ethnology* 16:147–166.

Johnson, A. W., and T. Earle

1987   *The Evolution of Human Societies: From Foraging Group to Agrarian State.* Stanford, Calif.: Stanford University Press.

Johnson, I. W.

1954   Chiptic Cave Textiles from Chiapas. *Journal de la Societé des Américanistes* 43:137–147.

John-Steiner, V.

1997   *Notebooks of the Mind: Explorations of Thinking.* New York: Oxford University Press.

2000   *Creative Collaboration.* Oxford: Oxford University Press.

Kleinman, A.

1996   General Discussion. Paper presented at the March colloquium "Culture and the Uses of the Body," Saint-Germain-en-Laye, France.

Lancy, D. F.

1996   *Playing on the Mother-Ground: Cultural Routines for Children's Learning.* New York: The Guilford Press.

Laughlin, R. M.

1975   The Great Tzotzil Dictionary of San Lorenzo Zinacantán. In *Smithsonian Contributions to Anthropology*, no. 19. Washington, D.C.: Smithsonian Institution Press.

Laughlin, R. M., and C. Karasik

1988   *The People of the Bat: Mayan Tales and Dreams from Zinacantán.* Washington, D.C.: Smithsonian Institution Press.

Lave, J., and E. Wenger

1991   *Situated Learning: Legitimate Peripheral Participation.* Cambridge: Cambridge University Press.

Loucky, J.

1988   Children's Work and Family Survival in Highland Guatemala. Ph.D. diss., University of California, Los Angeles.

Maynard, A. E.

1996   An Ethnomodel of Teaching and Learning: Apprenticeship in Zinacantecan Maya Women's Tasks. M.A. thesis, University of California, Los Angeles.

1999   Cultural Teaching. Ph.D. diss., University of California, Los Angeles.

2002   Cultural Teaching: The Development of Teaching Skills in Zinacantec Maya Sibling Interactions. *Child Development* 73:969–982.

Maynard, A. E., and P. M. Greenfield

2003   Implicit Cognitive Development in Cultural Tools and Children: Lessons from Maya Mexico. *Cognitive Development* 18: 489–510.

Maynard, A. E., P. M. Greenfield, and C. P. Childs

1999   Culture, History, Biology, and Body: Native and Non-Native Acquisition of Technological Skill. *Ethos* 27:379–402.

McVey-Dow, V.

1986   Indian Women and Textile Production: Adaptation to a New Environment in Chiapas, Mexico. Ph.D. diss., Department of Geography, University of Colorado, Boulder.

Modiano, N.

1973   *Indian Education in the Chiapas Highlands.* New York: Holt, Rinehart and Winston.

Molleson, T.

1996   The Physical Anthropology of Role Specialization from Neolithic Times. Paper presented in the March colloquium "Culture and the Uses of the Body," Fondation Fyssen, Saint-Germain-en-Laye, France.

Morley, S. G.

1946   *The Ancient Maya.* Stanford, Calif.: Stanford University Press.

Morris, W. F., Jr.

1984   *A Millennium of Weaving in Chiapas.* San Cristóbal de las Casas: Sna Jolobil.

1987   *Living Maya.* New York: Harry N. Abrams.

1996   *Handmade Money.* Washington, D.C.: Organization of American States.

n.d.   *Luchetik: El Lenguage Textil de los Altos de Chiapas (The Woven Word from Highland Chiapas).* San Cristóbal de Las Casas: Sna Jolobil.

Naranjo, T.

1992   Social Change and Pottery Making at Santa Clara Pueblo. Ph.D. diss., University of New Mexico, Albuquerque, N.M.

2000   Pueblo Pottery Remains Down to Earth: Old Beliefs Wrestle with New Influences. *Pasa 2000, Santa Fe New Mexican,* 1 January, pp. 8–9.

Nash, J.

1993   Introduction to *Crafts in the World Market: The Impact of Global Exchange on Middle American Artists,* edited by J. Nash, pp. 1-22. Albany: State University of New York Press.

Nash, M.

1967   *Machine Age Maya: The Industrialization of a Guatemalan Community.* Chicago:
[1958]   University of Chicago Press; originally published by the Free Press.

Ochs, E.

1988   *Culture and Language Development: Language Acquisition and Language Socialization in a Samoan Village.* Cambridge: Cambridge University Press.

O'Quin, K., and S. P. Besemer

1999   Creative Products. In *Encyclopedia of Creativity,* vol. 1, edited by M. A. Runco and S. R. Pritzker, pp. 413–422. San Diego: Academic Press.

Pérez Pérez, E.

1997a   Discussion held at the Regional Congress of Psychology for Professionals in the Americas, "Interfacing the Science and Practice of Psychology," Mexico City.

1997b   Los Maestros Bilingües Frente a un Conflicto Cultural: Criticas y Reflexiones. Paper presented at the Regional Congress of Psychology for Professionals in the Americas, "Interfacing the Science and Practice of Psychology," Mexico City.

Price-Williams, D., W. Gordon, and M. Ramirez

1967   Manipulation and Conservation: A Study of Children from Pottery-Making Families in Mexico, *Memorias del XI Congreso Interamericano de Psyicologia,* pp. 106–126.

Raeff, C., P. M. Greenfield, and B. Quiroz

2000 Conceptualizing Interpersonal Relationships in the Cultural Contexts of Individualism and Collectivism. In *Variability in the Social Construction of the Child, New Directions in Child Development,* edited by S. Harkness, C. Raeff, and C. R. Super, pp. 59–74. San Francisco: Jossey-Bass.

Rogoff, B.

1990 *Apprenticeship in Thinking.* Cambridge: Cambridge University Press.

Rogoff, B., and M. Gauvain

1984 The Cognitive Consequences of Specific Experiences: Weaving vs. Schooling among the Navaho. *Journal of Cross-Cultural Psychology* 15: 453–475.

Rogoff, B., and J. Lave

1984 *Everyday Cognition: Its Development in Social Context.* Cambridge, Mass.: Harvard University Press.

Rogoff, B., J. J. Mistry, A. Göncü, and C. Mosier

1993 Guided Participation in Cultural Activities by Toddlers and Caregivers. *Monographs of the Society for Research in Child Development,* vol. 58, series no. 236.

Rosch, E.

1973 Natural Categories. *Cognitive Psychology* 7:573–605.

Rus, D.

1990 La Crisis Económica y la Mujer Indígena: El Caso de Chamula, Chiapas. Instituto de Asesoría Antropológica para la Región Maya, A.C., San Cristóbal de las Casas, Chiapas, Mexico.

Saxe, G. B., and M. Gearhart

1990 The Development of Topological Concepts in Unschooled Straw Weavers. *British Journal of Developmental Psychology* 8: 251-258.

Sayer, C.

1990 *Arts and Crafts of Mexico.* San Francisco: Chronicle Books.

Schaefer, S. B.

2002 *To Think with a Good Heart: Wixarika Women, Weavers, and Shamans.* Salt Lake City: University of Utah Press.

1992 *Maya Textiles of Guatemala.* Austin: University of Texas Press.

Scribner, S., and M. Cole

1981 *The Psychology of Literacy.* Cambridge, Mass.: Harvard University Press.

Segall, M. H., D. T. Campbell, and J. M. Herskovitz

1966 *Influence of Culture on Visual Perception.* Indianapolis, Ind.: Bobbs-Merrill.

Segall, M. H., P. R. Dasen, J. W. Berry, and Y. H. Poortinga

1990 *Human Behavior in Global Perspective: An Introduction to Cross-Cultural Psychology.* New York: Pergamon/Allyn and Bacon.

Simmel, G.

1990 *The Philosophy of Money,* translated by
[1900] T. Bottomore and D. Frisby. New York: Routledge.

Stigler, J. W., R. A. Shweder, and G. Herdt

1990 *Cultural Psychology: Essays in Comparative Human Development.* New York: Cambridge University Press.

Stuart, G. S., and G. E. Stuart

1993 *Lost Kingdoms of the Maya.* Washington, D.C.: National Geographic Society.

Tapia Uribe, F. M., R. A. LeVine, and S. E. LeVine

1994 Maternal Behavior in a Mexican Community: The Changing Environments of Children. In *Cross-Cultural Roots of Minority Child Development,* edited by P. M. Greenfield and R. R. Cocking, pp. 41–54. Hillsdale, N.J.: Erlbaum.

Tedlock, B., and D. Tedlock

1985 Text and Textile: Language and Technology in the Arts of the Quiché Maya. *Journal of Anthropological Research* 41:121–146.

Turok, M.

1972 Handicrafts: A Case Study on Weaving in the Highlands. Manuscript on file, Harvard Chiapas Project, Department of Anthropology, Harvard University, Cambridge Mass.

1999 Le Geste des Tisserandes: Transmission et Renouvellement. In *Textiles Mayas: La Trame d'un Peuple,* edited by D. Dupiech-Cavaleri, pp. 34–49. Paris: Editions Unesco.

Vogt, E. Z.

1969 *Zinacantán: A Maya Community in the Highlands of Chiapas.* Cambridge, Mass.: Harvard University Press.

1979 The Harvard Chiapas Project: 1957–1975. In *Long-Term Field Research in Social Anthropology,* edited by G. M. Foster, T. Scudder, E. Colson, and R. V. Kemper, pp. 279–301. New York: Academic Press.

1994 *Fieldwork among the Maya: Reflections on the Harvard Chiapas Project.* Albuquerque: University of New Mexico Press.

Wagner, J.

2004 Constructing Credible Images: Documentary Studies, Social Research and Visual Studies. In special issue of *American Behavioral Scientist,* edited by Gregory Stanczak (in press).

Wasserstrom, R.

1983 *Class and Society in Central Chiapas.* Berkeley: University of California Press.

Wheeler, L. R.

1970 A Trans-Decade Comparison of the IQs of Tennessee Mountain Children. In *Cross-Cultural Studies of Behavior,* edited by I. Al-Issa and W. Dennis, pp. 120–133. New York: Holt, Rinehart & Winston.

Whiting, B. B., and C. P. Edwards

1988 *Children of Different Worlds: The Formation of Social Behavior.* Cambridge, Mass.: Harvard University Press.

Wood, D., J. S. Bruner, and G. Ross

1976 The Role of Tutoring in Problem Solving. *Journal of Child Psychology and Psychiatry* 17:89–100.

Wright, B.

1999 Colloquium on the Katsina Convocation, School of American Research, November, Santa Fe, New Mexico.

Zambrano, I., and P. M. Greenfield

2004 Ethnoepistemologies at Home and at School. In *Culture and Competence,* edited by R. J. Sternberg and E. Grigorenko, pp. 251–272. Washington, D.C.: American Psychological Association.

1999 From *Na'* to Know: Power, Epistemology, and the Everyday Forms of State Formation in Mitontik, Chiapas. Ph. D. diss., Harvard University, Cambridge, Mass.

Zukow-Goldring, P.

1989 Siblings as Effective Socializing Agents: Evidence from Central Mexico. In *Sibling Interaction Across Cultures,* edited by P. G. Zukow, pp. 79–105. New York: Springer-Verlag.

1997 A Social Ecological Realist Approach to the Emergence of the Lexicon: Educating Attention to Amodal Invariants in Gesture and Speech. In *Evolving Explanations of Development: Ecological Approaches to Organism-Environment Systems,* edited by P. Zukow-Goldring, pp. 199–250. Washington, D.C.: American Psychological Association.

© Lauren Greenfield/VII.

Index

mothers. *See* daughters; women
Motolinía, Fray Toribio de, 30, 90
motor activity, 30
"mountains" (zigzag designs), 114, 116, 152–153
museums, older-style weaving and, 83

Nabenchauk, 6; gender and schooling, 86; history of commerce, 92; as market for Guatemalans, 26, 27; outside world's influence, 21, 23; reconnecting with family, 5–9; social change in, 1–4, 16–21
Nachih, 93
na' (know), 52. *See also* knowledge
napkins *(servilletas),* 18, 79, 100–101
Naranjo, Tessie, 169–170
Nash, June, 120
Native Americans and change, 169–171
Navajo Indians, 171
"near" places, 24
neural activity, 44
Nibok, 13
"nichim" (flowers or embellishments), 112
nonverbal instruction in learning process, 62
nonweavers, 86
North American Free Trade Agreement (NAFTA), 73
notebooks of designs, 161

observation, learning by, 33, 36, 54, 60, 63, 75
Octagon, 23
Octaviana: Octaviana 172, 131; Octaviana Xulubte', 2, 33, 41, 54–55, 56
orange colors, 129, 142

Palas 213, 134, 135, 138
pants, 96, 117
paper patterns. *See* printed patterns
parades, 15

Paresvan, Loxa Hernandes, 100
patterns in weaving: 1970 styles, 8–9; American subjects in experiments, 132; basket weave, 89–90; beauty and, 140–142; colors and, 129; continuing patterns in stick representations, 127; cross-stitch, 160; experiments, 10, 123–126, 129–134, 132; light-dark stripes, 141; printed patterns (*See* printed patterns); representational tools, 160–165; "rules," 96; sources of designs, 113–115; Spanish flowers, 114; traditional patterns, 69
Pavlu family, 5, 7, 8, 9, 16–17
Pavlu, Loxa, xv, 8
Pavlu, Paxku', xvi, 33; on baptismal blouses, 117; at christening, 15–16; copying San Andrés embroidery, 119, 120; embroidery, 28, 120; learning by observation, 37; play weaving, 38, 43; on pyramid designs, 114; San Cristóbal journey, 76; stick construction, 140; stick pattern representations, 123, 124, 126; store-bought fabric, 117; teaching Ashley Maynard, 10, 49, 62; tracing system for designs, 161, 163; winding warp threads, 47
Pavlu, Petul, 8
Pavlu, Rosy: author's friendship with, 16; bad weaving errors, 82; on independent learning, 82; play weaving, 41, 47; toy looms, 37
Pavlu, Telex, 5, 10
Pavlu, Xun: on children, 21; *compadres* of, 11; dancing, 17; on driving, 24; photographs of, xv; on photography, 14; on schooling, 66, 78; on videocassette recorders, 23; on videotaping, 14; at videotaping sessions, 53–54; wife's passing, 5; at Xunka's christening, 16
Pavlu, Xunka': in baby carrier, 111; christening, 15–16; learning by observation, 33; photographs of, 28, 31, 47; play weaving, 43

Paxku'. *See also* Pavlu, Paxku': Paxku' 221, 58
Paxion Primero, 100
payments: changes in learning processes and, 81; for machine embroidery, 99; for videotaping weaving, 13; for weaving, 17, 116; for winding thread, 18
peer teachers, 79, 83
perception, 124–126, 140
Peres, Loxa Sanches, 14
Pérez Pérez, Elias, 86
Perez, Rosa Sanchez, 38
Petu': Petu' 201, 156, 160; Petu' 227, 139, 153–155
Petul: Petul 9, 136; Petul Pavlu, 8; Petul Vásquez, 14, 100; Petul Xulubte', 4
photographs: arrangements for, 14; permissions, 14–15; Polaroids, 11, 13
Piaget, Jean, 47–51
pink colors, 129, 142
pirik mochebales, 110, 112
play weaving and toy looms: constructing looms, 45–52; discovery of, 10; neural activity and, 44; photographs, 40; role of, 37–45, 80; tension in models of learning, 82; warp threads, 48, 49
pok mochebales. See shawls *(pok mochebales)*
Polaroid pictures, 11, 13
ponchos *(pok k'u'ul):* 1940's versions, 93; 1950's versions, 94; 1960's versions, 94–95, 101; 1980's versions, 96; 1990's versions, 96, 101; creativity in, 97–99; everyday wear, 117; floral designs on, 97; patterns in, 124, 125; stick pattern representations, 126, 129–131; tourist vs. native versions, 17; variability in, 102
pottery: Pueblo, 169–171; representations of looms, 29
pox, 14, 16
Price-Williams, Douglas, 126